D1119379

The Global Struggle for Human Rights

Universal Principles in World Politics

Debra L. DeLaet
Drake University

THOMSON

WADSWORTH

Australia • Canada • Mexico • Singapore • Spain
United Kingdom • United States

THOMSON

WADSWORTH

The Global Struggle for Human Rights: Universal Principles in World Politics
Debra L. DeLaet

Publisher: *Clark Baxter*
Executive Editor: *David Tatom*
Associate Development Editor: *Rebecca Green*
Editorial Assistants: *Reena Thomas/Cheryl Lee*
Technology Project Manager: *Michelle Vardeman*
Marketing Manager: *Janise Fry*
Marketing Assistant: *Teresa Jessen*
Advertising Project Manager: *Kelley McAllister*
Project Manager, Editorial Production: *Ryan Heal*

Art Director: *Maria Epes*
Print/Media Buyer: *Lisa Claudeanos*
Permissions Editor: *Joohee Lee*
Production Service and Compositor: *Scratchgravel Publishing Services*
Cover Designer: *Brian Salisbury*
Copy Editor: *Margaret C. Tropp*
Cover Image: *Getty Images/Marco Longari*
Printer: *Transcontinental Printing/Louiseville*

© 2006 Thomson Wadsworth, a part of The Thomson Corporation. Thomson, the Star logo, and Wadsworth are trademarks used herein under license.

ALL RIGHTS RESERVED. No part of this work covered by the copyright hereon may be reproduced or used in any form or by any means—graphic, electronic, or mechanical, including photocopying, recording, taping, Web distribution, information storage and retrieval systems, or in any other manner—without the written permission of the publisher.

Printed in Canada

2 3 4 5 6 7 09 08 07 06

For more information about our products, contact us at:
Thomson Learning Academic Resource Center
1-800-423-0563

For permission to use material from this text or product, submit a request online at http://www.thomsonrights.com.
Any additional questions about permissions can be submitted by email to thomsonrights@thomson.com.

Library of Congress Control Number: 2005920203

ISBN 0-534-63572-5

Thomson Higher Education
10 Davis Drive
Belmont, CA 94002-3098
USA

Asia (including India)
Thomson Learning
5 Shenton Way
#01-01 UIC Building
Singapore 068808

Australia/New Zealand
Thomson Learning Australia
102 Dodds Street
Southbank, Victoria 3006
Australia

Canada
Thomson Nelson
1120 Birchmount Road
Toronto, Ontario M1K 5G4
Canada

UK/Europe/Middle East/Africa
Thomson Learning
High Holborn House
50–51 Bedford Road
London WC1R 4LR
United Kingdom

Latin America
Thomson Learning
Seneca, 53
Colonia Polanco
11560 Mexico
D.F. Mexico

Spain (including Portugal)
Thomson Paraninfo
Calle Magallanes, 25
28015 Madrid, Spain

For my daughters, Edie and Daphne

About the Author

Debra L. DeLaet is an Associate Professor of Politics and International Relations at Drake University, where she teaches courses on human rights, peacebuilding and justice, gender and world politics, international law, and the United Nations. Her primary research interests are in the areas of international human rights, gender and world politics, and international migration. She is the author of *U.S. Immigration Policy in an Age of Rights* (Praeger, 2000) and several book chapters and articles on sexual orientation discrimination in international human rights law, gender and international migration, and gender and justice in war-torn societies.

Brief Contents

Contents

PART III: HUMAN RIGHTS AND THE QUEST FOR JUSTICE

11   PROMOTING HUMAN RIGHTS FROM THE BOTTOM UP   204

CONCLUSIONS   219

Preface

This book is a comprehensive introduction to the issue of human rights in world politics. The history of human rights is, at a very basic level, the history of world politics. This history has been rife with civil and international conflicts, ideological disputes over the proper role of government and the place of individuals in society, and interactions reflecting clashing cultures. All of these things involve fundamental questions of human rights. The civil and international conflicts that regularly erupt in world politics have often been based on conflicting conceptions of human rights, even if the language of human rights has not historically been used to describe these conflicts. Today, the language of human rights has become a prominent tool used by states, international organizations, nongovernmental organizations, and individuals in their global interactions, and these actors increasingly frame their disputes using this language. Ultimately, the very forces and events that have shaped world politics reflect an evolving conception of human rights.

The idea of human rights first achieved a prominent place on the international agenda of states in the aftermath of World War II. The United Nations, created at the end of the war, incorporates explicit references to human rights in its charter and states that one of the fundamental purposes of the organization is to promote respect for and to reaffirm faith in human rights. In 1948, the UN General Assembly adopted the Universal Declaration of Human Rights, which identifies a wide range of political and economic rights as basic human rights. Since that time, the international community has developed a significant body of international human rights law. Yet systematic violations of human rights continue to be a constant feature of world politics. One of the primary objectives of this book is to examine the question of why serious human rights abuses continue to be committed across the globe despite the dramatic advancements in international human rights law.

Two basic themes provide the organizational framework for this overview of human rights. First, the tension between state sovereignty and human rights is one of the book's organizing themes. State sovereignty, simply defined as a state's right to govern itself as it sees fit, is the core organizing principle of world politics. Designed to encourage states to respect the territorial integrity of other states and to refrain from intervening in their internal affairs, state sovereignty ideally serves to promote the values of peace, security, and stability in world politics. Because universal human rights represent an attempt to create a set of rights that transcend state borders, an obvious tension marks the relationship between the principle of state sovereignty and the ideal of human rights. The idea of universal human rights that belong to all human beings regardless of where they live clashes directly with the principle that states have the sole legal authority to determine how they will treat their own citizens and other individuals living within their borders. Indeed, sovereign states typically are the actors most responsible for perpetrating human rights abuses. At the same time, states are the primary actors responsible for promoting and protecting human rights. This paradoxical relationship between state sovereignty and universal human rights is at the heart of many of the most prominent issues and controversies in contemporary world politics. Thus, a focus on this theme throughout the book sheds light not only on the status of human rights across the globe but also on the essential workings of world politics.

Second, the book develops the theme that there is a crucial gap between lofty human rights rhetoric and the reality of human rights abuses in world politics. This gap between rhetoric and reality is built into the system of international human rights law that has evolved since the end of World War II. States across the globe have signed and ratified many treaties that assert that fundamental human rights are universal in scope and that states have obligations to uphold these rights. At the same time, international human rights law typically contains loopholes that allow states to deviate from these norms under certain circumstances. Moreover, international human rights law does not create strong enforcement mechanisms that would enable the international community to ensure that states uphold their commitment to promote and protect universal human rights. Thus, the progressive development of international human rights norms has not been matched by the actual advancement of human rights in practice. This gap between rhetoric and reality is explored throughout the book.

In addition to these organizing themes, this book is distinguished from other introductions to human rights in world politics in several ways. Unlike most books on human rights, this book incorporates the concept of gender throughout. In doing so, the book spends considerable time not only on feminist perspectives on human rights, as well as human rights issues that are of particular concern to women and girls, but also emphasizes the ways in which gender norms affect the ability of men and boys to fully enjoy fundamental human rights. The book also examines sexual orientation discrimination as a human rights issue. Finally, the book is distinct from many other introductions to human rights in that it devotes several chapters to examining various mechanisms for implementing human rights norms that are not typically covered in detail. Rather than focusing primarily on United Nations or foreign policy mechanisms for implementing human rights norms, though these topics are indeed covered, the book devotes an entire chapter to punitive justice and judicial mechanisms for promoting human rights and another chapter to restorative justice mechanisms, including truth commissions, reparations, and apologies. While the book, of course, covers all of the standard topics necessary in any book on human rights, its incorporation of these distinct features makes it a truly comprehensive introduction to the subject.

This book is organized into three parts. Part I: Human Rights in Theory and Law explores the legal and philosophical underpinnings of the concept of human rights. Chapter 1 considers philosophical, legal, and political problems associated with efforts to reach international consensus on a basic definition of human rights. Chapter 2 provides an overview of the development of and an introduction to the core body of international human rights law. It also considers feminist critiques of international human rights law. Chapter 3 explores various moral and philosophical arguments both for and against the concept of human rights. Chapter 3 also considers the question of whether human rights standards are or should be considered universal or whether different cultural standards or interpretations of human rights are acceptable.

Part II: Human Rights in Practice examines in detail the potential tension between state sovereignty and human rights by looking at concrete human rights issues and the way that states respond to them in practice. Chapter 4, which focuses on civil and political rights, highlights the tension between universal human rights norms and state sovereignty with a special focus on the "war on terror" and on the issue of self-determination. Chapter 5 provides an overview of collective rights and examines genocide as an extreme example of the breakdown of a moral order protecting basic human rights. Chapter 6 explores economic and social rights as basic human rights. Chapter 7 discusses gender equity and sexual orientation as these topics relate to human rights; it includes case studies of violence against women, sexual violence during war, and sexual orientation discrimination.

Part III: Human Rights and the Quest for Justice turns to an examination of the promotion and protection of human rights norms. Chapter 8 looks at foreign policy mechanisms used by states in an effort to promote and protect human rights norms, as well as elements of the United Nations system designed to monitor, prevent, and/or punish human rights abuses. Chapter 9 introduces the concept of punitive justice and evaluates various mechanisms for punishing human rights abuses, including trials, purges, and reparations. Chapter 10 examines the concept of restorative justice and discusses truth commissions, reparations, and apologies as mechanisms for fostering reconciliation in the aftermath of human rights abuses. Chapter 11 examines the role of nongovernmental organizations and individuals in promoting human rights norms. The book concludes with a review of the status of human rights at the dawn of the twenty-first century and challenges readers to consider the role that they might play as citizens, both of their nation-state and of the world, to further the advancement of human rights norms.

Each chapter contains discussion questions for classroom use, and most chapters include a list of web resources that instructors and students can consult for further information. The book's Web site (http://politicalscience. wadsworth.com/delaet01) contains additional information for instructors. In particular, the Web site describes possible classroom exercises that can be used in association with each chapter. The author has been teaching a course on human rights and world politics for nearly a decade and has shared a variety of exercises that she has used successfully in the classroom. Additionally, the Web site lists suggested films that correspond with each chapter's themes. The end-of-chapter discussion questions and Web site materials are designed to supplement what is intended to be a provocative and challenging introduction to the very important and typically controversial subject of human rights in world politics.

Acknowledgments

I would like to extend some brief but very important acknowledgments. I am very grateful to my colleagues and the administration at Drake University. I was able to complete most of the work for this book during my sabbatical leave and would like to thank Drake University for providing me with the opportunity to immerse myself in this project. I especially want to thank my colleagues in the Department of Politics and International Relations, Rachel Caufield, Dennis Goldford, Art Sanders, David Skidmore, and Eleanor Zeff, for their support of my professional development.

I also want to thank the many people who have given me feedback on drafts of the book. In particular, Charli Carpenter, Jaleh Dashti-Gibson, and Jeffrey Roberg provided me with invaluable insights and criticism that I considered carefully in revising the manuscript. I am very grateful to them for their incisive and constructive criticism.

I owe a debt of gratitude to my students at Drake University. Their persistent questions and thoughtful engagement with the topic of human rights in my courses over the years have brought to light questions I had not previously considered and have caused me to reevaluate fundamental assumptions on numerous occasions. I was initially motivated to write this book because of my interactions with students in my course on human rights, so I want to issue a general thank-you to the many students who have challenged me to think critically over the years. In particular, I would like to thank Marie Mainil for reading a draft of the manuscript and for offering a compelling critique of that early version.

Last but not least, I want to thank my husband Todd for his commitment to co-parenting and my young daughters for their patience (most of the time). Together, they have allowed me to continue to do the work that I love, and for that I am grateful.

Introduction

Suffering is not increased by numbers: one body
can contain all the suffering the world can feel.

Graham Greene, *THE QUIET AMERICAN*

WHY STUDY HUMAN RIGHTS?

I wanted to begin this book with a story of human suffering because, at the
end of the day, that is what proponents of human rights seek to prevent. I care
about the idea of human rights not primarily because the subject raises challenging philosophical, ethical, and political questions, though this is indeed the
case, but because real human beings suffer when human rights are not protected. The reality of human suffering that underlies human rights abuses across
the globe is what has motivated my commitment to the idea of human rights,
and it is why I want readers to learn and care about this topic. Thus, I wanted
to begin with a story of human suffering in an effort to stress from the outset
that the idea of human rights ultimately is about improving the lives of real,
ordinary human beings.

However, I encountered a dilemma in trying to decide what story of human suffering to tell. Whose story best conveys the importance of human
rights? Whose story most deserves to be told? The story of the Bosnian

Muslim prisoner who was ordered by Dusko Tadic, a Serbian guard at the Omarska concentration camp, to bite off the testicles of another Bosnian Muslim prisoner? Or the story of the man who was sexually mutilated in this case?[1] I could tell the story of the Zairian prisoner who was held incommunicado and beaten almost every other day for six months in the late 1970s on the charge that he had insulted then President Mobotu by saying that another prisoner had been beaten and tortured.[2] Perhaps I should begin with the story of the poor Indonesian man who lives with his wife and two children on blankets between two sets of urban railway tracks in Jakarta, literally inches from fast-moving trains, and whose legs were severed in a tragic train accident?[3] I could begin with the story of seventeen-year-old Fauziya Kassindja who fled Togo to escape forced polygamous marriage and forced genital mutilation only to end up in the American detention system where she faced inhumane conditions, abusive mistreatment, degradation, and despair.[4] Or should I begin with the story of the young, starving Sudanese girl who was so close to death as she literally dragged her emaciated body to a feeding center that she was stalked by a vulture?[5]

No, I cannot single out one story to tell. Telling only one story does not begin to capture the vast scale of human suffering in world politics: 6 million dead in the Holocaust; 2 million dead in Cambodia under the Khmer Rouge; more than half a million dead in 30 days in the Rwandan genocide in 1994; 11 million childhood deaths each year due to preventable illnesses. These staggering figures may provide a better sense of the scale of human suffering in world politics than a single individual's story, but they also risk numbing the reader and inducing a sense of paralysis about the possibility of change. And I have mentioned only a few examples of the countless numbers of human beings who have suffered through the ages as a result of genocide, political "disappearances," torture, and other forms of political repression and human degradation.

Moreover, to single out one story risks minimizing the human suffering that is encompassed in such a wide range of stories about victims and survivors of human rights abuses. It also risks suggesting that particular types of human rights abuses are worse than others, and the purpose of this book is not to "rank" human suffering. The difficulty of selecting a story for this introduction is compounded by the fact that we have not yet considered the challenges that impede global consensus on what types of human suffering should be classified as human rights abuses. Perhaps some of the stories I have already mentioned do not involve human rights abuses at all but instead represent inevitable human tragedies.

Thus, although I wanted to begin with a single story of human suffering, I find that I cannot. Nevertheless, I still want to draw attention to the centrality of human suffering to any exploration of human rights. Although this book will examine the idea of human rights in an abstract, rigorous, and sometimes critical manner, I do not want readers to lose sight of the humanistic impulse that ultimately drives the advancement of the idea of global human rights.

STATE SOVEREIGNTY
AND HUMAN RIGHTS

One of the central themes woven throughout this book is the tension between state sovereignty and human rights. State sovereignty is a core principle in both the study and practice of world politics and serves as one of the most significant obstacles to the advancement of global human rights norms. Scholars of international law typically define sovereignty as "the exclusive right of a State to govern the affairs of its inhabitants and to be free from external control."[6] State sovereignty is comprised of multiple elements, including territorial integrity, equality among sovereign states regardless of the size of the state, and noninterference in the internal affairs of other states.

Sovereignty is a legal principle, not necessarily a description of fact. History and contemporary world politics provide numerous examples of states violating the sovereignty of other states. These violations of state sovereignty illustrate a basic reality about world politics: States have a *legal* right to sovereignty though they do not always have the political power to exercise or to protect their sovereignty in practice. In particular, powerful states are more likely than weak states to be able to enjoy and protect their sovereignty.

Despite the reality that states historically have only imperfectly upheld and respected state sovereignty, it remains a preeminent organizing principle of international relations. All states claim the right to sovereignty and react defensively when it is threatened. State sovereignty has several advantages as a principle for organizing world politics. Historically, states came to accept sovereignty as the organizing principle of international relations as a way of minimizing interstate conflicts. By encouraging states to respect the right of other states to govern their own territory as they see fit, the principle of sovereignty discourages the use of force for the purpose of influencing the "internal affairs" of other states. In this way, the principle of sovereignty is designed to promote security, stability, and peace in international relations. Thus, the principle of sovereignty does not merely reflect the self-serving interests of governing elites within states but also promotes certain values in world politics.

While state sovereignty has played an integral role in promoting the values of security, stability, and peace in world politics, the principle of sovereignty works against other important values. In a global system organized according to the principle of sovereignty, a state's treatment of its citizens or residents is not a valid concern for other states or the international community. State sovereignty subjugates the basic rights of the individual human beings living within particular states to state interests as defined by governing elites within these states. In essence, state sovereignty trumps universal human rights. Thus, sovereignty may threaten the values of justice, fairness, equality, and freedom for individuals at the same time that it promotes the values of security, stability, and peace among states.

State sovereignty serves as an obstacle to the promotion of universal human rights because, by definition, universal human rights represent an attempt to create a set of rights that transcend state borders. The idea of universal human rights that belong to all human beings regardless of where they live clashes directly with the principle that states have the sole legal authority to determine how they will treat their own citizens and other individuals living within their borders. According to a human rights perspective, membership in the human community confers fundamental rights. In contrast, a state sovereignty perspective suggests that it is up to states to determine what rights, if any, are held by the individuals residing within their territory. In a world governed according to the principle of state sovereignty, states do not have the legal authority to intervene in the "internal affairs" of other states in an effort to promote or protect the rights of individuals living in that state. In short, the principle of state sovereignty places a higher priority on international order and stability, defined largely by the protection of the status quo respecting existing state borders, than on individual human rights.

Nevertheless, because sovereign states may choose to promote and protect fundamental human rights, it is not inevitable that sovereignty and universal human rights exist in tension. Indeed, the institutional resources and power of states may be required to ensure that human beings are able to enjoy fundamental human rights. For example, a state's resources may be crucial in meeting the basic economic rights of human beings, and a state may play an important role in preventing private actors from violating the basic rights of individuals. Nevertheless, the historical record has shown that sovereign states far too often violate basic human rights with impunity. Thus, the potential tension between human rights and state sovereignty is great.

As the previous discussion illustrates, the relationship between state sovereignty and universal human rights involves an important paradox. Sovereign states typically are the actors most responsible for perpetuating human rights abuses and are simultaneously the actors responsible for promoting and protecting human rights. In the absence of an effective international organization with the authority and power to implement human rights (an institution that will not be forthcoming unless states consent to it), sovereign states will need to play a crucial role if human rights are to be protected. This paradox will be explored throughout the book.

HUMAN RIGHTS AT THE DAWN
OF THE TWENTY-FIRST CENTURY:
THE GAP BETWEEN RHETORIC AND REALITY

A second important theme that is developed in this book is that there is a gap between lofty human rights rhetoric and the reality of human rights abuses in world politics. In *The Age of Rights*, Louis Henkin claims that universal human rights are "the idea of our time."[7] Writing after the fall of the Berlin Wall and as the Cold War was coming to an end, Henkin made this claim at a time of great optimism about world politics. With the demise of the Soviet Union at the end of the 1980s came hope for a "New World Order" that would usher in an era of idealism in international relations, an era that would be characterized by international cooperation and international norms promoting economic prosperity, political freedom, and human progress. However, it was not difficult to criticize the idealism of Henkin's claim, even amidst the heady optimism of the early 1990s. Torture, political repression, genocide, abject poverty, discrimination, and inequality have been a standard feature of life for many human beings throughout this century, before and after the Cold War. In short, a gap between rhetoric and reality characterizes Henkin's "age of rights."

This gap between rhetoric and reality is built into the system of international human rights law that has evolved since the end of World War II. The idea of human rights first achieved a prominent place on the international agenda of states in the aftermath of World War II. The United Nations, created at the end of the war, incorporates explicit references to human rights in its charter and states that one of the fundamental purposes of the organization is to promote respect for and to reaffirm faith in human rights. In 1948, the UN General Assembly adopted the Universal Declaration of Human Rights, which identifies a wide range of political and economic rights as basic human rights. However, the Declaration is not a binding legal document. Moreover, the UN Charter also codifies the principle of state sovereignty and makes interference in the internal affairs of sovereign states a violation of international law. Furthermore, states with egregious human rights records are often parties to major human rights documents, so critics point to this hypocrisy as evidence that international human rights law is an idealistic aspiration without power or force. Formal acceptance of human rights norms on the part of states means nothing insofar as states are able to act with impunity within their own borders and so long as human rights abuses continue across the globe. Thus, despite the important political and legal change represented by the passage of the Declaration and the inclusion of human rights provisions in the UN Charter, state sovereignty, as a general rule, has continued to trump the universalism of human rights norms in both law and practice.

The gap between the rhetoric and reality of the "age of rights" has characterized world politics during and after the Cold War era. During the Cold War, the bipolar structure of an international system dominated by two superpowers, the United States and the Soviet Union, constituted the overarching framework for understanding world politics. Within this framework, traditional national security concerns dominated both the study and practice of world politics. With the end of the Cold War, many analysts of international affairs believed that member states of the United Nations, freed from the constraining effects of bipolar ideological rivalry, might be more likely to take seriously the human rights dimensions of the United Nations mandate. Instead, the world witnessed an apparent increase in ethnic conflicts, civil wars, and widespread human rights abuses across much of the globe, in places like Rwanda, Bosnia, Kosovo, and Indonesia. Although it became involved in efforts to mitigate the violence, the United Nations, and the international community in general, failed to prevent large-scale violence and gross violations of human rights in each of these cases. The fulfillment of the human rights dimensions of the UN Charter remains an aspiration and not a reality.

Although violence and human rights abuses appeared to proliferate across the globe at the end of the Cold War, the truth is that such ethnic and civil conflict was a constant feature of world politics throughout the Cold War. During the Cold War, many individuals living in relative stability in Europe, North America, and elsewhere in the developed world were uninformed or unconcerned about civil violence and human rights abuses elsewhere across the globe. While it is true that civil conflict has indeed increased in certain regions, notably Europe, the post–Cold War era has simply raised global awareness of the smaller-scale violent conflicts that have been present throughout this century in much of the world, but that were previously ignored. For many scholars of world politics, these violent conflicts are cause for pessimism and are a sign that violence, in whatever form, is an inevitable feature of world politics. For other scholars, although these conflicts are a real cause for concern, the post–Cold War era also presents new opportunities for preventing violence in a war-torn world and for elevating the pursuit of principle over narrow national interest in world politics.

Given these conflicting viewpoints, what is the student of human rights and world politics to make of Henkin's claim that we are living in an "age of rights"? If by the "age of rights" we mean that human beings across the globe are able to enjoy fundamental human rights, then clearly Henkin's argument falls short. However, Henkin contends that human rights are the *idea*—not necessarily the reality—of our time. He argues that the idea of human rights, even if only recognized by hypocritical governments, remains important: "Even if it be hypocrisy, it is significant—since hypocrisy, we know, is the homage that vice pays to virtue—that human rights is today the single, paramount virtue to which vice pays homage, that governments today do not feel free to preach what they may persist in practicing."[8]

Despite its continued importance, state sovereignty does not have the unchallenged status that it once had in world politics, and states increasingly are constrained by human rights norms, at least rhetorically. Consider the following. At the end of World War II, the victorious powers were preoccupied with the question of how to deal with imprisoned Nazi leaders. Although ultimately Allied leaders decided to create the Nuremberg Tribunal to try Nazi leaders, the pursuit of this juridical solution was not a foregone conclusion. Stalin initially favored the option of summary execution, without trial, for Nazi leaders, and Henry Morgenthau Jr., then U.S. Secretary of State, proposed deporting several million Germans. Prime Minister Churchill and President Roosevelt even considered castration of German males as an option.[9]

Compare this situation with the debate over the "war on terror" in the wake of the September 11, 2001, terrorist attacks on the United States. One of the major questions in this debate has been whether or not the Bush Administration has the right to try alleged terrorists in military tribunals as opposed to the regular court system. While there are serious and legitimate concerns about the extent to which military tribunals adequately promote due process for defendants, it is notable that in this case military tribunals are criticized for not sufficiently protecting the basic rights of alleged terrorists. In contrast, in the aftermath of World War II, the military tribunal at Nuremberg represented *the* legalist option, as opposed to extra-judicial summary execution of Nazi leaders, deportation, or even castration of thousands of Germans. The "age of rights" may only have elevated the importance of human rights norms in state decision making in an imperfect way, but it appears to have changed the terms of debate and the available options for states to a considerable extent.

In another example of the way in which human rights norms are challenging the supremacy of state sovereignty as a governing principle in world politics, Augusto Pinochet, a former head of state in Chile, was arrested in England in 1998 as a result of a Spanish request to extradite him to Spain to face criminal charges of genocide, terrorism, torture, and forced disappearances during his rule in Chile. Although Great Britain ultimately released the elderly and ailing Pinochet on "humanitarian grounds," the initial arrest represented an unprecedented challenge to the sovereign immunity of former heads of state on the grounds of fulfilling universal human rights norms.

As these examples suggest, it is currently more likely than ever before that states will embrace human rights rhetoric, at least in principle. Rather than denying the validity of human rights claims, a state commonly will assert that its political and economic system does a better job of promoting human rights than competing states. When confronted with allegations of abuse, a state is likely to deny these allegations and, typically, will depict its own citizens as the real victims of human rights abuses. States commonly brandish the principle of human rights as a weapon against their strategic and ideological enemies. In this way, the rhetorical power of the principle of human rights, even if states do not always practice what they preach, represents a progress of sorts.

Henkin's argument reflects an increasingly prominent strand of thinking in the field of international relations which contends that ideas matter. The notion that ideas are important challenges mainstream approaches to the study of world politics which argue that interests, either political or economic, are the driving force behind world politics. Scholars of international relations who believe that ideas, and not just interests, matter counter that changes in ideas help to account for the ways in which individuals, groups, and states define their interests and, in this way, can shape policy in significant ways.[10] Yet even if one accepts that ideas matter, it seems reasonable to ask whether or not Henkin's claim still has value at the dawn of the twenty-first century. If the end of the Cold War signaled the triumph of the "age of rights," then did the terrorist attacks on the United States on September 11, 2001, usher in a new "age of terror"?

Clearly, these terrorist attacks have had a major impact on Americans' ideas about world politics. Concerns with national security are again at the top of the political agenda in the United States. Although the United States seeks to try some alleged terrorists that it has detained in military tribunals, as discussed above, there also is evidence that the United States has signaled its silent support of summary execution of alleged terrorists by our allies in the war on terror, including Pakistan, Egypt, and Malaysia.[11] The United States has increased aid to allies in its war on terror, regardless of the human rights records of these states. Additionally, the United States has sent suspected terrorists to countries known to use torture for interrogation as part of its "war on terror." More recently, the United States government has been scandalized by revelations of torture of Iraqi prisoners by American military personnel at the Abu Ghraib detention facility in Iraq as well as other prisons in Iraq and Afghanistan.[12] In the United States, then, there are signs that a new era of preoccupation with security in the face of terrorist threats has displaced the "age of rights," to the extent that this age ever existed.

Ultimately, students of human rights are faced with a daunting challenge as they begin to explore this topic: If the principle of human rights is powerful primarily as an idea and if the power of this idea has been trumped by concerns with national security in the face of new threats, then what merit is there in studying the subject at all? One can respond to this legitimate concern in two ways. First, one does not have to concede the point that the power of human rights rhetoric has been displaced by the war on terror. Citizens and residents of the United States have been understandably traumatized by the attacks on their fellow citizens and residents and on their country's soil. Yet proponents of human rights within this country remain undaunted in their support of universal norms. Human rights advocates who live in countries sadly more familiar with the terrorizing effects of violence against innocent civilians remain passionate about the importance of the principle of human rights and, indeed, see the advancement of human rights as a goal essentially related to, rather than separate from, the objective of living in a world secure from terrorist attacks. Second, ideas are not static. They are human creations, and citizens play a key role in determining which ideas have power. If students of human rights understand the power of human rights norms, they, as citizens, can play a role in giving these ideas the prominence they deserve.

ORGANIZATION OF THE BOOK

This book is organized into three parts. In each of these sections, the chapters will develop the organizing arguments articulated in this introduction. Specifically, the chapters develop and explore more fully the potential tension between sovereignty and human rights and the gap between idealistic human rights rhetoric and the reality of human rights abuses across the globe. In Part I: Human Rights in Theory and Law, students will explore the legal and philosophical underpinnings of the concept of human rights. Chapter 1 considers philosophical, legal, and political problems associated with efforts to reach international consensus on a basic definition of human rights. Chapter 2 provides an overview of the development of and an introduction to the core body of international human rights law. It also considers feminist critiques of international human rights law. Chapter 3 explores various moral and philosophical arguments both for and against the concept of human rights. Chapter 3 also considers the question of whether human rights standards are or should be considered universal or whether different cultural standards or interpretations of human rights are acceptable. The chapters in Part I provide ample evidence of the gap between the rhetoric and reality of human rights in world politics.

In Part II: Human Rights in Practice, students will have an opportunity to apply the theoretical insights from Part I as they explore the place of human rights in world politics through an examination of concrete issues. The chapters in Part II examine in great detail the potential tension between state sovereignty and human rights. Chapter 4 highlights the tension between civil and political rights and state sovereignty, with a special focus on the "war on terror" and on the issue of self-determination. Although this chapter emphasizes the tension between sovereignty and human rights, it also considers the potential contributions of state sovereignty to stability in world politics and the ways in which threats to sovereignty may make it more difficult for states to uphold certain human rights norms. Chapter 5 examines genocide as an extreme example of the breakdown of a moral order protecting basic human rights, and Chapter 6 explores economic and social rights as basic human rights. Chapter 7 discusses gender equity and sexual orientation as these topics relate to human rights through several case studies, including violence against women, sexual violence during war, and sexual orientation discrimination.

Students will turn to an examination of the promotion and protection of human rights norms in Part III: Human Rights and the Quest for Justice. These chapters illustrate the ways in which sovereignty, to date, has limited the promotion of universal human rights norms across the globe. Chapter 8 looks at foreign policy mechanisms used by states in an effort to promote and protect human rights norms, as well as elements of the United Nations system designed to monitor, prevent, and/or punish human rights abuses. Chapter 8 also includes a case study of humanitarian intervention. In Chapter 9, students will be introduced to the concept of punitive justice and will evaluate various mechanisms for punishing war crimes and human rights abuses, including trials, purges, and reparations. Chapter 10 introduces the concept of restorative justice and examines truth commissions, reparations, and apologies as mechanisms for fostering reconciliation in the aftermath of war crimes and human rights abuses. In Chapter 11, students will look at the role of nongovernmental organizations and individuals in promoting human rights norms. Although the chapters in Part III demonstrate that a gap between the rhetoric and reality of human rights still exists in world politics, they also discuss the ways in which this gap has narrowed and consider the ways in which human rights advocates might bring the reality of human rights closer to the ideal in the future. The book concludes with a review of the status of human rights at the dawn of the twenty-first century and challenges students to consider the role that they might play as citizens, both of their nation-state and the world, to further the advancement of human rights norms.

1

The Contested Meaning
of Human Rights

THE POLITICAL NATURE
OF HUMAN RIGHTS

For two weeks in June 1993, representatives of 171 governments met in Vienna for the World Conference on Human Rights. This widespread participation of state actors in global deliberations over human rights was unprecedented. In comparison, fewer than 60 states participated in the deliberations over the Universal Declaration of Human Rights, adopted by the UN General Assembly in 1948. Notably, because the General Assembly adopted the Universal Declaration prior to decolonization, not only were a smaller number of states involved in developing early international human rights law, but the states that created the Universal Declaration did not represent the range of political and cultural diversity across the globe. As a result, one can conclude that the work done at the World Conference on Human Rights more accurately reflects the degree of global consensus on the meaning and nature of human rights.

It is precisely this fact that makes it so remarkable that such a large number of politically and culturally diverse states adopted by consensus the Vienna Declaration and Programme of Action, the final report of the conference. The consensus that underlies the Vienna Declaration is especially notable because of the unequivocal endorsement the document gives to the universal nature of human rights. The Vienna Declaration affirms "that the human person is the central subject of human rights and fundamental freedoms, and conse-

quently should be the principal beneficiary . . . of these rights and freedoms."
In the first paragraph of Section I, the Vienna Declaration states: "The universal nature of these rights and freedoms is beyond question." In paragraph five
of Section I, the document notes that cultural, religious, and political differences must be taken into account but continues to stress the unquestionably
universal nature of human rights: "While the significance of national and regional particularities and various historical, cultural and religious backgrounds
must be borne in mind, it is the duty of States, regardless of their political,
economic, and cultural systems, to promote and protect all human rights and
fundamental freedoms."

The fact that states representing the cultural, religious and political diversity of every region of the world participated in a conference that produced
such unequivocal language about the nature of human rights suggests that the
meaning of human rights is beyond controversy. Yet if we look at the news
from across the globe, the reality of ongoing human rights abuses suggests that
universal acceptance of human rights rhetoric among states has not resulted in
universal interpretations of the meaning of human rights in practice. How can
states express unambiguous support for human rights while perpetrating and
rationalizing practices that constitute violations of fundamental human rights?
This chapter suggests that although states have moved toward consensus that
all human beings have fundamental rights, they continue to disagree on the
precise meaning and content of these rights.

In an effort to explain this gap between state rhetoric and the reality of
how states interpret and implement human rights in practice, this book begins
with a detailed examination of the contested meaning of human rights. While
students might think it unnecessarily tedious and overly analytical to delve
too deeply into definitional controversies, doing so is essential. Human rights
involve contested moral principles over which significant political struggles
occur. Efforts to define and categorize human rights are complicated and sus-
ceptible to political manipulation. Even with apparent agreement on the universality of human rights, global consensus does not exist on the precise
meaning and content of human rights in practice. In short, the process of defining human rights is inherently political. Students interested in understanding and furthering human rights as moral principles will be well served to
comprehend that to claim human rights is to engage in politics.

DEFINING THE CONCEPT
OF HUMAN RIGHTS

Human rights have been defined simply as "the rights one has because one is
human."[1] The simplicity of this definition is appealing, and most students can
grasp the essential meaning of the concept of human rights when they hear it.
Yet this definition technically is a tautology, in which the terms of the concept

"human rights" are repeated without providing any additional meaning. In order to understand more fully the concept of human rights, we need to delve more deeply into the meaning of its constitutive terms. When we examine these terms more closely, we gain insight into why the concept of human rights is at the center of many of the most widely disputed and contentious issues of our time.

What does it mean to be a human being? At first glance, the answer to this question seems to be so readily apparent that the question seems laughable. Webster's dictionary defines a human quite simply and straightforwardly as "a person." So, all persons—all human beings—have basic rights simply because they exist as humans. However, once again, simple definitions mask the complexities underlying the concept of human rights. Although most of us probably agree that any human being born to life on the face of the planet constitutes a person, history provides us with widespread evidence that such agreement on universal personhood has been widely contested across many cultures and historical periods. The denial of the essential humanity of African men, women, and children with dark skin underlie the violence of the transatlantic slave trade and the institution of slavery during the eighteenth and nineteenth centuries. Similar racist ideology is used to justify the continued existence of slavery across the globe today. A Nazi ideology that denied the humanity of Jewish people was used to rationalize the extermination of millions of Jews during the Holocaust. A hierarchy of personhood underlies the inequity and violence of the caste system in India. In many cultures, both historically and at present, women have been denied equal rights because they have been viewed as lesser persons than men. The contentious debate over abortion in the United States centers in large part on the question of when human personhood begins. As these examples illustrate, the essential meaning of personhood is contested. When people disagree on the meaning of personhood, disagreement on "the rights one has because one is human" inevitably follows.

Not only has there been a historical lack of consensus on *who* is a person, but variation has also marked various cultural and political perspectives on *how* human beings perceive and experience their humanity and, as a result, on how human rights should be fulfilled. Liberal democratic states and political cultures are more likely to view human beings as distinct and separate individuals who perceive and experience their humanity autonomously. Thus, in liberal democratic traditions, human rights are typically viewed as *individual* rights held by individual human beings that take priority over any obligations that individuals may have as members of larger groups, including their religion, culture, or state. In contrast, states and political cultures shaped heavily by communitarian traditions typically reject the idea of "autonomous individuals" as a fiction. According to a communitarian perspective, individual human beings cannot survive or flourish outside of the social structures in which they live. Communitarians believe that human beings perceive and experience their humanity first and foremost as members of groups. As a result, communitarian states and political cultures tend to view human rights, to the extent that they exist, as *group* rights and to stress the obligations that individuals have to the groups to which they belong. Clashing viewpoints over whether human rights are primarily individual or group rights signal that the basic meaning of human rights is contested, belying the simplicity of the definition of human rights as rights one has because one is human.

To define human rights as "the rights one has because one is human" also fails to give adequate consideration to the meaning of the term *rights.* Webster's dictionary defines a right as "that to which one is morally or legally entitled." In this case, the dictionary definition is helpful in highlighting a distinction that serves as an obstacle to global consensus on the precise meaning of human rights in practice. As this definition suggests, a right may be a moral or legal entitlement. A legal entitlement refers to rights that one has because they are codified in law. So, human beings have legal rights that are codified by the laws of their communities, states, and the international community. In contrast, a moral entitlement refers to rights that are claimed by human beings on moral grounds. Moral entitlements involve appeals made on the basis of moral philosophy. Individuals claiming moral rights are making normative appeals—human beings *should* have the human right in question—when the claimed right is being denied or abused. Typically, such normative appeals are made when formal legal entitlements protecting the claimed rights do not exist or when legal entitlements are not being upheld.[2]

Once again, a more detailed consideration of the meaning of the term *rights* helps to illustrate why it is so difficult to achieve global consensus on the meaning of human rights in practice. States concerned with protecting their sovereignty typically adhere to a concept of rights as legal entitlements. In this way, states believe they are only obligated to protect or provide those rights to which they have consented in the law, either domestic or international. Conversely, human rights activists and the victims of human rights abuses typically view them as moral entitlements, and the political discourse of human rights is grounded in moral appeals explicitly intended to expand the range of legal entitlements available to human beings across the globe. Indeed, most of the advances in domestic and international law in terms of extending basic rights to human beings have begun with moral appeals by activists and victims of human rights abuses. To the extent that the law represents the interests of the powerful, moral appeals have been the weapon of the weak in the global effort to advance human rights.

To define a right as "that to which one is morally or legally entitled" also does not clarify what it means to say a human being has basic "entitlements." Who is responsible for ensuring that human beings actually enjoy the rights to which they are morally or legally entitled? Presumably, if rights are legal entitlements, then the body that produced the law in question is obligated to ensure that humans enjoy these entitlements. For example, a state that adopts laws providing for certain basic legal entitlements is responsible for upholding them. However, what if an institution provides for legal entitlements on paper but does not implement them in practice? Does this failure in implementation suggest that the legal entitlements are not really rights at all? This problem is particularly vexing at the international level, where a wide variety of international laws provide for basic human rights but where there are few institutions with the authority to implement or enforce these norms. When institutions do not have the power or authority to enforce the rights that are supposedly provided by the law, can it truly be said that "legal entitlements" exist?

Moral entitlements raise even more difficulties because they involve normative appeals claiming that states (or the international community or other relevant actors) *should* uphold basic rights in the absence of any formal commitment on their part to do so. The fulfillment of moral entitlements depends on the will of the governmental body to which the appeal is being made. Because governments can choose to uphold or violate "moral entitlements" at will, we can question whether or not they should be considered "entitlements" in any meaningful sense of the word, if by entitlement we are referring to something individuals deserve and have a reasonable expectation of receiving. Moreover, the idea of moral entitlements is difficult because of widely varying cultural and ideological perspectives on morality. If proponents of human rights cannot point to concrete laws to validate human rights claims, then on what grounds can they "prove" that moral entitlements actually exist? Jerome J. Shestack, a philosopher of human rights, states the dilemma simply: "What makes certain rights universal, moral, and important, and who decides?"[3]

This exploration of the definition of human rights has complicated more than it has clarified. We began with a simple definition of human rights as "rights one has simply because one is human." We are left with a sense that it is difficult to define human rights in a way that generates global consensus. Global consensus continues to elude us both in terms of what it means to be human and what it means to have rights. Although it is frustrating to work with definitions that are not concrete, it is essential that students of human rights recognize the contested nature of the concept. Ultimately, human rights are not something concrete that we can simply define, identify, and implement, although human rights activists and scholars certainly wish for such simplicity.

Rather, human rights represent ideals over which conflicting groups will continue to struggle. Human rights activists and scholars will continue to push for a definition of human rights based on a broad and inclusive conception of what it means to be human and stressing a wide range of moral claims to which humans are entitled. States, groups, and individuals who are resistant to a progressive human rights agenda will commonly define humanity in more particular and limited ways and will be more likely to view rights simply as legal entitlements to which states must consent. In short, even if they agree on the universality of human rights, various states, non-state actors, and individuals continue to disagree on the precise meaning of human rights. Once again, the process of defining human rights is inherently *political*.

THE PHILOSOPHICAL ORIGINS
AND SOURCES OF HUMAN RIGHTS

As the preceding discussion illustrates, the process of defining human rights is inherently political. Accordingly, the arguments used to justify human rights have varied based on the historical context in which such claims have been advanced and the political interests and ideologies of the individuals and groups articulating these claims. The earliest human rights claims involved moral justifications grounded in religion. Religious justifications for human rights are based on the belief that a Supreme Being is the ultimate moral authority whose mandates override the laws of the state. This divine power considers all human beings sacred and, thus, requires that they be treated with equal dignity and respect.[4]

Two of the most important political documents first articulating claims for fundamental human rights, the U.S. Declaration of Independence and the French Declaration of the Rights of Man and Citizen, were clearly shaped by such religious overtones. In both the cases of the American and French revolutions, revolutionaries claimed certain inalienable rights as moral entitlements and pointed to God as the ultimate source of these fundamental rights. The U.S. Declaration of Independence claimed that "all Men . . . are endowed by their Creator with certain inalienable rights." Similarly, the French Declaration of the Rights of Man and Citizen asserted that there are "natural, inalienable, and sacred rights of man" that are enjoyed "under the auspices of the Supreme Being." Note the exclusionary language that does not explicitly provide that women enjoy the same rights as men, a criticism that we will take up in Chapter 2 and Chapter 7. For the purposes of our current discussion, the interesting point is that God or a Supreme Being was claimed as the ultimate source of fundamental rights in these cases.

Although this Supreme Being is not explicitly identified as a Christian God, the fact that the revolutionary thinkers who shaped these documents and movements were predominantly Christian may limit the power of this justification for non-Christian people and for individuals who do not believe in a "Supreme Being." Indeed, critics of the idea of universal human rights point to what they perceive as the Christian underpinnings of these particular claims as evidence that the idea of universal human rights reflects a "Western bias" that has limited applicability in the non-Western world. However, most religions include teachings that emphasize the sacred nature of human beings and a common humanity deriving from a shared divine "father."[5] Thus, religious justifications for human rights may provide the basis for a universal morality, at least to peoples of religious faith. However, because of the great religious diversity among people across the globe, religion as a universally accepted source validating human rights remains problematic. Moreover, the masculine identity of most religious visions of a higher power may help to explain why various religious traditions simultaneously claim that human beings are equal under the eyes of a Supreme Being at the same time that they sanction the denial of equal rights to women under religious laws and traditions.

Secular variants of natural rights theory also shaped early revolutionary movements claiming human rights. According to natural rights theory, articulated most prominently in the writings of John Locke, human beings in a "state of nature" lived in absolute freedom. However, when they came together to form social and political institutions out of self-interest, they voluntarily agreed to give up some freedom in order to gain the security of community. In doing so, they retained fundamental rights that they did not explicitly relinquish in the social contract. Indeed, according to natural rights theory, the primary purpose of government is to protect the natural rights of its subjects.[6] Natural rights theory profoundly shaped eighteenth-century revolutionary movements in the United States and Europe. Although these revolutions are marked by significant differences, the English, American, and French revolutions all represented at a basic level struggles against absolute monarchy. Drawing on natural rights theory, these revolutionary movements placed a high priority on individual liberties, particularly property rights.

Today, critics of universal human rights point to the emphasis on individual property rights in these early human rights movements as evidence that the concept of universal human rights is biased toward the economic interests of property-owning elites. Accordingly, these critics charge that the idea of human rights is ineffective as a tool for capturing the fundamental needs of most people across the globe. Nevertheless, it is important to bear in mind the historical context in which these early natural rights claims were articulated. These eighteenth-century rights movements were revolutionary in claiming that individuals had rights that absolutist governments could not violate and were bound to protect. They were egalitarian in the sense that they sought to reduce the privileges of the aristocracy and to broaden property rights. In many respects, they did represent the interests of economic elites, as upper-middle-class owners of capital sought to break down the state's monopoly on economic as well as political power. Yet, at a basic level, it is important to remember that the idea of property rights is not an inherently elitist one. When John Locke first wrote of the natural right to life, liberty, and property, he was not writing of the right of the wealthy to hoard riches. He was writing first and foremost of individuals' right to enjoy the fruits of their own labor; a human being's "personhood" and labor were the most important forms of property.[7] Thus, Locke's theory of natural rights has been used to argue against the evils of slavery as much as it has been used to justify the hoarding of riches by economic elites.

Natural rights theory remains a predominant influence in contemporary debates over the concept of human rights. Indeed, the Universal Declaration of Human Rights, adopted in 1948, was clearly shaped by a natural rights perspective. The appeal to natural law is evident in its Preamble, which speaks of the "inherent dignity and of the equal and inalienable rights of all members of the human family." Like the U.S. Declaration of Independence and the French Declaration on the Rights of Man and Citizen, the Universal Declaration of

Human Rights refers to "inalienable rights." However, it differs from these previous documents by using inclusive language (referring to the rights of "the human family" and not "the rights of man") and by eliminating references to God or a Supreme Being as the ultimate source of rights. In this way, it represents a variant of secular natural rights theory in that it argues that "equal and inalienable rights" for all humans serve as "the foundation of freedom, justice, and peace in the world."

Although natural rights theory has been a major influence on the growing body of international human rights law, it remains on philosophically shaky ground. Despite widespread formal acceptance of the idea that all human beings have "equal and inalienable rights" in the abstract, the reality that states continue to abuse human rights with impunity across the globe, often with the support of their populations, indicates that people across the globe continue to disagree on the rights that should be considered "inalienable." As long as this is the case, the idea of natural rights can be only an imperfect justification for human rights.

Utilitarianism represents a competing moral argument for rights that also originated during the period of the Enlightenment in Europe and profoundly shaped anti-absolutist revolutionary movements in eighteenth-century Europe and the United States. According to utilitarian philosophers, the justification for basic rights should be derived from a consideration of the general welfare. Jeremy Bentham, the most prominent early theorist of utilitarianism, identified the "general happiness principle" as the guiding moral principle in politics. Under the general happiness principle, the morality of a policy will be determined by a consideration of the greatest good for the greatest number. As a source of rights, utilitarianism suggests that human beings living within particular societies have rights only to the extent that the provision of such rights produces the greatest good for the greatest number. Bentham referred to claims that natural rights existed in the abstract as "nonsense on stilts." Instead, "both governments and the limits of governments were to be judged not by reference to abstract individual rights, but in terms of what tends to promote the greatest happiness of the greatest number. Because all count equally at the primary level, anyone may have to accept sacrifices if the benefits they yield to others are large enough to outweigh such sacrifices."[8]

In some respects, utilitarianism has made important contributions to the advancement of basic political rights in asserting that the legitimacy of governments should be based on its impact on the majority of people living within a polity. At the same time, utilitarian philosophy is limited in terms of providing a moral justification for human rights. Although utilitarianism represents a strand of liberal political thought that was influential in the struggle against absolutism and in the establishment of democracy in Europe and the United States in the eighteenth century, it can be consistent with violations of human rights. In contrast to a human rights perspective stressing the inviolability of fundamental rights under any circumstances, utilitarianism suggests that the ends can justify the means: Utilitarianism would justify violations of the fundamental human rights of certain individuals or minorities if such violations produced a greater good for a society as a whole. According to the logic of utilitarianism, the violation of the basic rights of some people is not only acceptable but also moral so long as the violation of such rights contributes to "the greatest good for the greatest number."

In contrast to religious, natural rights, and utilitarian justifications for human rights, positivism points to the law and not moral principles as the ultimate source of human rights. Positivism is a legal doctrine that assumes "that all authority stems from what the state and [its] officials have prescribed."[9] According to this doctrine, there is no moral or divine law that transcends the authority of the state. Historically, a positivist perspective on human rights has simply meant that human beings have only the rights that are provided by the legal system of the state to which they are subject. In this way, positivism historically has been consistent with a Marxist perspective on human rights. Marxists, like positivists in general, believe that the only rights that human beings may claim are conferred by the state and, as such, are historically contingent. Marxists view rights as collective, rather than individual, and, as a result, stress the obligations that individuals have to the state as coming before the rights that individuals may claim from the state.

Although Marxism and positivism share certain assumptions about the state as the ultimate source of human rights, positivism is not necessarily inconsistent with the concept of universal human rights. As a result of the creation of a large body of international human rights law in the aftermath of World War II, a positivist justification for human rights now exists. Proponents of human rights who wish to avoid the philosophical pitfalls involved in trying to justify human rights on moral grounds may simply point to the existence of a large body of international human rights law to which states have consented as evidence that universal human rights exist. The positivist perspective suggests that the only valid human rights are those rights agreed upon by sovereign states. In this regard, international human rights law is a product of sovereign states rather than an inherent challenge to state sovereignty.

The simplicity of the positivist perspective is appealing, and it is tempting to rely on positivist justifications for human rights because the existence of specific international human rights laws seems to settle the debate. As a result of the large body of international human rights law currently in existence, there appears to be no need to engage in the thorny and sometimes seemingly fruitless efforts to identify a universally accepted moral justification for human rights. If we can simply say that human rights are provided for in formal, legal documents, why do we need to engage in abstract arguments about the moral source of these rights? One response to this legitimate question is that the law, despite its political appeal, is an imperfect tool, especially at the international level. As we will see in Chapter 2, most laws providing for universal human rights represent statements of aspiration rather than concrete obligations for states. Even where concrete obligations do exist, very few mechanisms for enforcing international rights law exist. Sovereign states still exercise great discretion in determining whether or not human beings actually get to enjoy the human rights to which they are legally entitled. Ultimately, international human rights law means very little if it does not actually affect human beings' access to basic human rights. Thus, theorizing about the philosophical source of human rights remains an important component in any effort to identify compelling moral justifications for promoting the enjoyment of human rights in practice.

DEFINING AND CATEGORIZING
HUMAN RIGHTS IN PRACTICE

An exploration of the philosophical origins of human rights illustrates the profoundly political nature of the concept. Historically, human rights claims typically have been advanced by actors seeking to change broader political structures. The centrality of politics and ideology as forces shaping human rights claims is evident when one examines the way in which the content of human rights claims has evolved over time. Scholars commonly chronicle the evolution of human rights norms by distinguishing among "three generations" of rights.

The "first generation" of human rights claims, focusing on civil and political rights, emerged during the revolutionary era in Europe and the United States and was shaped by the struggle against absolutism. Specific examples of this first generation of human rights include the right to life, liberty, and security of person, the right to property, the right to freedom of speech and thought, the right to a fair trial, and the right to vote. First generation human rights also encompass prohibitions against slavery, torture, and arbitrary arrest and detention.

The "second generation" of human rights claims, stressing economic and social rights, emerged later and was shaped profoundly by twentieth-century revolutionary movements first in Russia and later in China. In the case of the Russian and Chinese revolutions, human rights claims had socialist origins and represented a reaction to the extremes of wealth and poverty that exist in capitalist societies. Despite the clear influence of socialist ideology on the "second generation" of human rights, this category is not exclusively a product of socialist revolutions. Indeed, U.S. President Franklin Delano Roosevelt identified the "freedom from want" (along with the freedom of speech and expression, the freedom to worship as one chooses, and the freedom from fear) as one of the basic four freedoms in his 1941 State of the Union Address. Specific examples of economic and social rights within this category include the right to work, the right to food, the right to housing, the right to medical care, and the right to education.

The "third generation" of human rights involves claims for solidarity rights that emerged out of mid-twentieth-century decolonization struggles across the globe, particularly in Africa. In this case, "third world" nationalism was a driving force behind claims for human rights as *collective* rather than individual rights. Specific examples of third generation solidarity rights include the right to self-determination, the right to economic development, the right to peace, and the right to a healthy environment. Interestingly, it should be noted that the right to self-determination and the right to economic development also have been claimed as individual rights.

Peter R. Baehr has noted that the use of the term *generations* is unfortunate in that it implies that each new generation takes the place of the former one. Instead, he claims that it is possible and desirable that "the three 'generations' exist and be respected simultaneously."[10] It is correct to note that each new generation of human rights did not displace previous generations. Moreover, it is true that the various rights claimed within the different categories are not necessarily in tension. For example, the Universal Declaration of Human Rights is based on the premise that universal human rights are the foundation for peace. If this premise is correct, then providing human beings with basic political rights, such as the right to vote, along with basic economic rights, including the right to a decent standard of living, will contribute to global peace. The assumption that the three categories of rights are interrelated in this way suggests that the protection of first generation political rights and the provision of second generation economic rights will contribute to third generation solidarity rights like the right to peace. According to this view, the generations of rights are connected and, indeed, can be seen as part of a seamless whole.

Nevertheless, it is important to note that the different generations of human rights *may* be in tension. For example, the first generation right to property and the third generation right to development commonly involve competing claims. The right to property has been categorized as a first generation civil right. The right to property suggests, of course, that *individuals* have a right to own property and to amass wealth. In contrast, the third generation right to development is claimed as a *collective* right. In the aftermath of decolonization, nationalist governments in newly independent countries commonly nationalized foreign-owned companies as a policy designed to foster national economic development. They justified these nationalizations as a means of fostering development as a *collective* right even though nationalization policies deprived foreign owners of their "property," not always with just compensation.

Not only may the different generations of rights conflict at times, but specific rights in each category may also be in tension with other rights claimed *within* the same generation. Within the first generation of civil and political rights, claims for freedom of religious expression may conflict with the right to be protected against discrimination. For example, claims that religious organizations should be compelled to adopt a nondiscrimination policy toward gay, lesbian, and bisexual persons in hiring practices are in tension with demands for freedom of religious expression that contend such policies would violate fundamental religious doctrines. The potential conflicts within as well as between the different generations of human rights highlight the political nature of human rights claims in practice.

In addition to categorizing human rights into different generations, human rights scholars often classify human rights as either "positive" or "negative." The terms *positive* and *negative* are not intended to signal that the rights labeled as such are either good or bad. Rather, they are used to indicate whether state action or inaction is required in order to fulfill the rights in question. Positive rights refer to the rights that individuals may claim from the state. Such rights require "positive" action on the part of the state; in other words, the state must take concrete steps to ensure that the rights in question are fulfilled. A claim for a positive human right typically is formulated as a "right to" something—for example, the right to life, the right to food, or the right to education. In contrast, negative rights refer to rights that are violated or abused by the state and, hence, that require inaction on the part of the state for their enjoyment. Because it requires the state to refrain from abusing the rights in question, a claim for a negative right is generally formulated as a "freedom from" something—for instance, freedom from torture, freedom from discrimination, or freedom from arbitrary detention.

Because there are differences between rights that require the state to take action and those that call for restraint on the part of the state, the distinction between positive and negative rights has some merit. Nevertheless, the categorization of rights as positive or negative has been misleading in an important respect. Commonly, the category of "negative rights" is used to refer strictly to civil and political rights that, it is assumed, simply require the state to refrain from acting in a rights-abusing manner. Conversely, the category of "positive rights" is applied primarily to economic and social rights that are believed to require positive state action to achieve their fulfillment. Ideological critics of economic and social rights often point to this categorization as a way of dismissing economic and social rights as goals that are too expensive and burdensome to implement and that will result in a state so large and powerful that it will be likely to violate civil and political rights. In this way, the categorization of rights as either negative or positive is used not only to signal that different rights require distinctive types of action for their enjoyment but also to suggest that different categories of rights are in tension and cannot be pursued simultaneously.

Despite the popularity of these assumptions, it is not necessarily true that civil and political rights are strictly negative rights and that economic and social rights are clearly positive rights. The state may have to take concrete actions to ensure that basic civil and political rights are fulfilled. For example, the right to vote typically requires significant involvement by state actors in order to ensure free and fair elections. In the United States, providing African Americans with the formal right to vote meant very little until the government adopted voting rights laws in the 1960s and provided human and financial resources directed at enforcing the right to vote. Charges of discriminatory practices in various states that are intended to suppress the vote of minorities continue to this day, and only concrete action on the part of the government will serve to eliminate such discrimination. In a federal system like the United States, the right to vote is both negative (it requires that the federal government and the various states refrain from adopting and implementing discriminatory voting requirements and procedures) and also positive (it requires the federal government and states to take action to ensure that other government actors—in this case, the various states or local governmental bodies—uphold the right to vote in a nondiscriminatory manner.) At the global level, the right to vote as a positive right is also demonstrated by the role that the United Nations has sought to play in providing election supervisors in an effort to ensure free and fair elections in newly independent countries or in countries emerging from conflict, such as Namibia, South Africa, Bosnia, and Cambodia, which did not have effective state institutions to serve this purpose.

Just as civil and political rights are not inherently negative rights, economic and social rights are not necessarily positive rights. Even though it is true that governments often need to take action to ensure that the basic economic and social rights of its citizens are met, there are times when inaction on the part of a government may better serve these ends. For example, in developing countries, governmental policies that have encouraged a shift from subsistence farming to cash crop production for export actually may have exacerbated poverty in these countries. In these cases, inaction on the part of the government might have been more likely to foster the achievement of basic economic rights. Similarly, development policies that encourage urbanization and industrialization have often had a detrimental impact on women and children to the extent that they make investments based on the often erroneous assumption that men will use new wage earnings to improve the welfare of their families. In reality, development policies with these gender-biased assumptions have disrupted traditional subsistence economies in ways that have had harmful effects on the basic needs of women and children. In these cases, governmental inaction might have better served the goal of promoting fundamental economic and social rights.

For the sake of clarity and simplicity, it would be nice if students of human rights could rely on simple categorizations in the effort to understand human rights. The work of human rights activists would be easier if they could simply state that certain rights require government inaction while other rights require action. Such simplicity also appeals to ideologues on both the right and left who want to make the case that either a small state or a large state is inherently more likely to provide and protect fundamental human rights. Reality is more complicated. Sometimes human rights require positive action on the part of the state, and other times the cause of human rights will be better served by state restraint. Certain rights, such as the right to vote, may actually require both action and restraint on the part of the state. Just as it would be easier if students of human rights could rely on simple categorizations, it would be nice if we could assume that good things always go together. In the real world, human rights claims sometimes reflect objectives that are in tension. Thus, the pursuit of human rights is an inherently political process that involves necessary trade-offs.

Moreover, precisely because of the political nature of human rights claims, the concept of human rights is often intentionally politicized and manipulated by actors using human rights rhetoric as a weapon toward entirely different political ends. For example, during the Cold War, human rights rhetoric was abused by both parties to this grand ideological conflict. The U.S. government decried Soviet abuse of fundamental civil and political rights as a way of discrediting claims for economic and social rights in the United States. Conversely, the Soviets pointed to extreme poverty and racial inequality in the United States as evidence that it was not possible to pursue civil and political rights simultaneously with economic and social rights and that economic and social rights should be given inherent priority. Neither government was inclined to look inward at its own inadequacies in terms of the fulfillment of basic human rights. Despite the employment of human rights rhetoric by both the United States and the Soviet Union during the Cold War, the foreign policy of each country was driven more by power considerations than a principled concern for fundamental human rights.

This section has highlighted how politics and ideology have fundamentally shaped the evolution of the concept of human rights. The way in which human rights have been defined and categorized in practice at various points in history reflects the different political and ideological priorities of the various political actors involved in this struggle. As this overview suggests, the divergent definitions of human rights among states sometimes represent genuine differences of perspective regarding the fundamental nature of rights. Other times, states employ critical human rights rhetoric not for genuinely principled reasons but because human rights rhetoric can be used to advance strategic interests. The complexities involved in defining and categorizing human rights illustrate why it is so important to study the topic of human rights carefully.

CONCLUSIONS

The basic purpose of this chapter has been to demonstrate that critical thinking about the meaning of human rights is essential for students interested in both understanding human rights in the classroom and promoting human rights in the real world. Proponents of human rights cannot propose appropriate policies intended to foster human rights without careful consideration of the best means of pursuing human rights objectives. Such careful consideration is not possible without critical thinking about the complexities involved in defining and categorizing human rights. Similarly, students of human rights cannot conscientiously evaluate the human rights policies of states unless they are aware of the political nature of these policies and the ways in which states may manipulate the idea of human rights.

Although this chapter has highlighted the importance of exploring the contested meaning of human rights as a means of understanding the dilemmas involved in efforts to advance the cause of human rights across the globe, abstract critical thinking alone will be insufficient in mobilizing political action designed to further human rights. Providing thoughtful definitions and philosophically sound justifications for human rights will be insufficient as a means of convincing policymakers, governing elites, and citizens of various states across the globe that the idea of human rights is a moral principle worth fighting for. In the aftermath of World War II, the philosopher Edmond Cahn suggested that philosophizing about justice represented a form of contemplation, and "contemplation bakes no loaves."[11] In contrast, he believed that exposure to the effects of real injustice would be more likely to provoke political action. In a similar vein, Richard Rorty has written that "the emergence of human rights culture seems to owe nothing to increased moral knowledge and everything to hearing sad and sentimental stories."[12]

As students of human rights, we are obligated to consider all of the definitional, philosophical, and political complexities raised by the claim that universal human rights exist. As advocates of human rights, it is incumbent on us to remember that the study of human rights should not just be an exercise in abstract thought. Rather, the issue of human rights is important and controversial precisely because it involves real human suffering, and it is a concern for this human suffering that ultimately motivates the study of human rights.

DISCUSSION QUESTIONS

1. What are some of the problems associated with defining human rights simply as "the rights one has because one is human"? Can you think of good reasons for relying on this simple definition?

2. To what extent does the fact that is difficult to define human rights in a universally accepted manner reduce the validity of the concept?

3. Which of the philosophical justifications for human rights do you find most persuasive? Which of the philosophical justifications for human rights do you find the least compelling? Why?

4. Utilitarianism suggests that the ends can justify the means. According to this perspective, a state could be justified in violating the basic rights of some people if doing so would produce a greater good for the majority of people in a society. Is this utilitarian logic persuasive? Why or why not?

5. Is it useful to categorize human rights into different generations? Why or why not?

6. Is the distinction between "positive rights" and "negative rights" helpful? Why or why not?

WEB RESOURCES

The Internet Encyclopedia of Philosophy: Human Rights (http://www.utm.edu/research/iep/h/hum-rts.htm)

A Short History of the Human Rights Movement: Early Political, Religious, and Philosophical Sources (http://www.hrweb.org/history.html)

Stanford Encyclopedia of Philosophy: Human Rights (http://plato.stanford.edu/entries/rights-human/)

2

The Development
of International
Human Rights Law

DOES INTERNATIONAL HUMAN RIGHTS
LAW MATTER?

Prior to World War II, international human rights law had not emerged as a distinct body of international law. Although states had adopted legal norms governing state conduct during war as well as norms prohibiting slavery, international laws asserting broad fundamental human rights for all human beings simply did not exist. Beginning with the adoption of the Universal Declaration of Human Rights by the United Nations General Assembly in 1948, the development of international human rights law since World War II has been prolific and impressive. The body of international human rights law now includes numerous binding treaties ranging from general treaties calling for the promotion and protection of basic civil and political as well as economic and social rights to treaties demanding human rights protections for particular groups, including women and children, to specialized treaties governing specific violations of human rights, such as torture and genocide. To say that development of international human rights law over the past fifty years has been impressive would be an understatement.

At the same time, gaps in the body of international human rights law still leave some individuals and groups, particularly sexual minorities, unprotected. Moreover, international human rights law is characterized by a significant gap between ambitious human rights norms codified in international law and weak enforcement mechanisms that reflect the continued importance of state sovereignty as the core organizing principle of international relations. In addition, states with egregious human rights records are often parties to major human rights treaties. This gap between idealistic rhetoric and reality helps to explain the continued existence of widespread human rights abuses across the globe. Thus, despite notable advancement in the development of international human rights norms, progress in the actual status of global human rights in practice has been less inspiring. Jeremy Bentham once called natural rights "nonsense on stilts," and skeptics who doubt the power of international human rights law might be tempted to dismiss it in a similar manner.

Nevertheless, this chapter suggests that international human rights law can be an important political tool in the global struggle for human rights. Both states and non-state actors increasingly employ international human rights norms in articulating their political views and demands. States have also drawn on international human rights law in developing national constitutions, policies, and legal decisions, a topic that will be covered in greater detail in Chapter 8 and Chapter 9. Thus, even with weak enforcement mechanisms, international human rights law retains the potential to dramatically shape the political behavior of states and non-state actors and, ultimately, the status of human rights across the globe. For this reason, it is incumbent upon students of human rights to have a clear understanding of the historical development and political underpinnings of international human rights law and its consequent strengths and weaknesses.

THE HISTORICAL FOUNDATIONS
OF INTERNATIONAL HUMAN RIGHTS LAW

Prior to World War II, the idea of human rights remained relatively obscure as a force in world politics. Eighteenth-century debates about "natural rights" fundamentally shaped revolutionary movements in Europe and the United States and served in large part as the foundation for the liberal democratic governments that emerged out of these conflicts. Despite the profound influence of natural rights theory on political development in the West, the idea of *human* rights did not play a major role in international relations across the globe in subsequent centuries. Instead, the principle of state sovereignty has been the core organizing principle of international relations since it emerged at the Peace of Westphalia in 1648.

Although state sovereignty was not significantly challenged as an organizing principle of international relations until World War II, important exceptions to this general rule exist. Transnational political movements seeking to abolish slavery drew upon the idea of "natural rights" to advance their cause. The first "success" of the antislavery movement came in 1885 when Europe states affirmed in the Berlin Treaty on Africa that trading in slaves was a violation of customary international law.[1] Notably, the Berlin Treaty only prohibited interstate slave trading and not slavery itself. Later, in 1926, the Slavery Convention, adopted under the auspices of the League of Nations, made slavery a violation of international law and called upon states to work toward bringing about its abolition.

Similarly, the laws of war that emerged during the late nineteenth and early twentieth centuries modestly challenged sovereignty as the core organizing principle of international relations. During this time period, the growing destructiveness and costs of modern warfare led states to codify basic customary legal norms governing state conduct during war. It should be noted that states were motivated largely by a desire to reduce the cost of killing during war due to the growing costs of new weaponry. The International Committee of the Red Cross, motivated by more humane impulses, was responsible for the humanitarian rhetoric that shaped the initial laws of war adopted by states.[2] These early state deliberations on the conduct of war produced important treaties, including the 1864 Geneva Convention regulating the treatment of wounded armed forces and the 1899 Hague Convention on the laws of war, which were intended to make war less expensive for the states waging it and, secondarily, more humane for those fighting it. These laws did not seek to limit the right of sovereign states to go to war.[3]

An additional legal challenge to sovereignty as the core organizing principle of international relations prior to World War II was embodied in the post–World War I peace treaties. These treaties included clauses mandating that defeated powers provide basic rights and protections to minorities living within their borders. For example, the Treaty of Peace with Turkey, signed in Lausanne on July 24, 1923, called upon Turkey to provide the full protection of life and liberty, religious freedom, and freedom of movement, and to provide the same civil and political rights to all of its inhabitants regardless of national, linguistic, racial, or religious background.[4] It is worth noting that the Lausanne treaty did not mention the genocide against the Armenians living in Turkey that had begun in 1915. Scholars estimate that nearly 80 percent of the Armenian population in Turkey, approximately 1.5 million people, was massacred between 1915 and 1921. Many of the surviving Armenians had been deported or were living in Armenian territory now occupied by the Soviet Union, but the few remaining survivors in Turkish territory continued to face violence and repression.[5]

Despite these legal challenges to a rigid adherence to state sovereignty, the idea of human rights did not become a central component of international law or the foreign policies of most states prior to World War II. A growing number of activists and nongovernmental organizations across the globe were beginning to speak with increased fervor about the need for fundamental human rights. Nevertheless, the nascent movement for human rights did not significantly erode the position of state sovereignty as the fundamental organizing principle of international relations.

It was not until the end of World War II that human rights rose to a place of prominence on the international agenda. Long before the war ended, a wide variety of non-state actors had urged states to adopt basic universal standards protecting human rights. However, the voices of these early human rights activists were lost amid the din of war and policy debates about national interests and power. By the end of the war, growing evidence of almost unfathomable atrocities committed by Nazi Germany became increasingly difficult for states and their citizens to downplay or ignore. Ultimately, belated acknowledgment on the part of major powers of the horrors of the Holocaust made broader segments of the public in many states across the globe more receptive to the idea of universal human rights.

Perhaps more important, foreign policy elites, especially in the United States, drew an important lesson from World War II—that peace and security were integrally related to human rights. Thus, the United States played a key role in pushing for the inclusion of human rights language in the UN Charter and, later, for the passage of independent legal instruments proclaiming basic human rights. As David Forsythe has explained, "That human rights language was written into the United Nations Charter had less to do with a western moral crusade to do good for others, than with the expediential concerns of particularly the United States."[6] It was in this historical context, then, that the core body of international human rights law emerged in the aftermath of World War II.

THE UNITED NATIONS CORE
OF INTERNATIONAL HUMAN RIGHTS LAW

Three primary documents comprise the United Nations core of international human rights law: the Universal Declaration of Human Rights, the International Covenant on Civil and Political Rights, and the International Covenant on Economic, Social, and Cultural Rights. Taken together, these three documents are often referred to as the International Bill of Rights. In addition to these specific human rights documents, the UN Charter includes significant references to the importance of human rights norms. An analysis of these UN documents highlights both the profound advancement in the development of human rights norms in the aftermath of World War II and the limitations of international law as an instrument for promoting and protecting fundamental human rights.

The Charter of the United Nations

The United Nations, created at the end of the war, incorporates explicit references to human rights in its Charter. The Preamble of the UN Charter proclaims the institution's determination to "reaffirm faith in fundamental human rights." In Article 1, the UN Charter states that one of the purposes of the organization is to "promote and encourage respect for human rights." Throughout the document, the Charter makes reference to the objective of reaffirming faith in and promoting basic human rights. The inclusion of human rights language in the UN Charter represents a fundamental shift in international law, which previously had treated individual humans merely as subjects and not objects. Nevertheless, the UN Charter represents the security interests of powerful states more than a principled emphasis on human rights. Ultimately, the human rights language in the UN Charter was formulated in very general language. Despite efforts by nongovernmental organizations for stronger provisions on human rights, the UN Charter neither proclaimed specific rights nor created concrete institutions for their enforcement.

At the same time, the UN Charter gives much more prominence to traditional notions of security. The Charter reaffirms the importance of nonintervention in international law. Article 2 of the Charter requires member states to "refrain in their international relations from the threat or use of force against the territorial integrity or political independence of any state." Traditionally, this principle of nonintervention has meant that one nation-state does not have the legal authority to intervene in the internal affairs of another state, even if those "internal affairs" include gross violations of human rights. The inclusion of this principle in the UN Charter essentially codifies the customary legal principle of sovereignty, which says that the nation-state is the highest authority within its borders and is legally entitled to govern as it sees fit.

The principle of sovereignty is not sacrosanct under the UN Charter. Chapter VII of the Charter gives the UN Security Council the power to authorize the use of force against nation-states that pose threats to international peace and security. However, the Security Council historically has considered a threat to international peace and security to exist only when one state violates the territorial integrity of another state. In other words, the United Nations has not typically treated human rights abuses as threats to international peace and security. The post–Cold War world suggests that this definition may be changing somewhat in cases where internal human rights abuses coincide with more traditional threats to international peace and security. For example, the Security Council authorized enforcement action in Haiti in 1994 partially on the grounds that the flight of refugees into the United States constituted a threat to international peace and security. Similarly, the Security Council adopted Chapter 7 enforcement measures in response to violent conflicts in Bosnia, Rwanda, and Somalia in the 1990s at least in part on the grounds that these violent "internal" conflicts involving widespread repression and human rights abuses threatened international peace and security.

Nevertheless, the UN's reluctance to take stronger actions to end the war in Bosnia or to stop genocide in Rwanda, and its inaction in the face of grave human rights abuses elsewhere, demonstrates that state sovereignty is alive and well. The international community still does not sanction strong action to protect human rights. It should be noted that an unwillingness to expend political, economic, and military resources, especially among permanent members of the Security Council, also contributes to the UN's reluctance to sanction intervention in other states for the purpose of preventing human rights abuses. The lack of political will to expend state resources and to sanction UN enforcement action to promote human rights reinforces the continuation of the status quo in world order and the ongoing importance of state sovereignty as a core organizing principle of international relations. Although its adoption raised the profile of the concept of human rights across the globe, the UN Charter ultimately gives greater priority to the principle of state sovereignty.

The International Bill of Human Rights

The UN General Assembly passed the Universal Declaration of Human Rights (UDHR) in 1948 by a vote of 48 to 0, with eight abstentions. Most of the abstaining votes came from the Soviet Union and eastern bloc states on the grounds that elements of the Declaration represented a challenge to state sovereignty. The UDHR sets out a range of basic human rights, including the right to vote, freedom of speech, prohibitions against the use of torture, the right to work and a decent standard of living, and the right to education. As a resolution passed by the General Assembly, the UDHR is a nonbinding document. Thus, it represents a statement of aspirations rather than a proclamation of enforceable legal norms. Many human rights scholars argue that the norms in the UDHR have attained the status of customary international law and, as such, are binding.[7] However, the continued lack of strong enforcement mechanisms reflects the reality that state sovereignty still trumps human rights in international law.[8]

After the General Assembly passed the UDHR, proponents of human rights within the United Nations and its member states almost immediately began to work on creating binding human rights laws. However, several political developments served to slow this process. The onset of the Cold War resulted in an ideological stalemate between the United States and the Soviet Union that led to their intransigence toward the creation of international human rights law. The Soviet Union insisted that the implementation of human rights was a matter of domestic jurisdiction, and the United States became reluctant to accept international legal obligations that might conflict with a foreign policy directed at containing or rolling back Communism. In addition, decolonization movements in Africa and elsewhere resulted in more than twice as many nation-states' being involved in the process of trying to create binding international human rights law. The addition of newly independent countries coming out of the oppression of colonial rule meant that new deliberations contained a greater emphasis on economic rights. Also, these newly independent countries brought a perspective that emphasized human rights as collective as opposed to individual rights. Though many European countries were supportive of the idea that basic economic needs constituted fundamental human rights, the United States and liberal democratic countries in general were resistant to conceptualizing human rights as collective rights. Ultimately, political and ideological conflict prevented the creation of a single, comprehensive human rights covenant.

Thus, the International Covenant on Civil and Political Rights (ICCPR) and the International Covenant on Economic, Social, and Cultural Rights (ICESCR) were adopted separately though at the same time. Both documents were signed in 1966 and entered into force in 1976 after the requisite number of nation-states had ratified the documents. As treaties that must be signed and ratified in order to enter into force, both covenants are binding under international law. Each covenant adds to the list of rights in the 1948 Declaration. Together, they provide a comprehensive list of basic human rights that represents the highest of human aspirations for many human beings across the globe. Unfortunately, it is primarily up to nation-states to protect these rights because there is no international body with the authority to do so in most cases. Thus, the list of human rights proclaimed in the International Bill of Rights represents noble aspirations that have not been realized in practice. The limitations of the International Bill of Rights as a mechanism for promoting fundamental human rights are demonstrated by the fact that many powerful states have not ratified the binding covenants on human rights. For instance, the United States did not ratify the Civil and Political Covenant until 1992 and still has not ratified the Economic, Social, and Cultural Covenant. Other states have ratified the covenants but have poor human rights records, leading critics to conclude that being a party to the treaty does not result in meaningful changes to states' human rights policies.

In failing to fulfill the norms set out in the International Bill of Rights, states are not necessarily flouting these laws. In fact, both covenants either explicitly allow states to derogate under specific circumstances from the human rights norms that they proclaim or fail to impose immediate and concrete obligations on parties to the treaties. Article 4 of the International Covenant on Civil and Political Rights authorizes states that have ratified the treaty to derogate from their obligations under the treaty "in time of public emergency which threatens the life of the nation . . . to the extent strictly required by the exigencies of the situation." The Article goes on to say that any derogation from human rights law must be consistent with other international legal obligations and must not be based on discrimination "solely on the ground of race, colour, sex, language, religion, or social origin." Moreover, the ICCPR specifies that states are not legally authorized to derogate from certain obligations under any circumstances. The ICCPR identifies the right to life and the right to freedom of conscience as inviolable and also mandates that parties to the treaty respect prohibitions against torture, slavery, and *ex post facto* legal punishment at all times. Thus, state parties to the ICCPR may only derogate from their legal obligations under limited circumstances. However, the ICCPR provides for only basic monitoring of the human rights records of parties to the treaty, as will be discussed further in Chapter 8, as a means of implementing the civil and political rights proclaimed therein. As a result, only weak enforcement mechanisms exist for seeking to ensure that parties to the treaty fulfill their legal obligations.

Article 4 of the International Covenant on Economic, Social and Cultural Rights says that states may limit the rights defined therein only to the extent that such limitations are compatible with these rights and that they promote the general welfare. Although this language seems to limit state discretion to violate the rights identified in this covenant, states are the actors that ultimately define whether or not particular policies contribute to "the general welfare." Moreover, the ICESCR defines state obligations under the covenant in a vague manner that gives states a great deal of discretion. For example, Article 2 of the ICECSR says that states that are a party to the treaty "must undertake to take steps . . . with a view to achieving progressively the full realization of the rights recognized in the present Covenant." This article also acknowledges that states do not all have the same resources for promoting economic rights, and the language "undertake to take steps" is quite flexible. Although such flexibility is necessary because states simply may not have the resources to provide all of the rights identified in the Charter, it also means that states to do not have immediate and concrete obligations under the Covenant. In its comments on the nature of states' obligations under the ICESCR, the Office of the High Commissioner for Human Rights suggests that Article 2 requires parties to the treaty to take deliberate and concrete steps to fulfill their treaty obligations within a reasonable amount of time.[9] Even if this interpretation is correct, it is notable that the ICESCR does not create institutional machinery with the power to effectively enforce these obligations.

As this overview has shown, the International Bill of Rights does an admirable job of proclaiming a wide set of universal human rights norms intended to apply to all individuals across the globe. Yet this section has also highlighted the limitations of international law as a mechanism for promoting and protecting rights in a world of sovereign states. Because states are the actors that create, sign, ratify, and, in the end, implement these norms, it should not be surprising that the International Bill of Rights does not fundamentally infringe upon state sovereignty in practice. The legal documents that comprise the International Bill of Rights contain loopholes that allow states to legally avoid implementing basic rights under certain circumstances. In addition to these legal loopholes, states at other times knowingly and willfully violate the human rights norms from which they are never supposed to derogate. The "enforcement" of international human rights law primarily involves monitoring, a topic that will be covered in greater detail in Chapter 8.

Despite its limitations in legal terms, the International Bill of Rights represents a very important development in the political development of human rights. State and non-state actors rely extensively on the International Bill of Rights as a way of defending the basic morality of the political agenda they favor, and the idea of universal human rights has widespread political appeal that states disregard altogether at their peril. To the extent that many states embrace human rights rhetoric, they may do so for cynical political reasons. Having done so, states cannot always control the power of this rhetoric, and the acknowledgment of the legitimacy of human rights in the abstract often generates concrete demands for human rights in practice. Although state sovereignty remains a dominant principle in international law, the development of international human rights law challenges the legitimacy of state sovereignty as a sacrosanct principle. Despite the fact that sovereign states often ignore their obligations under international human rights law, they cannot absolutely control the political effects of the International Bill of Rights or international human rights law in general.

Specialized Treaties in International Human Rights Law

The post–World War II era in politics also proved to be fruitful ground for the development of a number of specialized treaties dealing with specific human rights issues in addition to the general rights enumerated in the International Bill of Rights. With the political context of the Holocaust as a backdrop, the General Assembly adopted the Convention on the Prevention and Punishment of Genocide in 1948. This treaty, which entered into force in 1951, prohibited certain acts committed "with intent to destroy, in whole or in part, a national, ethnical, racial, or religious group." Under the Genocide Convention, prohibited acts include killing, causing serious bodily or mental harm, the infliction of conditions intended to bring about the physical destruction of a group in whole or in part, measures intended to prevent births, and the forcible transfer of children. Article 1 of the Genocide Convention describes genocide as a crime that state parties to the treaty undertake to prevent and punish. Article 6 says that persons charged with genocide shall be tried by either a competent tribunal in the state where the crime was committed or by an international tribunal whose jurisdiction has been accepted by parties to the treaty. Article 8 also says that parties to the treaty *may* call upon the United Nations to take action to prevent and punish genocide under the UN Charter. Although the convention specifies that parties will undertake to prevent and punish genocide and even uses peremptory language in Article 6, it does not create concrete mechanisms for ensuring that states actually respond to cases of genocide. In the end, the Genocide Convention creates a legal obligation to respond to genocide without creating any mechanism to ensure that parties to the treaty fulfill this obligation. Therefore, state prerogative ultimately determines whether or not states actually respond to cases of genocide. As in the case of the documents that comprise the International Bill of Rights, the Genocide Convention represents a tenuous effort to balance sovereignty concerns and human rights norms.

Also in 1948, the General Assembly passed the Convention Relating to the Status of Refugees. This convention, which entered into force in 1954, represented a response to the refugee crisis that plagued many European countries in the aftermath of World War II. Under the Refugee Convention, a refugee is defined as a person who "owing to well-founded fear of being persecuted for reasons of race, religion, nationality, membership of a particular social group or political opinion, is outside the country of his [or her] nationality and is unable or, owing to such fear, is unwilling to avail himself [or herself] of the protection of that country." The 1951 Refugee Convention initially applied only to refugees from World War II, but a 1967 Protocol modified the original language so that the Refugee Convention now applies to refugees across the globe. State parties to this treaty are obligated to process requests for refugee status made by persons within the state's territory. Thus, the Refugee Convention ostensibly signals a significant challenge to the principle of sovereignty because it diminishes the ability of states to regulate legal residence within their borders in any way they see fit. However, sovereign states still determine if an individual fulfills the criteria for being considered a refugee under the treaty, and ideological perspectives and national interests inevitably shape these determinations. As in the case of other international human rights treaties, the Refugee Convention seeks to protect state sovereignty at the same time that it challenges a rigid notion of state sovereignty by enunciating basic human rights norms.

In addition to the important human rights treaties adopted in the immediate aftermath of World War II, the UN General Assembly has continued to expand and modify the growing body of international human rights law. Important human rights treaties adopted in the decades following the war include the 1956 Convention on the Abolition of Slavery, the Slave Trade, and Institutions and Practices Similar to Slavery; the 1965 Convention on the Elimination of All Forms of Racial Discrimination; the 1979 Convention on the Elimination of All Forms of Discrimination Against Women; the 1984 Convention Against Torture and Other Cruel, Inhuman, or Degrading Treatment or Punishment; and the 1989 Convention on the Rights of the Child. The UN General Assembly continues to modify and expand the body of international human rights law to this day. Additionally, the International Labour Organization, an institution that is part of the United Nations system, has continued to develop treaties dealing with basic economic rights. Each of these treaties enumerates important human rights norms that challenge a rigid adherence to state sovereignty in international relations. Nevertheless, because states are the primary actors that create and implement international law, it is inevitable that international human rights laws ultimately protect sovereignty as a basic organizing principle of international relations.

THE DISTINCTION BETWEEN HUMAN RIGHTS LAW AND HUMANITARIAN LAW

Although international human rights law is the focus of this chapter, it is worth commenting briefly on international humanitarian law because these bodies of law overlap in some respects. Whereas international human rights law refers to the international legal norms claiming fundamental rights for all persons regardless of their race, sex, religion, nationality, or other status, international humanitarian law refers to the legal rules that call for the humane conduct of war. Humanitarian law has obvious implications for the treatment of both soldiers and civilians during wartime and, in this way, is related to the broader idea of human rights. However, humanitarian law does not call for fundamental human rights for all persons. In this way, it is quite distinct from international human rights law. Because students often confuse the two bodies of law, a brief overview of the historical development of humanitarian law and the ways in which it differs from international human rights law is in order at this point.

State efforts to regulate war have involved two types of regulations: efforts to limit the waging of war and rules calling for the humane conduct of war.[10]

One of the first prominent international legal efforts to limit the waging of war was embodied in the Covenant of the League of Nations. The Covenant sought to limit state recourse to war by calling upon member states to settle disputes through arbitration, judicial settlement, or other pacific means. Perhaps the most ambitious example of the effort to limit the waging of war is the Kellogg-Briand Pact of 1928. Under the terms of this pact, the United States and other major powers condemned the recourse to war, renounced war as an instrument of national policy, and called for the pacific settlement of disputes. Unfortunately, these efforts to limit the waging of aggressive war proved fruitless as they were followed just over a decade later by the onset of World War II. Following World War II, the UN Charter replicated the effort to limit aggressive war by codifying the principle of nonintervention. Although states retain the right to individual or collective self-defense under the UN Charter, Article 2 of the Charter affirms that it is illegal for one state to intervene in the internal affairs of another state.

The second method by which states have sought to regulate war is by creating rules governing the manner in which states may conduct wars. The laws of war encompassing norms for the humane conduct of war constitute the main body of what is also referred to as humanitarian law. In this case, the body of law is more expansive and detailed than the international legal efforts seeking to limit the waging of war. Humanitarian law governing the conduct of war is rooted in customary practices intended to limit the brutality of war. Certain Greek and Roman practices in antiquity suggest a customary prohibition on the targeting of civilians during war. Similarly, the Christian norm of condemning attacks on women and the wounded, along with norms prohibiting the infliction of unnecessary suffering, serves as a customary basis for limitations on the way in which war can be conducted.[11]

One of the most prominent examples of a state's effort to prescribe rules that regulate its conduct during war is the Lieber code in the United States. The Lieber code, formally known as the *Instructions for the Government of Armies of the United States in the Field*, was a set of rules put together by Dr. Franz Lieber in 1863 at the request of President Abraham Lincoln.[12] The Lieber code set out a wide variety of restrictions on the conduct of Union troops during the war, including the duty to spare innocent civilians "as much as the exigencies of war will admit" (Article 22), prohibitions on killing and "wanton violence" that are not justified by military necessity, the humane treatment of prisoners of war, and protection of public and private property to the extent possible. All of the Lieber code's restrictions on the conduct of war essentially rested on the notion that only killing and violence called for out of "military necessity" could be justified. The code firmly forbids killing or the use of violence for the purpose of inflicting suffering or executing revenge.[13] The Lieber code drew on customary practices of other states and has served, in turn, as a foundation for the ongoing development of customary humanitarian law.[14]

Although customary humanitarian law has roots that go back to antiquity, states did not begin to codify international laws governing the conduct of war until the nineteenth century. Codified international humanitarian law can be divided into two basic strands: law regulating the conduct of hostilities and law governing the treatment of protected persons, including detainees, the sick and wounded, and civilians. International humanitarian laws regulating the conduct of hostilities were first considered at an international conference in St. Petersburg in 1868. At the St. Petersburg conference, participants criticized the development of poison gases and explosive bullets. As discussed previously, states were motivated more by financial concerns about the costs of expensive armaments than the humanitarian impact of such weaponry. Nevertheless, under pressure from non-state actors, particularly the International Committee of the Red Cross, these early laws of war also came to be framed by humanitarian rhetoric: the St. Petersburg conference denounced weapons that "uselessly aggravate the sufferings of disabled men."[15] Similarly, the Hague Convention, adopted after an international conference at The Hague in 1899, condemned the use of "dum-dum bullets" and projectiles designed to diffuse poisonous gases.[16] A second Hague conference, held in 1907, produced another series of treaties governing the conduct of war. The 1907 Hague Convention calls for the humane treatment of prisoners of war and prohibits, among other things, the use of poisonous weapons, the infliction of unnecessary suffering, and attacks on undefended towns and public buildings not being used for military purposes, including hospitals, churches, and universities.[17]

International humanitarian law governing the treatment of protected persons, including detainees, the sick and wounded, and civilians, has been codified in a series of Geneva Conventions. The first Geneva Convention, adopted in 1864, regulates the treatment of wounded armed forces in the field. The 1864 Geneva Convention called for states to provide relief to the wounded without discriminating based on nationality and to respect the neutrality of medical personnel, equipment, and units, as identified by a red cross on a white background. The 1864 Convention was supplemented by two additional Geneva Conventions in 1929 and by the four Geneva Conventions of 1949 adopted in the aftermath of World War II. The 1949 Geneva Conventions, which remain the core treaties governing the treatment of protected persons during war, created humanitarian protections in four district areas. The First Convention calls for the humane treatment of sick and wounded combatants on land, and the Second Convention outlines requirements for the humane treatment of sick and wounded combatants at sea. The Third Convention contains regulations for the humane treatment of prisoners of war. Finally, the Fourth Convention regulates the protection of civilians during wartime.

The Fourth Geneva Convention provides various protections to civilians, including prohibitions on rape, forced labor, forced deportation, murder, and torture. However, a serious limitation of this convention in terms of providing humanitarian protection to vulnerable civilians is its limited definition of "protected persons." According to Article 4, "Persons protected by the Convention are those who, at a given moment and in any manner whatsoever, find themselves, in case of a conflict or occupation, in the hands of a Party to the conflict or Occupying Power of which they are not nationals." In essence, this restrictive definition means that only individuals in occupied territories or individuals being detained by a state of which they are not nationals are covered by the Fourth Convention's civilian protections. Civilians living in war zones or civilians suffering from non-international armed conflict are not clearly defined as "protected persons." In short, the Fourth Convention does not impose concrete obligations for states to treat all civilians humanely during war.

Although Article 3 of each of the Geneva Conventions does specify that even in non-international armed conflicts parties to the treaty are bound to treat innocent civilians humanely and to respect prohibitions on "violence to life and person" and "outrages upon personal dignity," the 1949 Geneva Conventions do not call upon states to create enforcement mechanisms in this regard. Whereas the Fourth Convention calls for states to undertake to "provide effective penal sanctions for persons committing, or ordering to be committed, any of the grave breaches" against protected persons in international armed conflicts, it does not call for enforcement mechanisms or punishments for states and individuals who violate these prohibitions in non-international armed conflicts.[18] This lack of enforcement mechanisms for non-international armed conflicts reflects state resistance to infringement on their sovereign right to deal with internal rebellion and conflicts as they see fit. Moreover, the civilian protections in the Fourth Convention are weakened by the lack of specificity in Article 3 about whether armed attack against civilian targets is prohibited. The prohibition against "violence to life and person, in particular murder of all kinds" would seem to forbid armed attack against civilian targets. However, the lack of concrete language limits the significance of the treaty in terms of providing broad civilian protections.

The 1977 Protocols to the Geneva Conventions were designed to expand upon the humanitarian protections available to civilians during wartime. Protocol I covers the protection of victims of international armed conflict and reiterates and elaborates many of the provisions from the 1949 Geneva Conventions. Unlike the 1949 Conventions, it clearly specifies that indiscriminate armed attacks against civilians, civilian populations, and objects or institutions necessary for civilian survival are unlawful. Importantly, Protocol I asserts that its provisions on armed attacks apply not only in foreign territory but in the national territory of a party to the treaty. It should be noted that the use of the word "indiscriminate" indicates that the unintentional killing of civilians during war is lawful. However, the Protocol makes clear that states are obligated to direct attacks at military targets strictly for military objectives. Despite its focus on international armed conflict, Protocol I specifies that its provisions explicitly apply to many civil conflicts, including anticolonial wars and struggles against racist governments. Nevertheless, Protocol I does not apply unless the conflict involves an international dimension—for example, the involvement of foreign governments.

The main objective of Protocol II is to supplement the civilian protections for victims of non-international armed conflicts asserted in Article 3 of the

1949 Conventions. Protocol II prohibits "violence to the life, health and physical or mental well-being of persons." Violence prohibited under this clause includes murder, torture, and corporal punishment. The Protocol further prohibits rape, enforced prostitution, slavery, and other humiliating and degrading treatment. It calls for special protection and care for children who are victims of non-international armed conflicts. Like Protocol I, it prohibits indiscriminate armed attacks against civilians, civilian populations, and objects or institutions necessary for civilian survival in non-international armed conflicts. Despite the expanded focus on civilians in the Geneva Protocols, they still lack strong enforcement mechanisms and reaffirm the priority of state sovereignty under international law by stressing that nothing in the Protocols can be used to justify intervention in a sovereign state.

As this brief overview of demonstrates, the continued importance of state sovereignty as an organizing principle in world politics characterizes international humanitarian law as well as international human rights law. Indeed, international humanitarian law does not go as far as international human rights law in asserting that individual human beings have fundamental rights at all times and in all places. Rather, international humanitarian law simply asserts that states are bound by certain obligations in the way in which they conduct hostilities during conflicts and in their treatment of prisoners of war, detainees, and civilians during wartime. Because human rights abuses commonly occur on a grand scale during violent conflicts, international humanitarian law has obvious implication for the status of human rights across the globe. Yet it is important for students to be aware of the fundamental differences between international humanitarian law, with its more limited focus, and the more ambitious and universal aspirations of international human rights law.

FEMINIST CRITIQUES OF INTERNATIONAL HUMAN RIGHTS LAW

In theory, international human rights law is gender neutral. Human rights are rights that all individuals should have regardless of their biological sex or gender. For example, Article 2 of the International Covenant on Civil and Political Rights says, "Each State Party to the present Covenant undertakes to respect and to ensure to all individuals within its territory and subject to its jurisdiction the rights recognized in the present Covenant, without distinction of any kind, such as race, colour, sex, language, religion, political or other opinion, national or social origin, property, birth or other status." The International Covenant on Economic, Social, and Cultural rights contains similar language.

In practice, many feminist scholars argue, international human rights law is biased against women in that it reinforces a "public–private" dichotomy that downplays human rights abuses that are of particular concern to women. The public–private dichotomy is based on a rigid separation of the public sphere, in which the state is the dominant actor, and the private sphere, where individuals live their lives outside the scrutiny of the state (at least in theory). Human rights law has traditionally condemned human rights abuses committed by states, such as torture, repression of the freedom of speech, or genocide. In other words, international human rights law focuses on human rights abuses perpetrated in the public sphere. Because many abuses of women's basic human rights, including rape, sexual harassment, and domestic violence, are perpetuated by private actors, feminist scholars of human rights argue that international human rights law does not bring enough attention to human rights abuses suffered by women.

Feminists further point out that nation-states often fail to prosecute or appropriately punish these crimes against women. For instance, many countries fail to prosecute or severely punish men who rape women, especially if a woman knows the man who raped her. Similarly, many countries have recognized the legitimacy of the "honor defense" which has been successfully used to defend men who have murdered their wives whom they believe to have cheated on them. This defense is still widely used throughout the world, in the developed as well as the developing world. Indeed, the "honor defense" was used successfully in a 1994 murder case in Maryland in the United States in which the judge sentenced a man who had murdered his wife after finding her in bed with another man to only eighteen months in prison.

In theory, violations of human rights committed by private actors should be punished and prosecuted under the criminal law of particular states rather than under international human rights law. However, because states so frequently fail to treat these human rights abuses in a serious manner, many feminists have suggested that international human rights law would be stronger if it explicitly condemned systematic human rights abuses committed by private actors. Moreover, feminists contend that states should be held accountable when they fail to prosecute human rights abuses committed by private actors. Of course, weak enforcement mechanisms for international human rights law in general mean that states typically are not even held responsible for the human rights abuses they directly commit. Therefore, proponents of human rights cannot reasonably expect that states will be held to a higher standard for punishing violations of human rights that they did not directly commit. Nevertheless, this feminist critique suggests that, at the least, the records of states in prosecuting and punishing crimes against women should be subject to the same scrutiny as their general performance in meeting human rights standards. Similarly, international agencies and nongovernmental organizations concerned with human rights should monitor human rights abuses against women, whether by public or private actors, and the response of states to these abuses in the same way that they monitor the human rights records of states in general.

Other feminist critics of international human rights law reject law altogether as a tool for promoting basic rights for women. In their view, international human rights law has been a failure in promoting and protecting basic women's rights. Moreover, they contend that the hierarchical, adversarial nature of legal institutions in general is inconsistent with, and indeed hostile to, women's needs. As an alternative to human rights discourse, some feminist legal theorists have advocated pursuing a "responsibility" approach as a more appropriate model for advancing the dignity of women that would be more consistent with women's experience. According to Gayle Binion, the goal of the responsibility model would be to focus on human needs rather than human rights and to "effect change and not to 'blame.'"[19] Assessing and achieving human needs, under this model, would replace the rights-based approach of establishing blame and guilt. Although this perspective is persuasive for numerous feminist scholars, many women's organizations and feminist activists involved in the effort to advance women's rights across the globe continue to view international human rights law as an important tool, albeit not a sufficient one, for their political movement.

In fact, as a result of efforts by women's organizations and feminist activists, a separate category of women's rights designed to condemn particular kinds of abuses to which women are especially vulnerable, such as rape and domestic violence, has emerged in international human rights law. The Convention on the Elimination of Discrimination Against Women (CEDAW) represents the most prominent example of international human rights law dealing specifically with women's human rights issues. One of the primary purposes of CEDAW is to reaffirm that all of the rights enumerated in the International Bill of Rights apply equally to women. Accordingly, CEDAW specifies that women have the right to vote and to hold public office and that women have equal rights to education and employment. CEDAW includes provisions directed specifically at women, notably rights to equal access to family planning information and services, to basic prenatal care, and to maternity leave with pay. The treaty also identifies child care as a fundamental human right. Notably, feminist efforts to raise awareness about these issues have had an impact, and the United Nations and other organizations have begun to monitor human rights abuses against women more effectively in recent years.

SEXUAL ORIENTATION DISCRIMINATION AND INTERNATIONAL HUMAN RIGHTS LAW

The treaties that comprise the body of international human rights law specify that human beings are entitled to fundamental human rights "without distinction of any kind, such as race, colour, sex, language, religion, political or other opinion, national or social origin, property, birth or other status." The Universal Declaration of Human Rights, the International Covenant on Civil and Political Rights, and the International Covenant on Economic, Social, and Cultural Rights each include this nondiscrimination clause in Article 2. Other international human rights treaties typically contain similar language. However, notably missing from the language in these human rights documents are clauses that specifically identify sexual orientation as an inappropriate basis for discrimination.

Arguably, the existing nondiscrimination clauses could be interpreted in a way that prohibited sexual orientation discrimination. For instance, proponents of human rights could argue that the categories of "sex" or "other status" cover gay, lesbian, and bisexual persons and thus that sexual orientation discrimination is already prohibited. However, the lack of specific language protecting gay, lesbian, and bisexual persons from discrimination is indicative of the lack of intent on the part of signatories to the major human rights documents to extend protection on these grounds. Moreover, the lack of specific protective language reflects and has contributed to the lack of attention to this issue on the part of most human rights advocates and organizations. Ultimately, international human rights law fails to set clear promotional standards and guidelines prohibiting discrimination on the basis of sexual orientation.

A variety of provisions in the core documents of international human rights law could provide protection for gay, lesbian, and bisexual persons if international human rights law were expanded to preclude discrimination on the grounds of sexual orientation. For example, the right to privacy under international human rights law would prohibit national laws that criminalized private sexual activity between consenting adults if sexual orientation were covered by the nondiscrimination clauses in international human rights treaties. Similarly, the right to marry, as proclaimed in both the Universal Declaration of Human Rights and the International Covenant on Civil and Political Rights, would protect same-sex marriages if sexual orientation were defined as a prohibited ground for discrimination under international human rights law. Any policy promoted by a state that allows various forms of sexual identity but prohibits their free expression or the systematic failure of a state to prosecute such discrimination by private actors would be violations of the rights to freedom of opinion and expression if sexual orientation discrimination were prohibited. The application of the rights to equal work and equal pay to all individuals regardless of sexual orientation would require states to take steps to safeguard gay, lesbian, and bisexual persons' right to work, equal pay, and promotion. [20]

In short, international human rights law could be used to promote fundamental human rights for gay, lesbian, and bisexual persons if nondiscrimination clauses prohibited sexual orientation discrimination. Because existing nondiscrimination clauses of the core documents in international human rights law do not explicitly list sexual orientation as an impermissible basis for discrimination, international human rights law fails to actively promote basic rights for gay, lesbian, and bisexual persons. Although it is true that international human rights law cannot alone prevent discrimination, it is a necessary tool in the struggle to promote human rights for all individuals. International human rights law provides persecuted groups with an important political symbol to use in the struggle against oppression. To the extent that gays, lesbians, and bisexuals are denied this symbol, they remain especially vulnerable to human rights abuses across the globe.

CONCLUSIONS

As this chapter has shown, a wide body of international human rights law proclaims an extensive set of fundamental human rights for all individuals across the globe. There are gaps in international human rights law that leave some individuals and groups vulnerable, and the process of creating comprehensive international legal norms proclaiming universal human rights for *all* people is ongoing. In addition to providing an overview of the body of international human rights law, this section has underscored the limitations of international law as a mechanism for promoting and protecting rights in a world of sovereign states. Because states are the actors that create, sign, ratify, and, in the end, implement these norms, it is inevitable that international human rights law is ultimately deferential to state sovereignty. As a result, it is tempting to conclude that international human rights law is not really "law" in any meaningful sense. Indeed, contemporary critics often describe it as "soft law" that does not impose the same obligations and is not enforceable in the way that the "hard law" of states is.

Nevertheless, students of human rights should not be too quick to dismiss international human rights law as irrelevant. States and non-state actors across the globe make frequent reference to the legal documents that comprise the International Bill of Rights as a rhetorical weapon in their efforts to advance their political claims. The new constitutions of countries either gaining independence or changing governments in the aftermath of the Cold War typically have made references to the rights enumerated in the International Bill of Rights. Recently, the practice of citing legal obligations under international human rights law in domestic courts has increased in many countries, a topic further discussed in Chapter 9. Regional organizations such as the Council of Europe and the Organization of American States have adopted language from the International Bill of Rights within their founding documents and have also created stronger enforcement obligations for their members. Finally, human rights nongovernmental organizations increasingly play a prominent role in shaping domestic politics in many states, and they rely extensively on the moral norms and legal obligations defined within the body of international human rights law.

Although international human rights law may not create institutions that directly enforce the obligations it creates, it remains a powerful force that can shape the behavior and policies of states. In this regard, it might be more useful to think of international human rights law in political rather than legal terms. Whether or not it directly creates concrete and enforceable legal obligations, international human rights law generates significant political effects. Students of human rights need to understand the complicated ways in which "soft law" can affect politics.[21] At the same time, recognition of the political nature of international human rights law will encourage human rights activists to embrace it as a powerful tool in the global struggle for human rights.

DISCUSSION QUESTIONS

1. Are human rights a priority in the United Nations Charter? Why or why not?

2. Under what circumstances may states derogate from basic human rights norms under international law? Does the fact that international human

rights law permits states to violate certain human rights norms under these circumstances undermine its importance?

3. Does international human rights law represent an important development in the protection of fundamental human rights in practice? Does it create meaningful constraints on states' behavior? Why or why not?

4. Is international human rights law an adequate tool for promoting and protecting the rights of women as well as men? Why or why not?

5. Is a separate category of "women s rights" in international human rights law consistent with the principle of universal human rights for all men and women? Why or why not?

6. Should the nondiscrimination clauses in the core international human rights documents be interpreted in a way that prohibits sexual orientation discrimination? Why or why not? Alternatively, should proponents of human rights push for the creation of new human rights documents that explicitly prohibit sexual orientation discrimination? Why or why not?

7. Should human rights activists focus their efforts on seeking to improve the implementation and enforcement of existing international human rights law or on revising and expanding international human rights law to proclaim basic human rights not currently protected under existing law?

WEB RESOURCES

UN Charter (http://www.un.org/aboutun/charter/index.html)

Universal Declaration of Human Rights (http://www.un.org/Overview/rights.html)

International Covenant on Civil and Political Rights (http://www.unhchr.ch/html/menu3/b/a_ccpr.htm)

International Covenant on Economic, Social, and Cultural Rights (http://www.unhchr.ch/html/menu3/b/a_cescr.htm)

Convention on the Elimination of Discrimination Against Women (http://www.un.org/womenwatch/daw/cedaw/econvention.htm)

International Law Guide IV: International Women's Human Rights and Humanitarian Law (http://www.law-lib.utoronto.ca/resguide/women2.htm)

3

Are Human Rights Universal?

DEFINING UNIVERSALISM AND RELATIVISM

Universalism refers to the belief that all moral values are fundamentally the same at all times and in all places. A universalist perspective on human rights suggests that basic human rights do not vary as a result of religious diversity, cultural difference, or historical context. In contrast, moral relativism stresses that moral values are determined by religion, culture, history, and other social contexts. Accordingly, a relativist perspective stresses that human rights are culturally and historically specific rather than universal.

These basic definitions suggest that there are two, dichotomous positions on the question of whether or not human rights are universal. However, it is more useful to think of these perspectives on the universality of human rights as existing on a continuum, with what Jack Donnelly calls "radical relativism" and "radical universalism" at either extreme.[1] We might also use the more neutral labels of "pure relativism" and "pure universalism" to describe the extreme points of the continuum. At one end of the continuum, "pure" or "radical" relativism essentially discredits the idea of universal human rights by suggesting that there are no rights that all individual human beings have simply because they are human. Rather, human rights, to the extent that they exist, are derived entirely from the groups and cultures in which humans live. At the other end of the continuum, "pure" or "radical" universalism suggests that universal human rights involve moral imperatives that must be upheld in uniform ways by nation-states across the globe at all times. According to a pure universalist perspective, any consideration of culture or historical context in the application of human rights standards would be invalid.

In practice, contemporary debate over the universality of human rights takes place somewhere in the middle of this continuum. Few foreign policy elites deny altogether that certain fundamental and universal human rights exist. Indeed, most nation-states endorsed a universal statement of human rights at the 1993 World Conference on Human Rights in Vienna, where they adopted a declaration reaffirming "the solemn commitment of all States to fulfill their obligations to promote universal respect for, and observance of, all human rights and fundamental freedoms for all in accordance with the Charter of the United Nations, other instruments relating to human rights, and international law. The universal nature of these rights and freedoms is beyond question."[2]

At the same time, most nation-states defend their sovereign right to rely on cultural interpretations and historical context in implementing basic human rights norms. The belief that universal human rights should be subject to cultural interpretation in their implementation is reflected in the declaration issued by Asian states as part of their preparation for the Vienna World Conference on Human Rights. Although reaffirming the universal nature of human rights, this declaration stressed that human rights "must be considered in the context of a dynamic and evolving process of international norm-setting, bearing in mind the significance of the national and regional peculiarities and various historical, cultural, and religious backgrounds."[3] As these statements from the Vienna World Conference on Human Rights indicate, contemporary political debates over human rights typically involve a delicate effort to balance universalist and relativist perspectives.

Although scholars of human rights and foreign policy elites characteristically speak of universalism and relativism in general, each perspective can also be broken down into either "descriptive" or "normative" variants.[4] Descriptive relativism points to the great diversity of viewpoints on human rights among cultures and nation-states as evidence that human rights clearly are *not* universal in practice. Conversely, descriptive universalism asserts that basic universal values, such as the value placed on human life, are common to all cultures, even if they are manifested in divergent ways.[5] Some scholars also suggest that the fact that states have consented to a growing body of international human rights law is evidence that universal principles indeed exist in practice.[6] Rather than debating the status of human rights in the real world at present, the normative variant of each perspective focuses on whether or not human rights *should* be universal. Normative relativism asserts that cultural and social contexts should be the primary determinants of the rights held by human beings, whereas normative universalism contends that individual human beings should have access to universal human rights regardless of where they live or the groups of which they are members.

The distinction between the descriptive and normative variants of each perspective is an important one. Obviously, the current descriptive status of human rights in the real world matters, and scholars of human rights and foreign policy elites often expend considerable energy debating whether or not the concept of human rights reflects universal principles widely accepted in practice by human beings across the globe. Despite the relevance of this debate, disputes over the status of global human rights in a descriptive sense often reflect more basic disagreements regarding the normative question of whether human rights *should* be universal. Because answers to this question shape whether and how states and non-state actors respond to atrocities and human suffering, it is ultimately the normative question that makes human rights one of the most contested global issues of our time.

ARE HUMAN RIGHTS A WESTERN CONSTRUCT?

According to relativist critics of human rights, efforts to implement ostensibly universal human rights represent an attempt on the part of Western states and societies to impose Western values on non-Western states and societies. In this way, relativists commonly dismiss the idea of universal human rights as a form of "cultural imperialism." Relativists often criticize proponents of universal human rights as ethnocentric elitists who assert the superiority of their own culture and values to non-Western cultures and values rather than respecting cultural diversity. The relativist position is reflected in the 1947 Statement on Human Rights issued by the American Anthropological Association in response to United Nations deliberations over the Universal Declaration of Human Rights. In this statement, the American Anthropological Association cautions against the imposition of Western values on non-Western societies in the name of universal human rights:

> Doctrines of the "white man's burden" have been employed to implement economic exploitation and to deny the right to control their own affairs to millions of peoples over the world, where the expansion of Europe and America has not meant the literal extermination of whole populations. Rationalized in terms of ascribing cultural inferiority to these peoples, or in conceptions of their backwardness in development of their "primitive mentality," that justified their being held in the tutelage of their superiors, the history of the expansion of the western world has been marked by demoralization of human personality and the disintegration of human rights among the peoples over whom hegemony has been established.[7]

The relativist position, as reflected in the American Anthropological Association's statement, does not necessarily deny that human rights exist. Instead, it contends that human rights are determined within cultures rather than being universal. Moreover, relativism suggests that efforts to impose universal values in the name of human rights may actually lead to the abuse and deterioration of human rights in practice.

The relativist criticism of human rights stems, in large part, from the history of colonialism. Defenders of colonialism often justified the subjugation of indigenous people in colonized countries by asserting the moral superiority of the colonizing countries. Colonizing elites characteristically defended colonialism as a mission that would bring civilization and Christianity to barbarian peoples and cultures. In the name of spreading "universal moral values," colonizing powers often systematically killed and maimed countless numbers of human beings that they had supposedly targeted for "salvation." Cultural relativists point to the Christian underpinnings of the universal moral rhetoric used to justify colonial expansion as grounds for skepticism about the genuinely universal nature of modern human rights claims.

An interesting example of the misuse of universal moral principles for self-interested and ultimately illiberal ends involves the effort by nineteenth-century European powers to justify their effort to colonize Africa by claiming that they were driven by a desire to stop the "Arab-dominated" slave trade.[8] As this example illustrates, Western powers have cynically used universal rhetoric in ways that have contributed to immeasurable human suffering. In this way, relativist skepticism about the universalizing moral rhetoric underlying the contemporary movement to promote universal human rights is justifiable.

As we saw in Chapter 1, no universally accepted philosophical justification for human rights exists. Relativists fear that despite its secular language, international human rights law is fundamentally shaped by Christian doctrine and values. Because the universal language of Christianity has been used to justify violence, as the historical case of colonialism illustrates, relativists are concerned that the universal language of human rights is more likely to be used to justify the commission of violence and the neglect of human suffering than to promote and protect human dignity.

In addition to reservations stemming from the confluence of universalizing moral rhetoric and colonial violence, relativists discount universalism simply because of the rich and complex variety of cultures that historically shaped and continues to mold the way different people across the globe live. For example, as we saw in Chapter 1, vastly different conceptions of what it means to be human impede global consensus on human rights. According to most relativists, Western societies share a conception of human beings as "autonomous individuals" who perceive and experience their humanity as distinct and separate individuals. In contrast, relativists believe that non-Western societies are more likely to have a conception of human beings as people who perceive and experience their humanity as members of the groups to which they belong. A striking example of a communitarian conception of humanity comes from Navajo and Hopi tribal cultures, in which the indigenous languages do not conceptualize humanity in an individualistic manner. These American Indian languages "construct humanness as belonging solely to those within the boundaries of the community, whose collective name means the 'people.' Outsiders are perceived to be non-human to a certain degree, particularly in origin myths."[9] The notion of human rights as something held by an autonomous individual certainly would be a foreign idea in such a culture!

As this example illustrates, genuine cultural differences complicate efforts to promote and implement universal human rights. Nevertheless, the characterization of the debate over whether or not human rights are or should be universal as a fundamental dispute between "Western" and "non-Western" cultures is misleading. Western philosophy has been marked by widespread and significant disagreement over the concept of human rights, and the liberal philosophical tradition that has been so influential in shaping the concept of human rights is by no means the only Western perspective on human rights. Indeed, the emphasis on freedom and individual rights is a relatively recent phenomenon in Western political thought, and support for authoritarianism was very prominent in ancient political thought in the West.[10] As Amartya Sen has remarked, "It is by no means clear to me that Confucius is more authoritarian than, say, Plato or Augustine."[11] Similarly, although communitarian philosophical perspectives have been prominent in many non-Western cultures, they are not the only non-Western perspective on human rights.

One of the most prominent historical criticisms of the idea of universal human rights comes out of Western philosophy in the writings of Edmund Burke. Criticizing the excesses of the French Revolution, Burke developed a classic, conservative critique of human rights. In his famous *Reflections on the Revolution in France*, Burke articulated a defense of "traditional" communities and depicted challenges to traditional values, such as loyalty, religion, and even love, as threats to the order and morality of the community. Burke's philosophy, an important part of the Western philosophical tradition, sounds very much like the communitarian criticisms of human rights that relativists tend to depict as the province of non-Western philosophy. Similarly, Marxist political thought has been a major force in shaping the view that rights are collective and are conferred by the state, rather than being individual and universal. Like Burke's conservative political philosophy, Marxism is a product of Western—not non-Western—political thought. The statist perspective that subordinates individual rights to the principle of state sovereignty is of Western origin and was "exported" to many non-Western societies through the process of colonialism. In addition, it should be noted that cultural relativism itself has been very prominent among Western scholars and foreign policy elites. In short, Western political thought has by no means been marked by clear and consistent support for the idea of universal human rights, either in theory or in practice.

Just as Western political thought has been and continues to be marked by diversity on the question of human rights, non-Western political thought is more diverse than relativists acknowledge. Although relativists commonly assume that non-Western societies have unambiguously downplayed the importance of individual freedoms and rights as values, the historical record is more complicated. Authoritarian perspectives have clearly played a prominent role in non-Western societies. However, as Amartya Sen has noted, "The real issue is not whether these non-freedom perspectives are present in Asian traditions, but whether the freedom-oriented perspectives are absent from them."[12] In his view, freedom-oriented perspectives are *not* absent in non-Western political thought. Rather, strains of Buddhist, Confucian, Hindu, and other non-Western political thought can be read as supportive of freedom, tolerance, and other values consistent with the idea of universal human rights. In support of his thesis, Sen cites an important statement calling for religious freedom made by the Moghul emperor Akbar in the late sixteenth century. Sen underscores the importance of Akbar's promotion of religious tolerance at that point in world history: "It may not be irrelevant to note, especially in the light of the hard sell of 'Western liberalism,' that while Akbar was making these pronouncements on religious tolerance, the Inquisition was in full throttle in Europe."[13]

In addition to disputing the idea that universal human rights represent "cultural imperialism" on the part of the West, proponents of universalism challenge relativism on numerous additional grounds. Fernando Téson, who has articulated one of the strongest defenses of universalism, enumerates several criticisms of relativism. First, he argues that relativists undermine their own argument that universal moral principles do not exist by identifying relativism as the one appropriate universal moral guideline. Second, he contends that relativists assume that because certain principles predominate in a culture, they are necessarily appropriate and moral. This perspective mistakes authority for morality. Finally, he asserts, in response to the charge that universalism is elitist and ethnocentric, that in fact relativists demonstrate a form of elitism and ethnocentrism when they deny minorities in "non-Western cultures" access to the same set of rights they promote for minorities in "Western cultures."[14]

Another fundamental problem with relativism is that the term *culture* is not analyzed sufficiently. What is culture? Must the boundaries of culture coincide with nation-states? If not, then why do some groups within a state, such as indigenous people, constitute a "culture" while other groups, such as religious minorities, women, or gay, lesbian, and bisexual persons, do not? And who gets to decide? Nation-states, cultural elites, or people who self-identify as part of a particular culture? These are difficult questions that relativists have not adequately addressed.

Rhoda Howard has labeled cultural relativists "cultural absolutists." According to Howard, "cultural absolutists" romanticize "primitive cultures" and stereotype "the inhabitants of non-Western geographical regions with the religio-cultural beliefs that these commentators believe must define the non-Westerners' lives and dominate their thoughts."[15] Howard cites an anthropological study in which the researchers accused members of an ethnic group in the Philippines of being "fake primitives" because they started to wear blue jeans and eat "Western" food. In reality, Howard believes that political elites often manipulate ideas of culture in self-serving ways that do not represent the interests or values of many members of the community, as was the case when Nazi Germany glorified the myth of an Aryan past with devastating results for the Jews, homosexuals, and gypsies who were targeted for repression and slaughter. For elites who benefit from defining culture in traditional ways, any external challenge to cultural norms represents an invalid effort by foreigners to impose culturally insensitive and destabilizing values. For individuals who experience traditional definitions of culture as oppression, access to universal principles can be experienced as liberation.

FEMINIST PERSPECTIVES
ON UNIVERSALISM AND RELATIVISM

Certain feminist perspectives have been instrumental in clarifying why relativist claims made by cultural elites need to be scrutinized carefully. Many feminists suggest that it is important to deconstruct the notion of culture by considering the extent to which people possess the ability to participate in shaping the values of their culture. One such approach is to examine the status of the individuals claiming to represent their culture. Because large numbers of people, especially women, are often excluded from shaping or speaking on behalf of their culture, the definition of culture has political content and is therefore used to protect the interests of specific groups within particular cultures, often at the expense of other individuals or groups within the same culture.[16] As a result, the relativist position that cultural beliefs and values are necessarily less political and, hence, morally superior to any "external" values can be called into question. In the words of Arati Rao, "the notion of culture favored by international actors must be unmasked for what it is: a falsely rigid, ahistorical, selectively chosen set of self-justificatory texts and practices whose patent partiality raises the question of exactly whose interests are being served and who comes out on top."[17] For feminists like Rao, it is clear that the interests of men and not women are being served when culture is used to justify repressive practices toward women.

Feminists point out that recognizing that the definition of culture is shaped by the political and economic interests of elites is especially important because cultural and relativist arguments seem to resonate across cultures most strongly when they are used to justify discrimination against vulnerable groups such as women. For example, some proponents of human rights accept cultural divergence with regard to rights that are viewed as less fundamental. Commonly, women's rights are categorized among norms that are not considered fundamental.[18] For example, although cases of genocide and torture are widely condemned across the globe, at least publicly, issues that involve the basic human rights of women, such as "female circumcision," forced marriage, and domestic violence, are less likely to generate cross-cultural agreement.

Thus, many feminists reject relativism as a perspective that justifies and perpetuates human rights abuses against women across the globe.[19] This feminist viewpoint treats universalism as a moral perspective that can be used to advance the cause of women's rights across the globe. Although to date international human rights law has promoted women's rights as human rights only imperfectly, universalism as a philosophy at least holds as a principle that *all* human beings deserve basic human rights. Thus, universalism suggests that all women, as human beings, deserve fundamental human rights. Feminists historically have drawn on universal arguments to make the case that basic rights should be extended to women.[20] For example, Mary Wollstonecraft, in her 1792 book *Vindication of the Rights of Women*, used the universal language of the Enlightenment to highlight the incomplete and imperfect nature of the American and French revolutions in that they articulated ostensibly universal rights that applied in theory and practice primarily to men. Wollstonecraft did not object to universal rights but argued instead that they should be applied in a *genuinely* universal way that encompassed women as well as men. As we saw in Chapter 1, feminists today continue to draw on universal language to try to shape international human rights law in a way that is more likely to encompass women's rights.

Although many feminists embrace a universal view of human rights, other feminists express reservations about universalism that are consistent in certain respects with relativism. In particular, postmodern feminism has been used to challenge the idea that human rights are or should be universal. Postmodern feminists bring gender, defined as the socially constructed traits and behaviors we characterize as masculine and feminine, to the center of their analysis. The concept of gender suggests that masculinity and femininity do not reflect essential or biological behaviors. Rather, they are behaviors created and reinforced by societies and cultures. So, what is considered masculine in one culture may differ in another culture. As the definition of gender suggests, postmodern feminists are concerned with the categories of "masculinity" and "femininity," not "male" and "female." This focus again reinforces the point that postmodernists are talking about learned behaviors, not biological traits. Postmodern feminists stress that there is not a single category of woman or man that applies across time and space. Rather, what it means to be a man or a woman will vary according to a variety of factors, including age, class, culture, religion, and ethnicity.

Because of their emphasis on the ways in which culture shapes the meaning of what it means to be a man or a woman in different societies, postmodern feminists are more likely to reject international human rights law as a means of promoting basic rights for women. Postmodern feminists have criticized international human rights law because of its philosophical foundations in "Western" assumptions about autonomous, rational individuals. According to this viewpoint, the concept of human rights is based on an understanding of human nature that adopts the male as norm. Thus, many postmodern feminists dismiss the idea of universal human rights as reflecting the biases of Western, white men. They contend that the individualistic assumptions on which a universal perspective on human rights is based are inconsistent with non-Western philosophical traditions and that human rights norms based on these assumptions disrupt traditional communities more likely to foster women's well-being.[21]

Different cultural viewpoints over the Muslim practice of veiling nicely illustrate why feminists have been unable to reach consensus on the notion that universal human rights are the appropriate mechanism for promoting and protecting basic women's rights. Western feminists often criticize the requirement in many Muslim societies that women wear veils in public as repressive and view this practice as a basic violation of human rights. However, many Muslim women argue that they experience veiling as protective and even liberating. Because the absence of a veil signals sexual availability in many Muslim societies, Muslim women frequently embrace the veil as something that allows them to participate in public life with a sense of modesty, personal safety, and security. Many Muslim women would wear some sort of veil or head covering in public even if not required to do so by the state. Indeed, some Muslim women contend that they would retreat to the private sphere rather than participate in public life if they were not able to wear the veil in public.[22] As this example illustrates, postmodern feminism suggests that the contexts of practices that appear to be repressive to outsiders must be carefully considered before such practices are condemned as violations of basic human rights.

Although many postmodern feminists have reservations about universalism, postmodern feminism is not necessarily inconsistent with the idea of universal human rights. Indeed, the concept of gender can be used to challenge relativism. It is indisputable that gender norms vary across culture in a descriptive sense, but that does not settle the normative debate. Because gender roles and values are socially constructed, they are not immutable. Rather, as social constructions, they are subject to change. Indeed, feminists who believe in universal human rights argue that static notions of culture are precisely the problem and that human rights advocates who are serious about promoting fundamental human rights for *all* human beings, women as well as men, need to challenge oppressive gender norms in an effort to advance women's rights and human rights in general.

CASE STUDY: FEMALE GENITAL MUTILATION OR FEMALE CIRCUMCISION?

"Female circumcision" or "female genital mutilation" involves the cutting and/or removal of part or all of the external female genital organs and has been practiced for thousands of years in a variety of countries and cultural contexts. The label "female circumcision" or "female genital mutilation" does not describe a single procedure but is actually used to refer to a wide range of practices that vary significantly in terms of their invasiveness. The least invasive practice involves a slight cut to the clitoris but does not permanently remove any part of the female genitalia. This practice has been referred to as "ritualistic circumcision."[23] At the other extreme, female genital mutilation involves infibulation, in which most of the external female genital organs are removed and "the remaining raw edges of the labia major are then sown together with acacia tree thorns, and held in place with catgut or sewing thread. The entire area is closed up by this process leaving only a tiny opening, roughly the size of a match stick to allow for the passing of urine and menstrual fluid."[24] In between these two extremes, the practice has involved the removal of the tip of the clitoris or the removal of most of the clitoris, referred to as a clitoridectomy. Clitoridectomy is the most common form of female circumcision or female genital mutilation.[25]

The debate over whether to refer to these various procedures as "female circumcision" or "female genital mutilation" illustrates the cultural obstacles that currently hinder global consensus on the idea of universal human rights. On the one hand, individuals who defend the procedure as a valid cultural practice refer to it as "female circumcision," a term that has clinical connotations and signals that it is benign in nature. Critics of the practice have embraced the label "female genital mutilation," a term with obvious negative connotations that captures the physical damage that the procedure does to the bodies of girls and women.

Despite a widespread popular misconception that this practice is limited to the Muslim world or to rural African tribes, female circumcision or female genital mutilation has been practiced in a wide variety of cultures across the globe. Historically, the practice has been followed by Christians, Muslims, and one sect of Judaism.[26] Although none of the texts of these religions requires female circumcision, it has been justified by religious elites in these traditions who have promoted the practice as a moral requirement intended to preserve the chastity of women.[27] Female circumcision or female genital mutilation has not been practiced solely by religious groups. A variety of African tribes has engaged in the practice historically and continues to do so to the present day. In these cases, the procedure is often part of a rite of passage for adolescent girls, though it has also been used to promote the value of chastity.[28] Myths, such as the belief that the procedure contributes to fertility, have also played a role in perpetuating the practice in many tribal societies.[29] As late as the 1940s and 1950s, doctors in the United Kingdom and the United States routinely used the practice as a "treatment" for "hysteria, lesbianism, masturbation, and other so-called female deviances."[30] In fact, doctors continued to perform the procedure in the United States into the 1970s.[31]

The practice of female circumcision or female genital mutilation continues across the globe. Currently, it is most prevalent in various parts of Africa as well as among immigrant women and girls in Europe, North America, and other industrialized regions. Because nation-states do not gather statistics on the procedure, estimates are imprecise. Nevertheless, the United Nations has estimated that perhaps 2 million women and girls are subjected to this practice annually.[32]

Critics of female genital mutilation, especially feminists, have initiated a global campaign to eradicate the practice as a fundamental human rights abuse. These critics highlight the physical pain and damage that is done to the girls and women who undergo the procedure to make the case that it constitutes a human rights abuse. The procedure is often carried out with "kitchen knives, old razor blades, broken glass, and sharp stones," and "anesthesia is almost never used in the process."[33] Even when the procedure is performed in health clinics with anesthesia, it can have lasting negative consequences for the girls and women on whom it is practiced. These medical complications include hemorrhaging, infections, shock, difficulties with urination, incontinence, menstrual problems, sexual dysfunction, complications with later childbirth, psychological trauma, and even death.[34] Dangerous health complications are most likely with infibulation. Many women who have undergone the procedure have noted a lack of sexual desire or sexual enjoyment. (It should be noted that for some proponents of the practice as a way of ensuring a woman's chastity, this sexual control of women is precisely the objective.) This range of negative consequences in both physical and emotional terms impinges on a variety of basic human rights, including the right to life, the right to be free from torture, the right to liberty and security of person, the right to privacy, and the right to enjoy the highest standards of physical and mental health. Critics of female genital mutilation have also pointed out that the practice especially constitutes a violation of the rights of children when it is performed on minors who do not have a meaningful choice in deciding whether or not to undergo the procedure.

Female circumcision has been defended on numerous grounds. In many cases, a majority of women in societies where female circumcision is the norm support the practice. For example, an interview conducted in the Sudan in 1983 indicated that more than 80 percent of women approved of female circumcision, even in its most severe form. This number was almost as high as the percentage of men supporting the practice.[35] The traditional importance of female circumcision as a rite of passage in many societies means that girls who have not undergone the procedure may not be considered good candidates for marriage. Because women's roles are often defined in very traditional ways in societies where female circumcision is practiced, a woman's ability to support herself and to meet her basic needs often depends very much on her marriage prospects. In these contexts, external efforts to eradicate the practice are seen as threats not only to social order in general but to the traditional paths of pursuing economic well-being and social status for girls and women.[36] Cultural relativists who defend female circumcision have pointed out that women in Western societies often undergo painful and risky physical procedures, including cosmetic surgery and breast implant surgery, to improve their "desirability" according to the cultural norms in the societies in which they live and to expand their economic prospects.[37] Human rights advocates have not initiated a global campaign to eradicate plastic surgery or breast implants. Why, relativists ask, should female circumcision be treated differently, especially if it is supported by most women in a society where it is practiced?

Even critics of female circumcision, especially individuals from the societies in which it is practiced, have expressed reservations about the way in which many Western feminists have gone about trying to eradicate it. According to these critics, external criticism of female circumcision is often perceived as arrogant and has shown insensitivity to the cultural settings that sustain the tradition. Criticism that dismisses the women and men who support the practice as ignorant or malicious will be highly suspect in cultures where female genital mutilation has been widely practiced. Accordingly, the reform efforts that have had the most success to date have involved grassroots activities designed to educate individuals about the potential negative health consequences of female circumcision rather than campaigns that condemn the practice as an immoral violation of basic human rights.[38]

As Gerry Mackie has written, "The followers of mutilation are good people who love their children; any campaign that insinuates otherwise is doomed to provoke defensive reaction."[39] For proponents of universal human rights who oppose female genital mutilation as a human rights abuse, it is imperative to understand that the people who engage in this practice are "good people who love their children." Without this awareness and sensitivity to the cultural context that drives female genital mutilation, there is little hope that any meaningful dialogue will occur between proponents of universal principles and defenders of cultural traditions and, as a result, that any progress will be made in reforming this practice.

CASE STUDY: MALE GENITAL MUTILATION OR MALE CIRCUMCISION?

A juxtaposition of the relative neglect of male circumcision in human rights scholarship and activism to the high-profile campaign against female genital mutilation sheds light on the cultural obstacles to global consensus on human rights as universal principles. Human rights activists in Western societies widely condemn female genital mutilation. In contrast, male circumcision has not been treated as a human rights priority. Even international human rights organizations do not categorize male circumcision as a human rights issue. For example, the Office of the High Commissioner for Human Rights identifies female genital mutilation as a harmful traditional practice affecting the health of women and children but does not include male circumcision on its list of harmful practices toward children.[40] Is the differential treatment of male circumcision and female genital mutilation in international human rights discourse warranted by the differences between these practices? Or should male circumcision be viewed as a violation of fundamental human rights? This case study explores preliminary answers to these questions. In doing so, it highlights the ways in which cultural relativism limits efforts to define and implement universal standards of human rights.

Male circumcision involves the removal of the male prepuce, the skin surrounding the glans, or head, of the penis. In this way, male circumcision is comparable in some respects to female clitoridectomy,[41] which involves the removal of the tip or most of the clitoris and is the most common form of female genital mutilation. The practices are also similar in that they remove the most sensitive parts of the sexual organs. Just as the clitoris is the most sensitive part of the female genitalia, the prepuce "contains the densest concentrations of the fine-touch neuroreceptors" on the penis.[42] Interestingly, even the few scholars and activists who write about male circumcision as a human rights issue typically refer to "male circumcision" rather than "male genital mutilation." Just as in the case of female circumcision, male circumcision has clinical connotations that suggest that the practice is benign in nature. However, if we conceive of male circumcision as a practice that does unnecessary physical harm to boys and men by removing a natural part of their bodies in the absence of a compelling medical reason and with harmful physical and mental consequences, might it be more appropriate to label the practice "male genital mutilation"?

Male circumcision or male genital mutilation is not widely practiced across the globe. Indeed, the global rate of male circumcision is only approximately 20 percent.[43] The United States has the highest rate of male circumcision—approximately 60 percent of male newborns in the United States are circumcised. Indeed, routine infant male circumcision is the most commonly performed surgical procedure in the United States, with roughly 3,000 male newborns circumcised each day.[44] Canada also has relatively high rates of male circumcision, with a rate of about 25 percent. Australia's national rate of male circumcision is approximately 15 percent.[45] Most other Western nations have much lower rates of male circumcision.[46]

Historically, male circumcision or male genital mutilation has been practiced in various regions of the world for thousands of years. Notably, the origins of the practice are cultural rather than medical. Male circumcision is a ritual practice in both Judaism and Islam. The procedure did not become widespread in the United States until the 1870s, when Victorian-era doctors adopted the practice as a "cure" for masturbation.[47] Over time, doctors added medical justifications to what began as a cultural practice. Claims of medical benefits have included, over time, the belief that the practice cured everything from epilepsy to bed-wetting.[48] Although the specific medical justifications for male circumcision have evolved over time, the belief that male circumcision is a procedure justified by medical necessity has become culturally entrenched.

Today, the best medical evidence supports more modest claims, including that male circumcision may somewhat reduce the risk of sexually transmitted diseases, urinary tract infections, and penile cancer. Although male circumcision had widespread support in the medical community throughout the twentieth century and is still defended by many doctors today, the medical community is moving toward increasing consensus that the potential benefits of male circumcision do not outweigh the potential risks.[49] Moreover, critics argue that the claimed benefits of the practice have been overstated.[50] On these grounds, medical organizations across the globe now argue that routine male circumcision is not medically warranted.[51] For example, the American Academy of Pediatrics no longer recommends routine male circumcision. Nevertheless, the Academy's guidelines on the practice suggest that the decision regarding whether or not to circumcise is up to the parents in consultation with their physician. Thus, the AAP's statement ultimately defers to cultural preferences rather than asserting the priority of health considerations, much less human rights.

Critics of male circumcision point out that the practice inflicts a variety of harms on boy children who undergo the procedure. Historically, male circumcision has most frequently been performed without analgesia. Thus, just like female genital mutilation, male genital mutilation inflicts pain on infant males undergoing the procedure. Because it is typically performed on newborn males, the procedure is inflicted on boy children without their consent. Male genital mutilation involves a variety of basic health risks, including hemorrhage, lacerations, infection, urinary retention, and in *extremely* rare circumstances, death (in these cases, usually as a result of complications from infection.)[52] Critics of male genital mutilation charge that these physical and emotional harms undermine a range of basic human rights, including the right to be free from torture, the right to liberty and security of person, the right to privacy, the right to enjoy the highest standards of physical and mental health, and, in very rare cases, the right to life. Just as in the case of female circumcision, opponents of male genital mutilation argue that it violates the rights of children because it is performed on infants who cannot give their consent to undergo the procedure. In cases where states ban female genital mutilation, it can also be argued that males suffer gender discrimination when male circumcision is not similarly prohibited. When the law codifies differential treatment for males and females, "males are being discriminated against on account of their gender, and because of a perception that male genitals are somehow less worthy of protection."[53] Similarly, when international organizations and human rights nongovernmental organizations condemn female genital mutilation but not male genital mutilation, they can be seen as contributing to gender inequity.

Defenders of male circumcision rely on numerous justifications for continuing the practice. As in the case of female circumcision, the "victims" of male circumcision typically view the practice as normal and support its continuation. Even if male circumcision is a cultural practice rather than a medically necessary procedure, cultural relativists argue that the international community should respect traditional cultural practices of groups that support the procedure. Indeed, Article 12 of the UN Convention on the Rights of the Child refers to "the importance of the traditions and cultural values of each people for the protection and harmonious development of the child." Relying on this clause, defenders of male circumcision could argue that even international human rights law ultimately remains deferential to traditional cultural practices.[54] In addition, because male circumcision is common among Jews and Muslims, defenders of the practice argue that restrictions on male circumcision would impinge upon the right to freedom of religion. Moreover, it should be reiterated that some doctors continue to believe that the potential benefits of male circumcision outweigh the potential risks.[55]

The disparate status of male circumcision versus female circumcision on the global human rights agenda highlights the importance of cultural norms as obstacles to a universalist perspective on human rights. Male circumcision is most widely practiced in the United States, a country that often espouses human rights as universal principles and where criticism of female genital mutilation is widespread.[56] In contrast, male circumcision has not been similarly prioritized, in the United States or elsewhere, by either human rights scholars or activists. In part, this differential treatment may be due to the genuine differences between the practices. Male circumcision most closely approximates clitoridectomy, a more "moderate" form of female genital mutilation than infibulation, the most severe form of female genital mutilation. Infibulation, as described in the case study of female genital mutilation above, would be the equivalent of removing the penis and testicles. If one uses infibulation as the point of comparison, it is not difficult to understand why the human rights community would give female genital mutilation greater attention than male genital mutilation.

However, differences between the two practices can be exaggerated. It is undoubtedly true that male circumcision is not nearly as invasive or threatening to men's health as infibulation is to women's health. Nevertheless, it is worth restating that clitoridectomy is the most common form of female circumcision or female genital mutilation. Thus, the type of female genital mutilation most likely to be experienced by women or girls is similar in many respects to male circumcision. Therefore, to the extent that this form of female circumcision warrants being treated as a violation of fundamental human rights, a human rights framework based on gender equity suggests that male circumcision should be condemned in the same manner.

To date, human rights organizations and activists have not widely embraced male circumcision as a human rights issue. Nevertheless, individuals and groups increasingly are seeking to make male circumcision a priority on the global human rights agenda. To the extent that they succeed, they will be well served to take lessons from the transnational movement against female genital mutilation. Critics of efforts to eradicate female circumcision have argued that the movement against the practice has been culturally insensitive and, indeed, that cultural arrogance has limited the effectiveness of the efforts to limit the practice. Opponents of male genital mutilation will likely be more successful if they show sensitivity to the cultural settings that have sustained the practice and if they recognize that, just as in the case of female genital mutilation, parents who support male circumcision are "good people who love their children."[57]

In the case of female genital mutilation, reform efforts framing the practice as a health issue have been more successful than campaigns that condemn the practice as an immoral violation of basic human rights.[58] A similar strategy may or may not work in the case of male circumcision. On the one hand, parents may be less likely to react defensively to campaigns that clearly lay out the relative costs and benefits of the practice in terms of health. On the other hand, male circumcision has been justified primarily in terms of health benefits and has become a deeply entrenched cultural belief, especially in the United States. As a result, it may be that a health framing strategy will be less successful in the United States and other Western countries with relatively high rates of male circumcision.[59] In the United States, then, because Americans widely embrace the ideal of human rights, framing male circumcision as a human rights issue *may* be a more successful strategy for eradicating the practice.

Regardless of the strategy adopted, an awareness of and sensitivity to the cultural context that drives male circumcision will be required for any meaningful progress to be made in reforming this practice. As both the case studies of female genital mutilation and male circumcision have shown, practices that advocates of human rights view as abusive are often deeply entrenched in culture. Even proponents of universalism need to be aware of and sensitive to the strength of cultural norms if they truly seek to advance global human rights as universal principles.

CONCLUSIONS

This chapter has provided an overview of two basic perspectives on the universality of human rights. Universalism suggests that human beings are entitled to fundamental human rights regardless of where they live or the groups to which they belong; relativism assumes that human rights, to the extent that they exist, are determined largely by history, religion, culture, and social context. In many respects, both universalism and relativism represent reactions to cases of violence and repression that have been justified by or perpetuated in the name of the other perspective. The assertion of universal values has been used by nation-states, both Western and non-Western, to justify intervention in the internal affairs of other states for self-interested reasons, as is starkly illustrated by the historical case of colonialism. Cultural relativists helpfully draw attention to the ways in which universal principles have been abused by states. At the same time, the rhetoric of cultural relativism has been used by states to legitimize the repression of individuals within these states, as proponents of universalism accurately point out. States also have used cultural relativism as an excuse to defend their own inaction and indifference to the suffering of human beings who happen to live in other cultures. In other words, nation-states have drawn on both universalism and relativism in the rhetoric they have used to defend policies and practices that have contributed to widespread violence and human suffering.

The global effort to promote universal human rights commonly involves a struggle to shape values and power relations both within and among cultures. Given the historical record of economic and political imperialism, the popularity of relativist arguments among non-Western elites is understandable, and it is important for human rights advocates to remain sensitive to cultural differences. At the same time, students of human rights are under no moral obligation to accept relativism without scrutiny. Relativists often assume that the concept of universal human rights is merely a new tool of domination on the part of "Western" states. In reality, nation-states are not the vanguard of the human rights movement. To the extent that they address human rights at all, most nation-states' foreign policies are likely to include more rhetoric than substantive content in terms of efforts to advance international human rights.

Instead, nongovernmental organizations and individuals are at the forefront of the struggle for universal human rights. To be sure, human rights advocates need to be more sensitive to cultural norms and more willing to work at the grassroots level if they hope to make progress in promoting universal human rights. Nevertheless, relativists should not dismiss individual or group claims for human rights on the grounds that they are "Western" in origin—a claim that is misleading, as this chapter has shown. Additionally, students and proponents of human rights do not need to accept certain cultural practices as legitimate simply because cultural elites justify them on the grounds that they are fundamental to their culture. Just as the effort to promote human rights is political, attempts to defend traditional practices as an inherent part of a culture are political as well. Students need to be aware of the explicitly political nature of both universalism and relativism in order to fully understand the complexities involved in the debate over whether or not human rights are or should be universal.

DISCUSSION QUESTIONS

1. What are the strongest arguments for a relativist perspective on human rights? What are the strongest arguments for a universalist perspective on human rights?

2. Article 23 of the International Covenant on Civil and Political Rights states, "No marriage shall be entered into without the free and full consent of the intending spouses." The practices of child betrothal and fixed marriages are still widespread in many non-Western countries. Do these marriages violate universal human rights norms? Why or why not?

3. As noted in this chapter, many women in Muslim societies do not experience the requirement that they be veiled in public as repressive. Does the fact that many if not most women accept this practice mean that it should be imposed on Muslim women in these societies who oppose the practice? Why or why not? Conversely, in societies that view veiling as a repressive practice, should it be acceptable to prohibit women from wearing the veil in the workplace, schools, or other places with dress codes? Why or why not?

4. Should the United Nations or individual nation-states pressure countries in which female genital mutilation is practiced to ban the procedure or to more rigorously enforce bans that are already in existence? Why or why not?

5. One of the major arguments against female genital mutilation is that it has detrimental effects on women's health. The latest medical research has found that the circumcision of males has detrimental health effects as well. Although male circumcision also has potential minor benefits, medical professionals now say that there are no net benefits from the procedure. As

this chapter has shown, other human rights norms are potentially threatened by male circumcision. Many parents continue to choose to have the procedure carried out on their sons for cultural reasons. Should human rights activists support a global campaign against male circumcision? Why or why not?

6. Even if one accepts the proposition that human rights are universal, disagreement remains over whether universal human rights are fundamentally individual or collective. If universal human rights exist, are they fundamentally individual or collective? Why?

4

Civil and Political Rights
in a World
of Sovereign States

CIVIL AND POLITICAL RIGHTS
AND STATE SOVEREIGNTY IN TENSION

As we saw in the Introduction, the relationship between state sovereignty and universal human rights involves a paradox. Sovereign states typically are the actors with legal responsibility for promoting and protecting human rights and, at the same time, are often the primary actors responsible for perpetuating human rights abuses. Indeed, states frequently justify human rights abuses on the grounds that deviations from human rights norms are essential to protecting state sovereignty. To explore this paradox, the present chapter provides an overview of civil and political rights as they exist in potential tension with state sovereignty, then illustrates this potential tension through detailed case studies of terrorism, torture, and the freedom of movement.

The potential tension between civil and political rights and state sovereignty is reflected in international human rights law. As we saw in Chapter 2, the International Covenant on Civil and Political Rights (ICCPR) codifies basic civil and political rights while making clear that states continue to retain their sovereignty. This continued emphasis on sovereignty in the ICCPR is most evident in Article 4, which authorizes states that have ratified the treaty to derogate from their obligations under the treaty "in time of public emergency which threatens the life of the nation . . . to the extent strictly required by the exigencies of the situation." In short, the ICCPR identifies security crises that potentially threaten the continued sovereignty of a nation-state as threats that justify derogation from human rights obligations. Because governing elites are the legitimate representatives of sovereign states, they exercise discretion in determining when a security crisis threatens state sovereignty and may do so in self-serving ways.

Although Article 4 goes on to say that any derogation from human rights law must be consistent with other international legal obligations and must not be based on discrimination "solely on the ground of race, colour, sex, language, religion, or social origin," the ICCPR does not create institutional mechanisms for enforcement. Similarly, although the ICCPR specifies that states are not legally authorized to derogate from certain obligations, including prohibitions against torture or slavery, under any circumstances, it once again does not provide for sanctions on states that do not comply with these obligations, nor does it create mechanisms for enforcement aside from basic monitoring. Thus, international human rights law reflects the tension inherent in proclaiming universal human rights that impinge upon the sovereignty of states that are the actors simultaneously capable of violating basic civil and political rights and most responsible for upholding them.

The tension between basic civil and political rights norms and state sovereignty is evident in practice as well as in law. To the extent that states openly acknowledge any deviation from their obligations to uphold basic civil and political rights, they justify such deviations from human rights norms as necessary to ensure national security. (More sophisticated state representatives might even cite Article 4 of the ICCPR as explicitly authorizing such deviations.) For example, states facing ongoing civil conflicts often adopt limitations on freedom of movement as a way of minimizing civil violence. A specific example of this type of response has been evident in the aftermath of urban race riots in the United States when city governments have commonly imposed curfews and other restrictions on freedom of movement as a way to quell immediate violence.

States also justify restrictions on freedom of speech and expression as measures intended to minimize violence and to enhance security. An interesting example is provided by the case of post–World War II Germany. During the war, the Nazi government adopted extreme limitations on the freedom of speech. After the war, the new German government restored freedom of speech in many forms but adopted new limitations on the freedom of expression, including prohibitions on the display of the swastika or the dissemination of Nazi propaganda, in an effort to prevent renewed anti-Semitic violence. Similarly, governments have justified restrictions on freedom of the press as necessary to prevent the inflammation of civil and political violence. In all cases of this nature, states appeal to implicit or explicit threats to sovereignty and security as justifications for limitations on civil and political rights.

Even when states engage in behavior explicitly prohibited under international human rights law during times of national security crises, such as the use of torture, governing elites either deny these abuses or justify them as necessary to fight subversive forces that threaten the very survival of the state.[1]

Students often provide justifications of this nature when discussing national security crises. For example, in the aftermath of the bombing of the Federal Building in Oklahoma City in 1996, many students in my classes suggested that torturing suspected bombers would be justified in an effort to extract information about potential additional planned attacks and even to punish the bombers. When governing elites throughout the world justify the systematic state practice of torture, they are engaging in similar logic. Indeed, rarely do states implement policies of torture because agents of the state enjoy torturing people, though sadly evidence suggests that officials responsible for torture often come to appreciate the sense of power they feel when engaged in the practice.[2] Rather, governing elites commonly believe that they are protecting national security when they implement policies that involve the systematic abuse of basic human rights.

The use of the "national security doctrine" by repressive Latin American governments during the 1970s and 1980s to justify the widespread use of torture and the killing of political "subversives" provides a striking example of the extent to which states are willing to justify systematic human rights abuses in defense of sovereignty. Under national security doctrines, military governments in various Latin American states identified a wide range of individuals and social groups—including nonviolent, generally apolitical groups such as the Rotary Club—as subversive threats to the state and targeted these groups for political violence and repression.[3]

The willingness of these states to identify potential political opponents as subversives went to unbelievable extremes. They did not seek to limit their use of political violence to individuals or groups who themselves practiced or espoused violence, against whom a violent reaction on the part of the state might be at least theoretically justifiable. Rather, they justified the use of political violence toward a wide range of innocent people as a means of terrorizing the population at large and discouraging political opposition. An official for the military regime in Argentina during the 1970s articulated the national security doctrine and its consequences for potential victims in stark terms: "First we will kill all the subversives; then we will kill their collaborators; then . . . their sympathizers; then . . . those who remain indifferent; and finally we will kill the timid."[4] Ultimately, the governing elites of these military regimes could not separate their own political interests from their conception of the national interest, with devastating consequences for the countless victims of human rights abuses by these repressive governments.

This discussion illustrates the practical difficulties inherent in any effort to negotiate an appropriate balance between the quest for universal human rights and the protection of state sovereignty. Certain circumstances seem to warrant restrictions on basic civil and political rights in the name of national security and sovereignty. Indeed, unstable states facing internal or external threats to their security are unlikely to be in a solid position to establish respect for and protection of fundamental human rights. Thus, it is not difficult to understand why states might seek to limit certain civil and political rights in order to protect their populations during a genuine national security crisis.

However, it is difficult to determine when such limitations are valid and when they merely represent the narrow political interests of governing elites. How do we know if governing elites are genuinely motivated by security concerns or if they are simply seeking to stifle political dissent?

Moreover, it is difficult to draw the line between restrictions on civil rights that are allowed under international law during times of public emergency, such as restrictions on freedom of movement or speech, and violations of basic civil and political rights that international law prohibits under any circumstances, such as torture. Although international law makes such distinctions, most states responding to national security crises do not. Thus, attempts to resolve the tension between sovereignty and universal human rights raise ethical and political challenges that have not yet been resolved. The political and ethical quandaries raised by efforts to negotiate an appropriate balance between universal human rights and state sovereignty are clearly illustrated by an exploration of case studies of terrorism, torture, and the freedom of movement in the following sections.

CASE STUDY: NATIONAL SECURITY AND TERRORISM

The Politics of Terrorism

Terrorism refers to the intentional and indiscriminate use of violence against civilian targets for the purpose of engendering fear among a population in an effort to achieve political objectives. The label *terrorism* is most commonly used to describe violence perpetrated by non-state actors against civilian targets. When adopted by non-state actors without access to the military resources and weapons of the state, terrorists typically use unconventional violent tactics, such as hostage taking, hijackings, and suicide bombings. Although the characterization of violence as terrorism is usually reserved for violence perpetrated by non-state actors, terrorists are often supported and trained by states. Moreover, states have used terrorist tactics directly to advance their security objectives. For example, when the United States dropped atomic bombs on Hiroshima and Nagasaki at the end of World War II, the U.S. government *intentionally* and *indiscriminately* targeted civilians with the objective of pressuring Japan to end its military campaign. Although defenders of this decision contend that it saved thousands of lives by bringing the war to an end more quickly, it nonetheless technically fulfills the definition of terrorism given here.

The application of the label *terrorist* to violence perpetrated by specific groups is political. In the words of a well-known saying, "one man's terrorist is another man's freedom fighter." Indeed, most groups and individuals who use terrorist tactics deny that they are terrorists. Rather, non-state actors labeled as terrorist often argue that they are using the only political tactics available to weak and oppressed groups and, thus, are justified in using violence to achieve legitimate political objectives. They also resist the notion that they target "innocent" civilians; they claim to use violence against individuals and groups who either collaborate with their oppressors or are otherwise implicated in their repression. Critics argue that terrorists are not necessarily motivated by oppression and point out that recent terrorist acts have involved middle-class or upper-middle-class individuals motivated by greed, power, or even bloodlust rather than repression.[5]

It is not the purpose of this chapter to resolve the question of whether or not terrorists are motivated by legitimate political aims or whether certain groups or states should be labeled terrorist. Instead, the objective of this case study is to explore the potential tension between state sovereignty and human rights when states respond to what they perceive (legitimately or not) as terrorist threats. Political theorists discuss what is known as the liberty–security trade-off. Liberty and security are both important values, and it is widely believed that these values exist in tension. Enhanced security may require limitations on liberty and, similarly, an expansion of liberty may lead to reduced security. State responses to terrorism are shaped by this "liberty–security" trade-off. Sovereign states, influenced by different cultural, ideological, and political contexts, will resolve this trade-off in different ways. In general, however, governing elites in states are understandably highly preoccupied with security in the face of terrorist threats and typically crack down on civil liberties and rights in an effort to avert terrorist violence. Whether or not individuals or groups view these restrictions on civil rights as legitimate will depend on the extent to which they are directly harmed or inconvenienced by these limitations and whether or not they believe the limitations genuinely promote security.

State policies directed at fighting terrorism involve a wide range of tactics that impinge upon basic civil and political rights. The negative consequences of state responses to terrorism for civil and political rights occur at both the domestic and the international level. Domestically, state policies designed to fight terrorism limit freedom of movement, contribute to discrimination, and violate basic due process procedures. Internationally, state efforts to fight global terrorism may lead states to aid repressive governments that violate the basic civil and political rights of their citizens and residents. Even when states do not actively aid civil rights–abusing governments, they may be reluctant to exert political pressure on behalf of human rights against states whose cooperation they rely on to combat terrorism. We will now examine two cases that clearly illustrate the tension between state efforts to combat terrorism and civil rights: Israel's response to Palestinian violence and the U.S. "war on terror" in the aftermath of the September 11, 2001, terrorist attacks on U.S. soil.

Israel's Security Dilemma and Responses to Terrorism

Israel's response to Palestinian terrorism provides a number of examples of the ways in which state efforts to fight terrorism hinder civil rights norms. The Israeli government has imposed curfews on Palestinian residents in the occupied territories in an effort to crack down on the mobility of potential terrorists.

Israel has also detained approximately 600,000 Palestinians since the country gained control of the West Bank and Gaza in 1967. According to the Israeli government, this policy of detainment is an essential component of the state's effort to gather intelligence on terrorist networks. [6] Israel's policy is based on the detention of all Palestinian males of a certain age, regardless of whether concrete reasons for suspicion exist.[7] Similarly, Israel has denied work permits to Palestinians fitting the profile of potential terrorists, thus frustrating the ability of Palestinians to fulfill their basic economic needs.

Israel has also erected physical barriers to restrict the entry of Palestinians into Israel proper. The Israeli Parliament recently voted in favor of a law that denies citizenship or legal residence to Palestinians who marry Israeli citizens, a restriction that it does not place on other noncitizens who marry Israelis. According to its supporters, the purpose of this policy is to prevent the infiltration of terrorists into Israel.[8] In these ways, Israeli policy engenders discrimination based alternatively on biological sex, age, and ethnicity, which further inflames political resentment among Palestinians and serves, in turn, as an additional impetus to future terrorist attacks.

Israeli policy also hinders due process norms by failing to provide detainees with information about the reasons for their arrest or access to lawyers, by detaining Palestinians without charging them for up to six months, and by trying suspects in military courts with secret evidence.[9] Additionally, Israel violates a fundamental tenet of a civil rights approach to justice that says that punishment and justice for crimes should be *individualized*. According to this approach, only individuals who are directly responsible for perpetrating crimes shall be held responsible for those crimes. In contradiction to an individualized approach to criminal justice, Israel razes the homes of the families of Palestinian terrorists as a method for deterring further terrorism. Despite its civil rights implications, the Israeli Supreme Court recently upheld the government policy of destroying without notice homes of families related to suicide bombers.[10] Israeli security forces also take large numbers of Palestinians into custody not because of individualized suspicion but because of their location in areas known to harbor suspected militants.

The growing use of suicide bombers by Palestinian militants demonstrates the complex nature of the security dilemma faced by Israel. In the past, Israel's policy of detaining and denying work permits to Palestinian males of a certain age was based on the reality that this profile fit the individuals likely to engage in suicide attacks—namely, young unmarried males.[11] Today, potential suicide bombers have a more diverse profile, with middle-aged and married individuals, children, and increasingly women serving as suicide bombers. Suicide bombers have even disguised themselves as Orthodox Jews in order to circumvent Israeli security measures.[12] From the point of view of the terrorists, changing the profile of suicide bombers makes sense because this change enables them to circumvent Israeli security measures designed to obstruct their efforts. From Israel's point of view, the changing nature of the threat of suicide bombers creates an incentive to develop new and more widely applied restrictions on civil liberties rather than eliminating these restrictions altogether.

Ultimately, innocent Palestinian civilians suffer as a result of the militarization of the occupied territories that Israel pursues as a security measure. At the same time, innocent Israeli civilians are targeted with violence because they are viewed by the Palestinians as complicit in their oppression. Thus, Israel's response to its security dilemma helps to perpetuate the cyclical nature of the Israeli–Palestinian conflict.[13] In the end, Israeli efforts to bolster its security with measures that violate basic civil rights and liberties are experienced as oppression by the Palestinians, and the cycle of violence and repression continues to spiral.

The U.S. "War on Terror"

The U.S. response to terrorism in the aftermath of September 11 has also involved basic restrictions on civil and political rights and is driven by similar political dynamics. After September 11, the United States adopted new rules leading to the increased detention of individuals in the United States in violation of the country's immigration laws and providing for secret deportation hearings. The new rules also allow for the prolonged detention of citizens and legal residents as well as illegal immigrants accused of "being material witnesses to terrorism, or fighting for the enemy."[14] U.S. courts have challenged many of these detentions but upheld the indefinite detention of two U.S. citizens, Yasser Esam Hamdi and Jose Padilla, as "enemy combatants" without charges, without an opportunity to challenge their detention before a judge, and without legal representation.[15] A federal district court judge ruled that the identities of most detainees should be made public under the Freedom of Information Act. Another federal district court in Virginia ruled that Mr. Hamdi be allowed to consult a lawyer, but a federal appeals court reversed the decision.[16] However, the U.S. Supreme Court recently ruled in regard to Mr. Hamdi's case that enemy combatants must be permitted to challenge their designated status and indefinite detention before a judge or "other neutral decision-maker."[17]

U.S. efforts to fight terrorism within the country's borders have also involved an assumption of guilt by association. Under the Antiterrorism and Effective Death Penalty Act, passed by Congress in 1996, it is a crime to provide "material support" to terrorist groups. Obviously, individuals who knowingly and intentionally provide support to terrorist groups are legitimate targets of antiterrorism measures. However, the Bush Administration's application of this legislation in the aftermath of September 11 is based on a broad interpretation of "material support." Individuals may be regarded with suspicion for paying dues or making contributions to organizations that do not openly espouse terrorism and that have other purposes. Thus, individual contributions to these groups may not be based on an awareness of or support for the group's terrorist activities. Critics charge that detaining individuals who unknowingly support the terrorist activities of such groups as terrorist suspects for prolonged periods without trial represents an unjust application of "guilt by association."

In addition to restricting civil and political rights domestically, the "war on terror" by the United States has contributed to a foreign policy that is dismissive of and sometimes downright hostile to civil and political rights in other countries. In its milder versions, U.S. foreign policy simply tolerates repression abroad. For example, after an Egyptian court sentenced a pro-democracy advocate to a seven-year prison sentence for promoting democracy in what critics have called a sham trial, the State Department did nothing more than express its "disappointment" out of fear that they might alienate a U.S. ally in the "war on terror."[18] In more extreme cases, U.S. foreign policy actively contributes to repression in other countries. For instance, the Bush Administration resumed direct military training assistance to Indonesia in the aftermath of the September 11th terrorist attacks against the United States for the purpose of fighting terrorism in the region despite the objection of human rights groups who pointed to the repressive nature of the Indonesian government. The U.S. Congress had cut aid to Indonesia in the 1990s because of concern about systematic human rights abuses in the country.[19]

Not only has the United States aided repressive governments in the "war on terror," but it has also intentionally taken advantage of repressive political environments in other countries to bolster its efforts to fight terrorism. For example, after the September 11th attacks, the U.S. government began sending suspected Al Qaeda terrorists to other countries, including Egypt, Syria, and Jordan, for interrogation. One justification for these policies is that the governments of these countries have a greater understanding of Islamic groups. However, critics suggest that the United States preferred to have Al Qaeda suspects interrogated in these countries because they use torture to extract information.[20] Indeed, the U.S. "war on terror" involves implicit if not explicit endorsement of gross violations of human rights abroad, including prolonged detentions and imprisonment without trial, torture, and summary executions.[21]

A foreign policy that intentionally encourages restrictions on civil and political rights abroad can obviously be criticized on moral grounds because it leads to violations of the fundamental human rights of individuals who have the misfortune of living under repressive governments. In addition, a foreign policy leading to repression can be criticized on pragmatic grounds. Although it may be tempting to support repressive measures as an effective method for preventing terrorism, such policies may have the unintended consequence of exacerbating terrorism if human rights abuses committed by governments supported by the United States generate anti-American sentiment and lead populations in foreign countries to sympathize with terrorist forces.[22] Ultimately, a repressive foreign policy of this nature may fail to promote security at the same time that it violates fundamental human rights.

In addition to condoning torture and political repression abroad through its foreign policy, recent revelations suggest that the United States may have actively embraced torture as a strategic tool in its "war on terror" abroad. The recent prison abuse scandal at Abu Ghraib detention facility in Iraq, which the United States invaded in 2003 partially due to allegations that there were links between Al Qaeda and Saddam Hussein, involved the torture and mistreatment of Iraqi prisoners. Abuses at Abu Ghraib included sexual humiliation, forced sexual acts, sleep deprivation, extended isolation, the pouring of chemicals and cold water on naked prisoners, and severe beatings. Notably, most of the detainees at the facility were civilians who had been detained in random sweeps by the U.S. military and did not pose a threat to society.[23] U.S. government officials in the Bush Administration contend that the Abu Ghraib scandal represents the acts of isolated individuals and has moved to try and punish violators through the U.S. military justice system. However, several of the soldiers on trial for their roles in the prisoner abuse scandal contend that they were merely following the directions of military intelligence officers at Abu Ghraib who wanted them to "soften up" prisoners so that they would be more likely to cooperate during interrogation sessions.[24]

Trials of six soldiers for their involvement in perpetrating abuses at Abu Ghraib are ongoing so, to date, no judicial pronouncement has been made on the validity of these prisoners' defense. Nevertheless, a recent government memo that appears to signal support of the use of torture lends some credence to their claims. In August 2002, the U.S. Justice Department issued a memo indicating that interrogators could use "extreme techniques" on prisoners being detained in the "war on terror." Without specifying particular techniques that could be considered legitimate, the memo suggested that the president had the authority to approve a wide range of coercive techniques without violating international or national legal prohibitions on the use of torture.[25] Administration officials deny that the United States engages in or condones torture. However, there are written records documenting the government's support of interrogation techniques "including hooding, nudity, stress positions, 'fear of dogs' and physical contact" as well as "sleep and dietary manipulation."[26] Defenders of such practices might argue that aggressive coercion is necessary to gain crucial information to prevent future terrorist attacks. Indeed, the Pentagon was motivated to approve aggressive interrogation techniques out of concern that Al Qaeda and Taliban detainees had information on future terrorist attacks.[27] In this context, the government's determination to aggressively seek to prevent such attacks is understandable. However, proponents of human rights contend that such tactics are unlikely to produce reliable intelligence and, in any case, represent unacceptable violations of fundamental human rights.

Furthermore, the Abu Ghraib prisoner abuse scandal, coupled with allegations of torture and other abuses at detention facilities elsewhere in Iraq and Afghanistan, has generated moral outrage throughout much of the Middle East and, indeed, across the globe. Not only do such abuses undermine the legitimacy of U.S. claims that it stands for human rights and freedom across the globe, but they also may generate increased support for Al Qaeda and other terrorist groups that threaten U.S. national security. In short, repression of civil and political rights intended to enhance national security may backfire by generating political animosity toward the United States and by increasing the numbers of individuals and groups who wish to perpetrate violence against the country and its citizens.

Do Restrictions on Civil and Political Rights
Enhance National Security?

The U.S. and Israeli cases illustrate both the logic and the limitations of policies designed to fight terrorism with restrictions on civil and political rights. On the one hand, such policies represent rational responses to real security threats that target both states and innocent civilians. Curfews, ethnic profiling, limitations on due process, collective punishment, and collaboration with repressive governments all may serve the ends of deterring or thwarting at least some terrorist attacks and, as a result, may enhance national security.

On the other hand, such policies risk inflaming political resentments among targeted individuals and groups who may become more inclined to embrace the ideology and tactics of terrorists. Indeed, critics of restrictions on civil and political rights as a mechanism for fighting terrorism argue that, in fact, there may be a positive relationship between civil and political rights and national security. According to this perspective, enhancing the civil and political rights of repressed groups will undercut the forces that drive terrorism and, in the long run, enhance national security. Because states responding to immediate security threats tend not to take this long-term perspective, whether or not the protection of civil and political rights enhances national security remains an open question.

CASE STUDY: FREEDOM OF MOVEMENT, CIVIL RIGHTS, AND SOVEREIGNTY

Freedom of Movement under International Law

The ability to regulate who may legally enter and reside in a state's territory is a fundamental component of state sovereignty. At the same time, international human rights law identifies freedom of movement as a fundamental human right. According to Article 12 of the International Covenant on Civil and Political Rights, all human beings have a right to leave any country, including their native land. Although this language suggests that human beings have a fundamental right to freedom of movement, international law also protects the right of sovereign nation-states to regulate their borders and to decide who may legally enter their territory. Thus, there is an inherent tension between individuals' right to freedom of movement and the right of countries to regulate immigration and emigration.

What is the appropriate response to the tension between these two goals? Some people argue that freedom of movement is a basic individual liberty that allows individuals to pursue equal opportunities. Restrictions on freedom of movement may condemn individuals to political, economic, and social injustice merely by accident of birth.[28] Indeed, proponents of freedom of movement argue that national borders are arbitrary in many respects. Thus, proponents of this view contend that it would be more appropriate to define political community based on a commitment to national norms than by accident of birth. Defenders of the right of states to restrict freedom of movement point to territorial control as a fundamental legal right of the sovereign state. These individuals generally assume that the state represents the interests of society as a whole and, therefore, that the state is justified in controlling its borders in order to pursue national interests.[29]

Although scholars continue to debate whether individuals should be able to move freely throughout the global system or whether states should have an essentially unlimited right to control their borders, the debate has been settled in law and practice. Despite the fact that individuals have a right to leave their country under the ICCPR, states are not bound by a corresponding obligation to allow individuals to enter or reside in their territory. (International refugee law, discussed in the next section, modifies this claim to some extent.) States continue to claim the sovereign right to restrict freedom of movement, and the preponderance of public and elite opinion across the globe tends to support state sovereignty on this issue. Nevertheless, national borders are growing increasingly porous in an era of globalization, thus ensuring that the debate over how to balance the right of sovereign states to regulate their borders with the individual right to freedom of movement will continue.

International Refugee Law and Sovereignty

The development of international refugee law in the aftermath of World War II seems to challenge the notion that state sovereignty is sacrosanct. The UN General Assembly passed the Convention Relating to the Status of Refugees in 1951. This convention, which entered into force in 1954, represented a response to the refugee crisis that plagued many European countries in the aftermath of World War II. Under the Refugee Convention, a refugee is defined as a person who "owing to well-founded fear of being persecuted for reasons of race, religion, nationality, membership of a particular social group or political opinion, is outside the country of his [or her] nationality and is unable or, owing to such fear, is unwilling to avail himself [or herself] of the protection of that country." The 1951 Refugee Convention initially applied only to refugees from World War II, but a 1967 Protocol modified the original language so that the Refugee Convention now applies to refugees across the globe.

International refugee law potentially creates an important mechanism for advancing basic political rights. In theory, refugee law calls for states to provide sanctuary to individuals who face political persecution in their countries of origin. Although international human rights law ostensibly prohibits states from violating the basic civil and political rights of citizens and residents to begin with, it does not create concrete mechanisms for enforcing these prohibitions. In this context, international refugee law represents a safety net of sorts. When states threaten citizens or residents with political persecution, international refugee law suggests that persecuted individuals may seek to protect themselves from political repression and violence by seeking asylum elsewhere.

In practice, international refugee law has not created a reliable method for protecting individuals from political persecution in their countries of origin. Despite the fact that state parties to the Refugee Convention obligate themselves to process requests for refugee status made by persons within the state's territory, sovereign states still determine if individual applicants fulfill the criteria for being considered a refugee under the treaty. In an international system organized according to the principle of sovereignty, it is inevitable that the ideological perspectives, foreign policy concerns, and political values of governing elites shape national decisions regarding whether or not to admit particular individuals as refugees. Thus, although the Refugee Convention ostensibly signals a significant challenge to the principle of sovereignty, it ultimately reflects the reality that state sovereignty continues to fundamentally shape world politics in practice.

Illegal Immigration and Civil and Political Rights

An exploration of state responses toward the issue of illegal immigration clearly illustrates the ways in which state sovereignty and civil and political rights exist in tension. In developing this argument, this section will focus on examples from U.S. immigration policy. The choice of examples from the United States is instructive *not* because U.S. policy is especially restrictive. U.S. immigration policy is quite open in comparison to the immigration policies of most states across the globe and, indeed, has been fundamentally shaped by ideas stressing the importance of basic civil and political rights.[30] Because it is generally less restrictive than the immigration policies of many states, U.S. immigration policy is an illustrative case that highlights the ways in which restrictive immigration policies can threaten civil and political rights even when such policies are, by global standards, comparatively sensitive to fundamental human rights.

Tension between efforts to restrict illegal immigration and the protection of basic civil rights can be manifested in several ways. First, policies designed to restrict immigration often lead to discrimination against ethnic minorities. When employers face penalties for hiring undocumented workers, they may be reluctant to hire ethnic minorities even if they are citizens or have authorization to work legally in a country. Additionally, policies allowing for the detention or deportation of suspected illegal immigrants may lead to discrimination against citizens or legal residents of a country who happen to be ethnic minorities. For example, police in Chandler, Arizona, acting under the authority of U.S. legislation authorizing local authorities to take actions to enforce immigration law, worked with federal immigration officials to round up illegal immigrants in the area. During this process, which included stopping cars and detaining suspected illegal immigrants in restaurants and churches, the police detained many U.S. citizens without probable cause.[31]

Second, restrictive immigration policies may contribute to brutality against suspected illegal immigrants and ethnic minorities. Traditionally, U.S.

efforts to restrict illegal immigration have prioritized preventing illegal entry along the U.S. border with Mexico over identifying and removing immigrants who have entered the country with fraudulent documents and are already residing in the country. The emphasis of a punitive policy along the U.S. border with Mexico has led the immigration bureaucracy to treat this policy problem as a threat to U.S. security that warrants an aggressive and sometimes violent response. As a result, U.S. immigration officials have been accused of engaging in brutality along the border, including verbal insults, physical intimidation, and brutality.[32] Indeed, one scholar reported that it was once common for Border Patrol agents to refer to suspected illegal immigrants as "tonks," for the sound made when their batons hit the heads of the suspects.[33]

Third, U.S. deportation policies have violated the due process rights of undocumented immigrants. Immigrants entering or residing in the United States illegally are subject to deportation or removal. On its face, this policy represents a clear effort to exercise state sovereignty and does not seem controversial. However, critics charge that the due process rights of illegal immigrants subject to deportation are often violated. For example, prior to the passage of the Illegal Immigration Reform and Immigrant Responsibility Act of 1996, only a trained immigration judge had the authority to order the deportation of an undocumented immigrant. However, the 1996 law gave expedited removal authority to Immigration and Naturalization Service inspectors who had the power to order the deportation of an undocumented immigrant on the spot at designated points of entry based on their own judgment that these migrants do not fulfill the criteria for asylum. In addition, these inspectors have frequently failed to inform potential candidates for asylum of their rights, to provide interpreters, or to ask required questions regarding whether undocumented immigrants have a fear of returning home.[34] Immigrant advocacy groups charge that this policy has led to the deportation of numerous undocumented immigrants who fulfill the criteria for receiving asylum in the United States.[35]

Finally, the U.S. government's immigration policies have involved arbitrary and prolonged detention for immigrants who face deportation. The 1996 Illegal Immigration Reform and Immigrant Responsibility Act mandated that the Immigration and Naturalization Service detain without bail all immigrants facing removal for criminal offenses, even minor criminal offenses committed years ago for which the immigrants had already fulfilled their punishment, until receiving the final judgment on deportation. This mandatory detention provision led to the indefinite detention of legal residents facing removal, and these immigrants were denied the same due process rights as U.S. citizens. As of June 2001, approximately 3,000 immigrants, both undocumented migrants and legal residents, were being detained by the U.S. immigration bureaucracy under this policy.[36] The 1996 Illegal Immigration Reform and Immigrant Responsibility Act also provided for the mandatory detention of individuals who have been granted asylum hearings until their cases are decided. Thus, asylum applicants typically are detained pending the decision in their cases; these decisions may take months or even years. Civil rights and refugee advocacy groups charge that to imprison individuals who are guilty of nothing but seeking asylum from persecution in their countries of origin is inhumane and unjust.

Notably, the U.S. government has adopted even more restrictive policies on detention and deportation in the aftermath of the September 11th terrorist attacks on U.S. soil, as discussed previously in the section on terrorism. Indeed, the Immigration and Naturalization Service has been disbanded, and its functions have been placed under the authority of the Department of Homeland Security, created in 2002 in the aftermath of the September 11th attacks. This administrative shift signals that the civil and political rights problems discussed here are likely to be exacerbated by the U.S. "war on terror." Because the Department of Homeland Security has responsibility for providing security in the interior of the United States, illegal immigration is even more likely than before to be framed as a security threat rather than a civil and political rights issue.

CONCLUSIONS

The potential tension between civil and political rights and state sovereignty is reflected both in international human rights law and in the practice of states across the globe. When states deviate from their obligations to uphold basic civil and political rights, they tend to justify such deviations from human rights norms as essential for protecting national security or the national interest more generally. State efforts to defend repressive policies in their efforts to combat terrorism provide a stark example of such justifications. Because the threat of terrorism is so great—in terms of individual lives as well as the very survival of states—states have not only justified restrictions on freedom of movement and freedom of expression, which can be valid under international law, but also tolerated the use of torture and summary executions, violations that international human rights law does not sanction under any circumstances. Similarly, when states adopt restrictive immigration policies, governing elites typically are unconcerned about the civil rights implications of restrictions on the freedom of movement. In their view, a state has a sovereign right to maintain the integrity of its borders and to protect its security with restrictive immigration policies. The basic civil and political rights of asylum seekers, undocumented workers, and even legal immigrants can be subjugated to the national interests of sovereign states, as defined by their governing elites.

When governing elites violate fundamental human rights in the name of national security, typically they genuinely believe that they are acting in the national interest by fighting subversive forces that threaten the very survival of the state. In the same vein, when states implement limitations on freedom of movement, elites generally view these limitations as legitimate expressions of sovereignty and the national interest. Unfortunately, it is difficult to draw the line between legitimate attempts to protect national sovereignty and the cynical manipulation of the concept of sovereignty by governing elites for their own self-aggrandizement. Too often, governing elites are unable to recognize that the national interest may not correspond exactly with their own political interests. The tendency of elites to conflate the national interest with their own political interests and ideological commitments leads too often to devastating consequences for countless victims of human rights abuses across the globe.

This chapter has illustrated the practical difficulties inherent in any effort to negotiate an appropriate balance between the quest for universal human rights and the protection of state sovereignty. Clearly, there are instances in which limitations on basic civil and political rights may be appropriate. Security, stability, and peace are important values, and state sovereignty is an important mechanism for pursuing these objectives. At times, limitations on basic civil and political rights may seem entirely legitimate and appropriate for securing these ends. Indeed, the International Covenant on Civil and Political Rights acknowledges this fact by specifying that states have the right to derogate from certain basic civil and political rights obligations "in time of public emergency which threatens the life of the nation." Moreover, it is important to note that civil and political rights often are most threatened in unstable political environments when the security situation in particular nation-states is deteriorating. Under immediate conditions of instability and violence, restrictions on basic civil rights, such as limitations on freedom of movement or freedom of speech that might otherwise incite violence, may be appropriate mechanisms for seeking to prevent explosive societal violence from erupting.

At the same time, the historical record of repressive regimes demonstrates the ways in which deviations from basic human rights obligations have been abused by governing elites in the name of national security and sovereignty. What governments initially justify as temporary restrictions on basic civil rights as a means of preventing immediate violence may evolve into permanent efforts to silence political opponents and critics of repression. Additionally, restrictions on civil and political rights justified in the name of national security and sovereignty have a way of evolving from generalized security measures that affect a population in general to discriminatory measures that target specific groups, especially racial, ethnic, and gender minorities. Perhaps most disturbing, when states violate prohibitions against torture and other civil rights norms that are *never* justified under international human rights law, they often engage in political violence against individuals who are clearly innocent and have done absolutely nothing to warrant a violent response. In doing so, they often exacerbate the security crises they claim to be seeking to resolve. Ultimately, states that abuse civil and political rights in the name of sovereignty may undermine the values of peace, security, and stability that they are ostensibly trying to promote.

DISCUSSION QUESTIONS

1. Is the tension between sovereignty and civil and political rights inevitable? Why or why not? Can you think of ways that sovereignty could be used to promote basic civil and political rights? Are there ways in which the protection of basic civil and political rights might enhance sovereignty?

2. Are restrictions on basic civil and political rights ever justified? Why or why not?

3. If restrictions on basic civil and political rights are justified, which rights would it be acceptable to restrict? Under what circumstances?

4. Are there any basic civil and political rights that states should never restrict or violate under any circumstances? Why or why not? If there are such rights, which ones should never be violated or restricted?

5. When states restrict basic civil and political rights in the name of sovereignty, what criteria can we use to evaluate whether governing elites are doing so for valid reasons or whether they are acting out of narrow political self-interest?

6. Is it ever valid to use torture to gain information from suspected terrorists? Why or why not?

7. Should states have an obligation to accept refugees fleeing repression or deprivation in their countries of origin as a means of protecting basic human rights? Why or why not?

WEB RESOURCES

International Covenant on Civil and Political Rights (http://www.unhchr.ch/html/menu3/b/a_ccpr.htm)

Amnesty International (http://www.amnesty.org)

Human Rights Watch (http://www.hrw.org)

United Nations Web Resources on Human Rights (http://www.un.org/rights/index.html)

5

Collective Rights in a World of Sovereign States

HUMAN RIGHTS AS COLLECTIVE RIGHTS

Collective rights refer to human rights claimed by human beings as part of groups. As discussed in Chapter 1, collective rights evolved as part of the "third generation" of human rights that emerged out of mid-twentieth-century decolonization struggles across the globe. For example, newly independent African countries in the aftermath of decolonization framed human rights as "peoples" rights rather than individual rights. In doing so, these African states adopted the "Western" framework of human rights while rejecting the assumption that human rights belong first to individuals rather than groups. Because "third world" nationalism was a driving force behind claims for human rights as collective rather than individual rights, demands for collective rights have focused prominently on self-determination and the right to economic development. In fact, Western critics of collective rights have often dismissed the concept of collective rights as reflecting a rigidly Marxist perspective on economic rights that is ultimately dismissive of civil and political rights.

However, collective rights are *not* limited to economic rights. Human beings experience fundamental abuses of civil and political rights as members of groups. For example, ethnic or religious minorities often suffer political persecution and are denied basic civil and political rights simply because of their status as members of these minority groups. As a result, members of such groups commonly frame their demands for basic civil and political rights as collective rights. An individual who has been denied the right to vote because of her ethnicity does not typically simply demand that she as an individual be given the right to vote—rather, she decries the discrimination against her ethnic group and asserts the right to vote for all members of the community whose basic political rights have been denied.

Violations of civil and political rights aimed at specific groups go beyond issues of voting and other forms of political participation. Indeed, the very survival of some groups is often threatened by violations of fundamental civil and political rights, as illustrated starkly by cases of genocide. Thus, collective rights involve a wide range of demands for civil and political as well as economic and social rights, including the right to self-determination, the right to economic development, the right to be free from discrimination, the right to political participation, and even more recently claimed rights to peace and to a healthy environment.

In an examination of human rights as collective rights, it is crucial to explore the relationship between state sovereignty and collective rights. States are often asked to resolve competing rights claims, both between groups and individuals and between different communities. For example, states often must address competing claims between women seeking equality with men in a society and minority religious or cultural groups that believe different, and often unequal, gender roles are an essential part of their culture or religion. Interestingly, such conflicting political claims between women and religious or cultural minorities can be framed either as competing collective rights (if we conceive of women as a collective group) or as a conflict between individual and collective rights (if we conceive of individual women as the primary holders of equality rights.) Either way, these competing rights claims raise complicated political and moral questions. Because competing rights claims are rarely easy to settle, the concept of state sovereignty is an important factor in explaining why states resolve these conflicts in different ways.

Not only do states have to address competing rights claims between different individuals and groups, but they also are frequently implicated in disputes over collective rights. On the one hand, state elites frequently adopt the language of collective rights to reinforce state sovereignty as a norm. To this end, states not only claim that state sovereignty is an important principle in and of itself but also reframe the argument to suggest that state sovereignty is a mechanism for promoting human rights as collective rights. In doing so, states typically take for granted that the state represents the interests of its citizens and residents and, thus, claim that respect for state sovereignty is essential for protecting the collective rights of its people. On the other hand, states deny the importance of collective rights when dissenting groups within the state make claims for group rights that threaten the survival or sovereignty of the state.

Thus, state sovereignty is often at the center of disputes over collective rights. Ultimately, sovereignty as a principle can either coincide with or be in tension with collective rights depending on how the idea of collective rights is interpreted and applied. As we saw in the Introduction, the relationship between state sovereignty and universal human rights involves a paradox. In the case of collective rights, this paradox is evident in the fact that states laud sovereignty as the best means for protecting collective rights and, at the same time, violate and repress collective rights in the name of state sovereignty. This chapter provides an overview of collective rights as they exist in potential tension with state sovereignty. In particular, it explores the relationship between collective rights and sovereignty through detailed case studies of self-determination and genocide.

COLLECTIVE RIGHTS
AND INDIVIDUAL RIGHTS

Demands for collective rights often involve fundamental *individual* rights, such as the right to equal opportunity or political freedom. Thus, critics of the idea of collective rights often dismiss the concept as redundant—in their view, if a state genuinely protects basic individual rights, then rights for various groups should follow.[1] However, although this perspective has some validity, it does not sufficiently consider the merits of claims for collective rights. It is, in fact, true that groups demanding collective rights represent individuals whose basic political and economic rights have been denied. Because these individuals experience human rights abuses as members of particular groups, it should not be surprising that they would seek to demand basic rights *as members of these groups* rather than as isolated individuals. In other words, proponents of group rights turn the arguments of critics around. Whereas critics contend that if states protect individual rights then group rights will follow, proponents of collective rights argue that states must promote collective rights if individual members of various communities are to be able to enjoy fundamental rights.

This discussion rightly suggests that individual and collective rights are *not necessarily* in tension. The promotion of basic political and economic rights for individuals can ensure that members of previously repressed groups enjoy fundamental rights. Similarly, the extension of rights to formerly oppressed groups simultaneously represents an expansion of individual rights. Thus, in many respects, debates over the relative merits of individual and collective rights often involve a sort of "chicken or egg" dilemma, with arguments focusing on which set of rights needs to be prioritized first in an effort to promote both in the long term. In these cases, the argument is not over *whether* individual rights or collective rights are more important but, instead, over *how* to best promote both. In essence, individual rights and collective rights can be seen as complementary, and the only question is how best to protect them—by prioritizing individual rights first or by ensuring basic rights protections for groups.

Although it is true that individual and collective rights can be complementary, they can also be fundamentally in tension with each other. In these cases, group demands for collective rights can conflict with other individual human rights claims. For example, a religious group might claim that dress codes for women are required by its theology, represent an expression of its collective right to self-determination, and should be upheld by the state. In contrast, individual women from within this group might argue that such dress codes violate their right to freedom of expression, a right that should be protected by the state. Similarly, an indigenous people might argue that states should respect its restrictions on marriage outside of the group or on the job or social mobility of youth as legitimate expressions of its collective rights. At the same time, individual members of this indigenous population might protest that such restrictions violate their fundamental human rights and seek state intervention on their behalf. As these examples illustrate, fundamental tension often separates claims for individual and collective rights.

Additionally, it is important to note that different sets of collective rights might conflict with each other. We can revisit the previous examples to illustrate this point. In each case, we can reconceptualize the political disputes as involving two sets of collective rights rather than collective rights versus individual rights. In the first case, disputes over religious dress codes involve two collectivities, a religious community and women *as a group*. In the second case, two collectivities, an indigenous people and youth *as a group*, are involved. Thus, even if one concludes that collective rights should take priority over individual rights, it does not necessarily settle the debate. Individual members of a community who wish to assert their own rights against the collective rights of the larger community might simply define themselves as part of a separate group also deserving of collective rights, such as women, youth, or a religious or ethnic minority. In such cases, we do not have clear criteria for resolving which human rights claims should take priority.

CASE STUDY: SELF-DETERMINATION

Self-Determination under International Law

The right to self-determination is set out in both the International Covenant on Civil and Political Rights (ICCPR) and the International Covenant on Economic, Social, and Cultural Rights (ICESCR). Both of these covenants share a common Article 1 that articulates and defines the right to self-determination as follows: "All peoples have the right to self-determination. By virtue of that right they freely determine their political status and freely pursue their economic, social, and cultural development." Notably, the right of self-determination is discussed in Part I of each treaty separate from other substantive rights, which are identified in Part III in both the ICCPR and the ICESCR. Before moving on to a discussion of other rights, each covenant includes articles describing states' general implementation obligations in Part II.

The placement of the discussion of the right to self-determination as a preeminent human right separate from and prior to other human rights in each treaty indicates the great importance states attach to this right. According to the UN Human Rights Committee, the right of self-determination receives such prominence in the International Covenant on Civil and Political Rights because states must be able to realize this collective right in order to promote and protect basic individual rights.[2] Similar logic can be used to explain the prominence of self-determination in the International Covenant on Economic, Social, and Cultural Rights. A more cynical interpretation suggests that states intended to signal a conception of self-determination that would reinforce, rather than challenge, state sovereignty when they gave the principle of self-determination such prominence in these documents.

Despite the prominence of the right to self-determination in international human rights law, no global consensus exists regarding how to interpret and apply the right to self-determination. Perhaps the thorniest issue involves the question of which "peoples" may make valid claims for self-determination. Traditionally, two viewpoints have dominated the debate. A territorial perspective suggests that "peoples" who have the right to self-determination are defined by their citizenship status. According to this perspective, states may claim the right to self-determination on behalf of their citizens. Conversely, an ethnic perspective defines "peoples" as groups who share a common history, language, religion, racial identity, or other social and cultural factors that distinguish them from other groups. According to the ethnic perspective, a group's self-perception of itself as a distinct people is the crucial factor that enables it to make legitimate claims for the right to self-determination.[3] An interpretation of self-determination that uses the first definition of "peoples" reinforces the principle of state sovereignty. In contrast, a definition of "peoples" based on ethnicity fundamentally challenges state sovereignty because of the reality that ethnicity and citizenship do not correspond neatly in most states across the globe.

Moreover, if self-perceived identity is the standard that should be used to define "peoples" for the purposes of self-determination, one could argue that even the ethnic perspective does not sufficiently capture the diverse cultural, political, social, and economic identities of peoples across the globe. For example, groups of women might self-identify themselves as a "people" for the purposes of self-determination. As a case in point, some women's rights groups in the United States have argued that the right to reproductive choice is essential for women's self-determination. Similarly, gays, lesbians, bisexuals, transsexuals, and transgendered individuals might perceive themselves as distinct peoples deserving the right to self-determination. These examples illustrate the conceptual difficulties of defining self-determination based on self-perception of identity.

Carried to a logical extreme, such a broad interpretation undermines the notion of self-determination as a collective right in that the possible permutations of identity are almost endless and might end up reflecting nothing more than narrow *individual* preferences. In this case, an individualized approach might be more appropriate to advancing basic political and economic rights. Moreover, a very broad definition of "peoples" threatens state sovereignty in very dramatic ways and will not be accepted by states. However, a complete rejection of self-perceived identity as a criterion for identifying a "people" risks rendering the principle of self-determination meaningless. If "peoples" are nothing more than citizens of particular states, then asserting a right to self-determination merely becomes a redundant way of saying that states have a right to sovereignty.

Another controversy that arises in debates over how to interpret and apply the right to self-determination involves the question of whether or not this principle implies that "peoples" have a right to independence. In this case, greater consensus among both scholars and policymakers exists. The preponderance of evidence indicates that the right to self-determination does *not* mean that all peoples have a right to independence under international law. Rather, international legal norms and state practice suggest that autonomy for groups within sovereign states as well as the provision of basic political and economic rights are valid means for promoting self-determination.

Self-Determination in Historical Context

The historical evolution of the right of self-determination under international law demonstrates the way in which state interests and politics have shaped the concept. A right to self-determination was first enunciated in the aftermath of World War I as a justification for the Allied division of the territories and colonies of the defeated powers in World War I—namely, the Austro-Hungarian and Ottoman empires and Germany. Although neither the Treaty of Versailles, the Treaty of Sevres, nor the Covenant of the League of Nations proclaim the right to self-determination, Allied leaders asserted that a right of self-determination motivated their efforts to create new states out of the former colonies and territories of the defeated powers, as embodied in these postwar settlement treaties.[4] (For the purposes of clarity, it is worth noting that the Covenant of the League of Nations comprised the first thirty articles of the Treaty of Versailles and the first twenty-six articles of the Treaty of Sevres.) U.S. President Woodrow Wilson articulated perhaps the most famous defense of an emerging right to self-determination in his Fourteen Points speech when he said that "peoples and provinces must not be bartered about from sovereignty to sovereignty as if they were chattels or pawns in a game" and that questions involving territorial borders and governing authority should be settled "in the interests of the populations concerned."[5]

Self-determination under the post–World War I settlement led to the creation of six new nation-states out of the Austro-Hungarian empire: Austria; Czechoslovakia; Hungary; Poland; the Kingdom of Serbia, Croatia, and Slovenia (which later became Yugoslavia); and Romania. (Interestingly, two of these nation-states, Czechoslovakia and Yugoslavia, broke apart in a new wave of self-determination at the end of the Cold War. In the case of Czechoslovakia, the division of the country into Slovakia and the Czech Republic proceeded relatively peacefully; Yugoslavia disintegrated in a wave of civil and international violence, as will be discussed later in this chapter.) Similarly, the peace treaties carved new nation-states out of the religiously and culturally diverse Ottoman Empire. The borders of these new states typically reflected the interests of the war's victors more than political, social, and cultural realities of the people living in this region, and the reverberations of this exercise in state creation are still being felt throughout the Middle East. The Covenant of the League of Nations created a mandate system for the former colonies of the Ottoman Empire and of Germany under which the Allies were authorized to administer these territories with the objective of eventually moving the people living in the new mandates towards self-governance.

Despite claims by Allied leaders that they sought to promote the right of self-determination, the historical record suggests that they were motivated by more narrow political and ideological considerations. Notably, the postwar peace settlement did not apply the concept of self-determination to the overseas colonies of the victorious powers. Moreover, despite Wilson's grand claims about the necessity of acting in the interests of the people concerned, the Allies did not typically hold referenda to determine the preferences of the affected populations in making decisions about the creation of borders for new states. In general, the Allies did not stress the importance of creating democratic forms of governance for ascertaining the will of the people in the states they were creating. Moreover, although the Covenant of the League of Nations did call for basic protections of minority groups, efforts to draw borders in a way that would maximize self-determination for groups that perceived themselves as a distinct people were minimal. Instead, political and strategic calculations played a much greater part in shaping Allied decisions about drawing borders.[6] Because their efforts represented the political interests of the victors more than a principled commitment to the self-determination of peoples, the Allies attached less importance to the right to self-determination in their foreign policies after they had settled (at least temporarily) territorial questions raised by the end of World War I.

The right to self-determination reemerged on the global agenda in the aftermath of World War II. However, at this time, the victorious powers attached less prominence to the principle than they had after World War I. Instead, the Allies stressed peace and security as the ultimate values after World War II. Although the victors also emphasized the importance of human rights, they did so because they viewed the pursuit of human rights as integral to the broader goals of peace and security, as we saw in Chapter 2. Moreover, to the extent that they placed importance on human rights, they did not identify self-determination as a core human right. The UN Charter makes only brief references to the principle of self-determination, and it was not even identified as a right in the UN Declaration of Human Rights. This omission is striking given the place of prominence the right of self-determination receives in the binding covenants on human rights.

What explains this dramatic shift in perspective between the 1948 Declaration on Human Rights and the UN General Assembly's adoption of both covenants on human rights in 1966? In short, decolonization across the globe explains the change in perspective. As a result of decolonization movements in Africa and elsewhere, more than twice as many nation-states were members of the United Nations in 1966 than in 1948. Coming out from under the oppression of colonial rule, these newly independent countries stressed human rights as collective rather than individual rights. In particular, these newly independent countries viewed self-determination as a crucial vehicle for asserting their right to be free from oppression and external interference.

This shift in perspective was first evidenced when the UN General Assembly adopted the Declaration on the Granting of Independence to Colonial Countries and Peoples in 1960. In paragraph 2, this declaration first articulated the language on self-determination that was later incorporated, verbatim, in Article 1 of both covenants on human rights. Because of its centrality in all of these documents, it is worth repeating the language here: "All peoples have the right to self-determination; by virtue of that right they freely determine their political status and freely pursue their economic, social, and cultural development." The Declaration goes on to proclaim, in paragraph 6, "Any attempt aimed at the partial or total disruption of the national unity or territorial integrity of a country is incompatible with the purposes and principles of the Charter of the United Nations" and further asserts, in paragraph 7, "the sovereign rights of all peoples and their territorial integrity."[7]

The direct evolution of the language calling for the right to self-determination out of the Declaration on the Granting of Independence to Colonial Countries and Peoples makes it absolutely clear that the right to self-determination under international law was intended to *reinforce* and not to challenge state sovereignty outside of the context of decolonization. Although the language in the human rights covenants proclaims that "all peoples" have the right to self-determination under international law, states in practice historically have limited their recognition of a right to self-determination to colonized peoples and have not generally recognized self-determination for ethnic or other identity groups that would threaten the sovereignty of territorially contiguous states. For example, the international community did *not* recognize a right to self-determination for the Ibo tribe living in the Biafra region of Nigeria in the 1960s despite the Nigerian government's oppression of this group. Similarly, the United Nations sent a peacekeeping force to the Congo in 1960 to prevent secession of the Katanga region from the country that had just gained its independence from Belgium.

As these examples indicate, in practice, states historically have used the concept of self-determination as shorthand for state sovereignty. A literal reading of the legal language articulating a right to self-determination suggests that this narrow application of the concept is too limited even though it may be understandable when placed in historical context. Given the myriad ways in which colonialism victimized the populations of colonized countries, it should not be surprising that newly independent states would stress the importance of their right to be free from external interference. The history of colonialism, often perpetuated in the name of humanitarian impulses, suggests the need to scrutinize with great care claims made by states that they are intervening in other states in the name of human rights. Governing elites in decolonized countries typically have demonstrated an understandable preoccupation with independence as a means of promoting genuine self-governance and economic independence. At the same time, these same governing elites too often use the rhetoric of sovereignty and self-determination to quash political dissent and to exploit the economic resources and people they now govern for self-interested ends. In short, they engage in the very forms of oppression for which they have justifiably condemned colonizing powers, and they have commonly done so in the name of self-determination.

Self-Determination and Indigenous Peoples

An examination of self-determination for indigenous peoples provides an excellent illustration of the ways in which demands for collective rights can simultaneously challenge state sovereignty and conflict with other individual rights. Indigenous peoples can be defined as "ethnically distinct communities who usually reside in remote hinterlands and who have resisted, or been denied, assimilation into the dominant modernizing culture."[8] The term *indigenous peoples* is typically used to refer to communities of people that lived in a territory prior to its colonization. Despite often having been forcibly displaced from their original land by colonizing groups, they often view the land on which they currently live as a sacred ancestral trust and seek to preserve it for future generations. Even though these groups have typically been shaped by the modernization of the broader societies in which they live, they often maintain deep connections to their cultural roots and hold many premodern values.[9]

Indigenous peoples perceive themselves as distinct peoples. In this way, they clearly fulfill the criterion for self-determination if one defines "peoples" by ethnicity. Nevertheless, states typically resist the notion that indigenous people have a right to self-determination because of the fundamental challenge that recognition of such a right would pose to state sovereignty. The 1993 World Conference on Human Rights provides a striking example of state resistance to the right of self-determination for indigenous peoples. At this conference, participating states decided to use the term *indigenous people* rather than *indigenous peoples* so as not to signal that these groups were entitled to claim the right to self-determination.[10]

Of course, states are reluctant to endorse the right to self-determination for indigenous peoples because they do not intend to grant independence or to relinquish territory to these groups. They fear, perhaps correctly, that conceding a right to self-determination would indicate a willingness to make such concessions not only to indigenous peoples but also to other distinct ethnic groups who might make self-determination claims against the state. Thus, even when they adopt policies that accommodate some of the demands of indigenous peoples, states typically do not acknowledge that these policies are directed toward the objective of self-determination.

Another difficulty that complicates state efforts to foster self-determination for indigenous peoples is that doing so typically means providing these groups special rights that are not available to the population at large or granting them immunity from national laws. When states grant special rights to indigenous peoples, they violate the principle of nondiscrimination that suggests all *indi-*

viduals are to be treated equally under the law. In this way, an inherent tension between individual rights and collective rights exists. State efforts to protect the "natural heritage" and ancestral lands of indigenous peoples have significant potential to generate conflicts between individual and collective rights—for example, competing individual rights claims involving the right to private property.

Self-determination movements involving Native American tribes in the United States and Canada illustrate the potential tension between individual and collective rights. Indigenous tribes in each of these countries have sought and received exemption from national laws in their efforts to pursue self-determination:

> Instead of insisting on equal treatment as Americans and Canadians and full integration (if not assimilation) into the majority cultures, the dominant thrust of the contemporary rights movements of Native Americans (on the U.S. mainland) and of the Inuits (in Canada and Alaska) is toward restoring the authentic dignity, including the political autonomy, of their own cultures. To many of the new leaders, self-determination means immunity from, rather than equal protection of, the laws of the dominant Euro-American political systems to which their communities have been subordinated (often forcibly) during the past 300 years.[11]

A specific example of the differential treatment of indigenous tribes in the United States and Canada involves exemptions for these groups from hunting or fishing restrictions imposed on other U.S. and Canadian citizens. These special usage rights are provided as a means of granting these tribes access to ancestral lands and allowing them to support themselves through traditional practices. However, other U.S. and Canadian citizens who fish or hunt for either commercial purposes or sport often resent this differential treatment.

Whereas critics of collective rights have claimed that they are redundant and that the provision of basic individual rights should be sufficient, this example illustrates the shortcomings of this perspective. For example, disputes over special hunting and fishing rights for indigenous peoples reflect differing perspectives on how to fulfill the basic human right to food. Article 11 of the International Covenant on Economic, Social, and Cultural Rights provides that all human beings have a right to an adequate standard of living, including adequate food. A perspective stressing the preeminence of individual rights says only that a human being must have guaranteed access to food. A state that provides a social safety net ensuring that all of its citizens have access to food would be considered to have fulfilled its obligations. However, a collective perspective on human rights might suggest that guaranteed access to food is not enough. From the point of view of an indigenous tribe, having guaranteed access to food is *not* the same thing as being able to gather food in the traditional manner of one's community. Proponents of self-determination for indigenous peoples contend that it is not just the content of individual rights that matters. Rather, self-determination implies a group's right to determine the appropriate means by which it will pursue and enjoy its basic rights.

In general, proponents of self-determination for indigenous peoples contend that states need to protect collective rights in order for members of various communities to truly be able to enjoy fundamental rights. According to
Christian Bay, the collective right to self-determination is crucial for the survival of indigenous peoples, and states should allow for reasonable exemptions
to national laws in an effort to ensure that these cultures are able to survive. In
his view, the cultural survival of these traditional communities is essential if
individuals truly are to have genuine freedom in choosing how to live their
lives. Ultimately, Bay likens the extinction of indigenous cultures to genocide:

> This is not as bloody as outright genocide, but the result is the same: the
> extinction of yet another culturally distinct people. Ethnocide is like
> genocide on the installment plan . . . it destroys the cultural dignity and
> identity of all members of a people, and very likely destroys their mental
> and physical health to boot, as well as their unique worldviews and tradi-
> tional knowledge, and it often terminates their ability or motivation to
> produce their own kind.[12]

Bay acknowledges that tension between collective self-determination and individual rights is inevitable and does not sanction the violations of certain basic
individual rights, such as infanticide, in the name of self-determination. Nevertheless, he contends that exempting indigenous peoples from national laws,
even at the expense of infringing on some basic individual rights such as the
right to private property, is a small price to pay to ensure the survival of culturally distinct indigenous peoples.[13]

Self-Determination after the Cold War

A new wave of self-determination began at the end of the Cold War when
groups demanding political autonomy or independence sought to stretch the
historically narrow interpretation of this principle. To some extent, states indicated growing acceptance of a broader interpretation of self-determination
when they recognized the independence of new states representing people
who did not fit the traditional definition of a colonized people and, thus, did
not fulfill the historical criteria for self-determination. At the same time, state
behavior during this period continued to stress the importance of state sovereignty. In the end, although the post–Cold War period witnessed an expansion
of the way in which states applied the concept of self-determination in limited
cases, states generally reinforced the preeminence of state sovereignty as a norm
and applied this principle in a way that did not challenge existing state borders.
A comparison of the international community's response to self-determination
movements in the former Yugoslavia and the Chechen struggle for independence in Russia illustrates the evolution of the right to self-determination in
the aftermath of the Cold War.

Prior to its collapse, the federal state of Yugoslavia was comprised of six
constituent republics: Bosnia-Herzegovina, Croatia, Macedonia, Montenegro,
Serbia, and Slovenia. At the end of the Cold War, the ruling Communist Party

in Yugoslavia, dominated by Serbs, began to foment ethnic nationalism as a means of consolidating power in the aftermath of the collapse of global Communism. In response, nationalist movements in the various constituent republics began to grow.[14] In 1991, the republics of Slovenia and Croatia declared their independence from Yugoslavia. In a deviation from the historical practice of limiting self-determination to colonized peoples, the European Community recognized Slovenia and Croatia as independent states in 1992. Macedonia also declared independence from Yugoslavia in 1991, though international recognition was not immediately forthcoming because of Greek opposition, for various cultural and political reasons, to its use of the name Macedonia. Also in 1992, Bosnia-Herzegovina declared its independence after a referendum for independence received majority support, although Bosnian Serbs abstained from the referendum. Subsequently, the European Community and the United States recognized Bosnia's independence.

Critics of the U.S. and European decisions to recognize the independence of the former Yugoslav republics argued that this recognition exacerbated violence in the former Yugoslavia by fomenting nationalist fervor and ethnic conflict among the diverse groups in each republic. Bosnia-Herzegovina was especially marked by diversity, with a population comprised of a plurality of Muslims, followed by a large Bosnian Serb population and significant numbers of Croats.[15] Thus, it is not surprising that nationalist conflict was especially violent in the ensuing Bosnian war. According to critics, international recognition of the independence of the former Yugoslav republics ensured that what should have been a civil conflict emerged into a major international crisis and threatened to disrupt stability in the entire region. Moreover, critics suggested that U.S. and European recognition of the independence of the former Yugoslav republics would give minority groups across the globe an incentive to demand self-determination and would lead to the eruption of communal violence in states with large minority populations.

In contrast, proponents of self-determination for the peoples of the former Yugoslav republics pointed to the Yugoslav government's repression of ethnic minorities and denial of basic human rights in what ultimately constituted a case of genocide against the Bosnian Muslims as a justification for the U.S. and European recognition of the independence of the former Yugoslav republics. In their view, promoting the self-determination of Bosnian Muslims and other minorities within the former Yugoslavia was the only means of guaranteeing fundamental human rights to the peoples living there. According to this perspective, the recognition of the right to self-determination for national groups in the former Yugoslavia was *not* the cause of chaos and disorder but a principled response to ugly Serbian nationalism that ultimately was the driving force behind violence in the region.[16]

Although the United States and Europe recognized the independence of the former Yugoslav republics, the international community was unwilling to back up a principled commitment to a broader interpretation of self-determination with any meaningful political or military resources. Instead, as will be discussed in the case study of genocide that follows, the international community did very little to prevent Serb efforts to "ethnically cleanse" Bosnian Serb areas of Bosnia in what amounted to a contemporary case of genocide.[17] Although they had apparently endorsed a broad conception of self-determination by recognizing the independence of the former Yugoslav republics, powerful states did not intervene to prevent genocide against Bosnian Muslims, let alone to ensure their political autonomy. In this case, the inaction of the international community spoke louder than its words. Nevertheless, the former Yugoslav republics continue to exist as independent states, though in the case of Bosnia-Herzegovina, the government lost significant amounts of territory during the war. In this way, the case of the former Yugoslavia suggests an important shift in the balance between state sovereignty and the principle of self-determination as a concept that applies to *peoples* rather than states.

The international community's response to the conflict in Kosovo also suggests a shift in the balance between state sovereignty and self-determination under international law. The Federal Republic of Yugoslavia was made up of several constituent republics—Bosnia-Herzegovina, Croatia, Macedonia, Montenegro, Serbia, and Slovenia—before it disintegrated in the mid-1990s. At this time, Kosovo was an autonomous province located within Serbia. Roughly 90 percent of the population in Kosovo was Muslim ethnic Albanian, and the remainder of the population consisted primarily of Christian Orthodox Serbs and Montenegrins. In 1989, Yugoslavia revoked the autonomous status of Kosovo. In the process, the Yugoslav government fired thousands of ethnic Albanians from state jobs. Moreover, Yugoslavia instituted police rule in Kosovo characterized by torture, arbitrary arrests, and killings.

Yugoslav repression in Kosovo contributed to a pro-independence movement in this province. In a 1991 referendum, conducted "underground" without the permission of the Yugoslav government, 99 percent of those voting favored independence for Kosovo. The majority of the population in Kosovo practiced peaceful resistance in order to push for independence and to protest repression. The Democratic League of Kosovo (LDK), the ruling ethnic Albanian party at the time, represented this political viewpoint. Conversely, the Kosovo Liberation Army (KLA), which came into existence in the mid-1990s, used violent methods in making its claims for independence.

The Yugoslav government labeled the KLA a "terrorist" group and used the threat of terrorism as justification for further repression. Indeed, after several KLA attacks on Yugoslav authorities in Kosovo, Yugoslavia initiated a military crackdown in Kosovo in which Yugoslav forces killed Albanian civilians as well as suspected members of the KLA. In the face of escalating violence, the Contact Group on the former Yugoslavia, consisting of ministers from Britain, France, Italy, Germany, Russia, and the United States, began to work on forging a consensus on how to respond to the crisis in Kosovo. Early in March of 1998, the Clinton Administration warned that the United States would intervene if the Serbs used "massive force" in Kosovo. Nevertheless, the Yugoslav government escalated its military campaign in Kosovo. Ultimately, in the face of growing refugee flows out of Kosovo and reports of Yugoslav atrocities in the province, the North Atlantic Treaty Organization (NATO) initiated a bombing campaign against Yugoslav forces in Kosovo as well as targets within Yugoslavia proper.

Notably, the UN Security Council did not approve of the NATO bombing campaign, a sign that the international community in general resisted interpreting the right to self-determination in a way that would legitimize military intervention in sovereign states. Nevertheless, the United Nations ultimately endorsed a form of intervention in this case when the UN Security Council established the UN Interim Administration Mission in Kosovo (UNMIK) in 1999. UNMIK's mandate included the following objectives: overseeing municipal elections within the province; appointing judges and prosecutors for municipal courts; guaranteeing basic rights for all populations within Kosovo; and developing an interim legal framework for autonomy and self-governance for Kosovo. The fact that the United Nations, in the end, sanctioned a mission that involved intervention within the sovereign territory of Serbia is a striking example of the expansion of the right to self-determination in the aftermath of the Cold War.

However, neither NATO nor the United Nations insisted on independence for Kosovo. In the end, the NATO intervention represented a dramatic shift in the approach of the United States and Europe toward self-determination for threatened minority groups. At the same time, NATO and the United Nations refrained from endorsing independence for Kosovo because the international community still viewed the province, which had never been an independent republic, as an essential part of Serbian territory. In this way, the international community reinforced a conception of self-determination that was at least somewhat deferential to state sovereignty.

The case of the Chechen struggle for independence from Russia provides a stark contrast to the international community's reaction to self-determination movements in the former Yugoslavia. During September 1999, Russia responded with military force to an invasion by Chechen rebels into neighboring Dagestan. This military campaign represented a renewed Russian effort to reassert control in Chechnya following an unsuccessful military campaign to put down the Chechen secessionist movement in the mid-1990s. According to the Russian government, Russian military actions in Chechnya constitute an "antiterrorist" operation against Chechen separatist guerrillas.[18] In recent years, radical Islamic theology has exerted growing influence on the Chechen separatist movement, which increasingly is adopting terrorist tactics such as suicide bombing, though most Chechens reject both radical Islam and terrorism.[19]

Human rights organizations have charged that Russia has committed war crimes and crimes against humanity in carrying out its military operation in Chechnya. Testifying before the U.S. Senate Committee on Foreign Relations in March 2000, Human Rights Watch asserted that Russia has committed grave atrocities against the civilian population in Chechnya, including the intentional bombing of civilian targets, the refusal to allow safe passage of civilians out of areas of active hostilities, the massacre of civilians, rape, and looting. Human Rights Watch has also received reports that Russian forces have arrested civilian men and detained them in undisclosed locations; victims who have escaped from these "detention centers" have testified that Russian soldiers beat, tortured, and raped men and women detainees in this camp. Human Rights Watch also reports that it has documented violations by Chechen rebels, including the placement of military positions close to populated civilian areas, beating and shooting of civilians, kidnappings, and hostage taking. Nonetheless, Human Rights Watch has concluded that Russian forces have committed the majority of abuses it has documented.[20]

The international community has done little in response to alleged Russian atrocities in Chechnya. In contrast to the NATO bombing in Kosovo, the United States and other NATO allies, despite periodic criticism, have continued to pursue a generally friendly relationship with Russia. These countries have avoided labeling Russian atrocities war crimes and, in general, downplay the significance of the Russian military campaign in Chechnya. In April 2000, the United Nations Commission on Human Rights did pass a resolution expressing "grave concern" about the Russian military campaign in Chechnya, but the United Nations has not taken stronger measures to protest the alleged war crimes and atrocities. In general, the international community has not demonstrated significant support for Chechen self-determination. As this example illustrates, in most cases, states continue to apply a narrow interpretation of the right to self-determination that remains deferential to state sovereignty and that reflects the security interests of powerful states.

This overview of self-determination clearly illustrates the complex relationship between state sovereignty and collective rights. On the one hand, the status of self-determination under international law reinforces traditional notions of state sovereignty. Despite the fact that international human rights law theoretically accords "all peoples" the right to self-determination, states, in practice, have applied this right in a restrictive manner, limiting it primarily to colonized peoples.[21] More recently, as the conflicts in Bosnia-Herzegovina and Kosovo illustrate, demands by minority groups within states for self-determination have been recognized to varying degrees by powerful states in the international community. In this way, recent state interpretations of self-determination challenge a rigid adherence to state sovereignty.

Nevertheless, states have not engaged in a wholesale reinterpretation of self-determination. Powerful states do *not* consistently support demands for self-determination and certainly do not intervene consistently on behalf of oppressed minority groups. Indeed, from the perspectives of states, such resistance to a broad interpretation of self-determination is entirely rational. If states were to apply a broad standard of self-determination for other countries, they would run the risk of having this precedent come back to haunt them with respect to minority groups within their own borders. On precisely these grounds, critics contend that a broad interpretation of self-determination engenders civil conflict and political instability. Growing fear of terrorism in many countries after the September 11th terrorist attacks on U.S. soil has contributed to a backlash against self-determination. For example, after September 11, the United States became more sympathetic to

Russia's perspective on the conflict in Chechnya, which the Russian government depicts as an internal security threat rather than a movement by an oppressed minority group fighting for self-determination. Even in Kosovo, the international community, in the end, deferred to state sovereignty by refusing to support demands by Kosovars for territorial independence from Serbia. Thus, in spite of recent exceptions to the rule, states continue to uphold a concept of self-determination that ultimately respects the territorial integrity of sovereign states.

CASE STUDY: GENOCIDE

If self-determination serves as the most appropriate vehicle for realizing basic group rights, then genocide represents the most egregious denial of fundamental collective rights. Genocide not only denies basic rights of political expression, autonomy, and economic opportunities to specific communities but also threatens the very existence of these groups. Genocide inevitably involves the denial and abuse of fundamental *individual* rights, including the right to life, the right to be free from discrimination, the right to freedom of movement, and the right to equality of opportunity. However, genocide adds a *collective* dimension to these individual human rights abuses. At the most basic level, genocide threatens a *group's* fundamental right to life.[22] The purpose of genocide is to destroy particular groups, and the violation of individual human rights is used as a means toward this end. Thus, genocide simultaneously involves violations of both individual and collective human rights.

What we now call genocide has occurred throughout history, though the term itself was not coined until the mid-twentieth century as a response to the Holocaust. Raphael Lemkin, an international lawyer and passionate proponent of human rights, coined the term *genocide* during World War II. As a young man, he had been horrified by the international community's failure to respond to Turkey's efforts to annihilate Armenian Christians during World War I.[23] In 1921 in Berlin, a young Armenian survivor named Soghomon Tehlirian assassinated the former Turkish interior minister, Talaat Pasha, who had overseen the Turkish slaughter of Armenians. Tehlirian was subsequently put on trial in Berlin and was ultimately acquitted. Nevertheless, Lemkin remained troubled that Tehlirian was put on trial while Talaat, who had orchestrated the murder of more than a million Armenians, escaped judicial scrutiny on the grounds that he had not violated any international laws that would have justified his prosecution. Lemkin was astounded at the moral inconsistency: "It is a crime for Tehlirian to kill a man, but it is not a crime for his oppressor to kill more than a million men?"[24]

Lemkin's outrage was founded on an accurate sense that the international community did not condemn collective crimes committed by states in the name of state sovereignty. This outrage grew when the international community failed to respond to growing evidence of Nazi atrocities against the Jews during the 1930s. Lemkin, who happened to be Jewish, fled Poland in order to save his life after Germany's invasion. As he agonized over the fate of his family who had remained in Poland, he became increasingly convinced that it was essential to give a name to state efforts to destroy particular ethnic groups in order to convey the gravity of such moral crimes and to create legal consequences for states that perpetuated such violence.[25] Ultimately, Lemkin settled on the term *genocide,* which "was a hybrid that combined the Greek derivative *geno,* meaning "race" or "tribe," together with the Latin derivative *cide,* from *caedere,* meaning "killing."[26] Although the term initially generated great controversy, politicians and human rights advocates across the globe have adopted this term so that it is now a part of common usage. As Lemkin had hoped, the term *genocide* immediately conjures a sense of moral gravity about state efforts to destroy particular groups.

After coining the term, Lemkin lobbied tirelessly for the international community to adopt it as a legal concept. In the aftermath of World War II, in a belated acknowledgment of the scope of Nazi atrocities that came too late for millions of Holocaust victims, the international community embraced Lemkin's vision. In 1948, the General Assembly adopted the Convention on the Prevention and Punishment of the Crime of Genocide, which came into force in 1951. Article 2 of the Genocide Convention defines genocide as

> any of the following acts committed with the intent to destroy, in whole or in part, a national, ethnical, racial, or religious group, as such: a) killing members of the group; b) causing serious bodily or mental harm to members of the group; c) deliberately inflicting on the group conditions of life calculated to bring about its physical destruction in whole or in part; d) imposing measures intended to prevent births within the group; e) forcibly transferring children of the group to another group.

This legal definition illustrates the *collective* nature of the crime of genocide. Whereas other international human rights laws prohibit states from depriving *individuals* of basic human rights, the Genocide Convention makes it illegal for states, or other actors, to seek to destroy national, ethnic, racial, or religious communities.

Notably, the concept of genocide highlights the importance of the motivations that drive state efforts to destroy particular groups. In order for an act to constitute genocide, it must be committed with an *intent* to destroy a particular group. In this way, genocide differs from violations of individual human rights that are committed for other reasons—for example, for political or ideological reasons. At first glance, it may not seem to matter whether or not killing innocent civilians is part of a larger plan to destroy a specific community—the victims are dead or otherwise harmed regardless of the state's motivation. Nevertheless, Raphael Lemkin and other proponents of the idea argued that genocide constituted a distinctly important form of "state terror that . . . caused the largest number of deaths, was the most common, and did the most severe long-term damage—to the targeted groups themselves and to the rest of society."[27] Of course, human rights advocates do not condone state terror in any form. Yet the idea that a state would intentionally seek to destroy a group of individuals solely because of their membership in a particular national, ethnic, religious, or racial group is especially offensive to supporters of human rights across the globe. The concept of genocide draws attention to the multiple layers of human rights abuses involved in state efforts to destroy particular groups and signals that the international community considers such crimes to be of especially grave concern.

While the concept of genocide appropriately draws attention to state motivations in engaging in mass violence, the Genocide Convention's emphasis on intent also complicates efforts to condemn and punish genocide. Mass violence perpetuated by states does not constitute genocide under international law unless *intent* can be demonstrated. In Germany, *Mein Kampf* provided evidence of Hitler's long-standing intentions toward the Jews, as did public Nazi statements and written records. In 1988, Human Rights Watch responded to the Iraqi gassing of the Kurds by finding that Iraq had committed genocide, on the grounds that the Iraqi government kept records that explicitly documented its intent. However, a government's intent to destroy a particular group is not always easy to document. States frequently justify mass killings in the name of national security, as we saw in Chapter 4. Indeed, repressed groups often employ violence as a means of fighting against oppression, and states typically justify the use of violence as a legitimate response. Moreover, states often claim that they cannot be held responsible for "random" violence perpetuated by military forces and, indeed, that irregular military forces are often responsible for violence directed at innocent civilians. Thus, it can be difficult to document that states orchestrate violence and discrimination against specific groups with the intent of destroying them.

In addition to defining and prohibiting genocide, the Genocide Convention, in Article 1, commits states that ratify the treaty to "undertake to prevent and to punish" genocide. Article 5 calls upon states to provide penalties for persons found guilty of genocide, and Article 6 calls for the trial of accused persons in appropriate judicial bodies. Article 9 authorizes, but does not require, parties to the treaty to call upon the competent bodies within the United Nations to take actions to prevent genocide. (Although the Genocide Convention does not spell out what these steps might entail, Chapter 7 of the UN Charter, which allows the Security Council to authorize the use of force for the purpose of preventing threats to international peace and security, provides the basis for the strongest response.) An analysis of its basic provisions indicates that despite the inclusion of both "prevention" and "punishment" in the full title of the treaty, the Genocide Convention places greater emphasis on punishment than prevention. Only Article 9 makes reference to preventive measures and, in this case, the provision's language simply gives permission for states to urge preventive measures by the United Nations. The Genocide Convention does not require states to address genocide within the United Nations, nor does it authorize states to take unilateral action to prevent genocide. In this way, the Genocide Convention reinforces the traditional emphasis on state sovereignty in international law. In theory, the Genocide Convention challenges the right of sovereign states to commit mass violence against specific national, ethnic, racial, or religious groups within their borders. In practice, the law does not create meaningful enforcement mechanisms that would give states the authority to take strong action to prevent genocide.

Consistent with the emphasis on sovereignty in international law, states typically fail to respond with concrete measures to prevent genocide. The international community's response to "ethnic cleansing" in the former Yugoslavia in the early 1990s clearly illustrates this point. Although defenders of the international recognition of the independence of the former Yugoslav republics made their case on principled grounds, the actual response of the international community to the violence that followed reflected a mix of principle and pragmatism. Once the international community had recognized the independence of Bosnia-Herzegovina and the other former Yugoslav republics, the violent conflict between Serbia and these republics by definition was an *international* and not a *civil* conflict. As such, the international community had a legitimate stake in the conflict and could have intervened under Chapter 7 of the UN Charter to protect international peace and security.

Nevertheless, despite Security Council authorization for enforcement action, the international community responded with only limited means to prevent the extensive violence that followed the independence of the former Yugoslav republics. In general, international involvement emphasized medical aid and humanitarian relief to victims of violence rather than prevention. The United States and its allies, acting with Security Council authorization, did implement a naval blockade to enforce an arms embargo, but proponents of self-determination argued that this worked to undermine self-determination for Bosnian Muslims, who were significantly disadvantaged in terms of access to weapons because the Serbs exercised control over Yugoslav military resources. The United States and Europe also engaged in limited air strikes against Serb targets that threatened "safe havens" designed to protect Bosnian Muslims. However, on the whole, the international community did very little to protect the Bosnian Muslims from Serb efforts to "ethnically cleanse" Bosnian Serb areas in Bosnia-Herzegovina of Muslims, in what amounted to a modern case of genocide.[28] As a result, the settlement eventually negotiated in the Dayton Peace Accords rewarded Serb aggression by granting Serbia control over territories from which they had "cleansed" Bosnian Muslims by expelling or killing them.[29]

The international community's failure to respond to the 1994 genocide in Rwanda also demonstrates that the adoption of the term *genocide* under international law represents a moral advance in rhetoric more than reality.[30] In 1994, the plane of Rwandan president Juvénal Habyarimana was shot down. The Rwandan government, dominated by members of the Hutu ethnic group that constitutes a majority of the Rwandan population, blamed the shooting on Tutsi rebels. (Later, allegations would surface that Hutu extremists had shot down the plane in an effort to inflame the genocide that followed.) United Nations peacekeepers in Rwanda immediately became concerned that the incident would spark Hutu mass violence against the Tutsi minority population and communicated these warnings to the UN Secretariat.[31] Major General Romeo Dallaire, who served as commander of the UN mission in Rwanda, learned that Hutu officials had prepared lists of victims to be targeted for killing, and Radio Mille Collines, the official state radio, disseminated propaganda intended to incite violence and even broadcast the names and addresses of targeted Tutsi and moderate Hutus.[32] Despite growing evidence of a Hutu plan to destroy Tutsis and moderate Hutus, the United Nations denied Dallaire's requests for reinforcements and relaxed rules of engagement that would enable the UN peacekeepers in Rwanda to take stronger actions to prevent the genocide.[33] In fact, after Hutus killed Belgian peacekeepers, the United Nations eventually withdrew most of the remaining UN peacekeepers and left the Tutsis to their fate. In the end, Hutus killed an estimated 800,000 Tutsis in only 100 days.[34]

The Rwandan genocide represents a failure not only of the United Nations but also of powerful states to respond to the genocide. In the United States, the Clinton Administration refused to label what was happening in Rwanda genocide out of concern that doing so would create political pressure for the government to respond to a crisis in which the United States had no clear interest.[35] After the genocide ended when Tutsi rebels recaptured Rwandan territory and drove out Hutu extremists, President Clinton belatedly called what had happened "genocide" and, during a brief visit to Rwanda in which he never left the Rwandan airport, made a speech in which he apologized for the failure of the United States and the international community to take stronger preventive measures.[36]

The United States was not the only country that failed to take action to prevent the genocide. France, an ally of the Hutu government, did contribute peacekeeping troops whose objective was to provide a safe zone in the southwest region of the country. However, they did not take strong preventive measures. French troops failed to capture Hutus responsible for inciting genocide or to dismantle the propaganda machinery that the Hutus actually set up within the safe zone.[37] In fact, critics argue that the French safe zone may actually have impeded the effort of Tutsi rebels to take back Rwandan territory. This policy may have saved Hutus from Tutsi revenge killings but did not serve to stop Hutu efforts to continue genocidal killings against Tutsi. Indeed, during the height of the genocide in Rwanda, French President Francois Mitterand reportedly said, "In such countries, genocide is not too important."[38]

France was not alone in this attitude. Few countries were willing to endorse, let alone commit troops to, a UN peacekeeping force that would have had the authority to use military force to prevent the genocide. As both the cases of Bosnia and Rwanda indicate, the international community's condemnation of genocide under international law falls short of a genuine commitment to take meaningful measures to prevent state efforts to destroy national, ethnic, racial, or religious communities. As Philip Gourevitch sadly concludes, the premise underlying the Genocide Convention was the novel idea that the protection of humanity was in every state's interest, and it was well understood in the aftermath of World War II that action against genocide would require a willingness to use force and to risk the lives of one's own. The belief was that the price to the world of such a risk would not be as great as the price of inaction. But whose world were the drafters of the Genocide Convention . . . thinking of?[39]

While the idea that states will seek to prevent and punish genocide is a noble one, the reality is that states are reluctant to take strong preventive measures because of an unwillingness to risk the lives of their own citizens in the name of humanity as well as out of deference to the norm of state sovereignty. Notably, states do not shy away from risking the lives of their own citizens in the name of the national interest, and powerful states willingly violate the sovereignty of other states when they believe crucial national interests are at stake. In the end, states typically are motivated more by considerations of power, interest, and pragmatism than principle when it comes to responding to genocide.

CONCLUSIONS

This chapter has highlighted the complicated relationship between the principles of state sovereignty and collective rights in world politics. As we have seen, sovereignty as a principle can either coincide with or be in tension with collective rights depending on how the idea of collective rights is interpreted and applied. The relationship between state sovereignty and collective rights involves an important paradox. At times, states embrace the concept of collective rights as something that reinforces and enhances state sovereignty. At other times, states justify the violation and repression of collective rights in the name of state sovereignty. In short, states use the rhetoric of collective rights when they believe it is in their interest do so and abuse collective rights when they are deemed to threaten the state.

The examination of self-determination in this chapter illustrates the complicated relationship between state sovereignty and collective rights. Although international human rights law ultimately subordinates self-determination to the principle of state sovereignty, self-determination continues to pose a fundamental challenge to state sovereignty as an ideal. If all peoples genuinely have a right to self-determination in principle, this norm undermines the validity of state sovereignty as a moral concept. Clearly, "all peoples" do not correspond neatly with the territorial boundaries of existing nation-states. So long as there is a disjunction between state borders and group identities, states will be vulnerable to challenges to their political authority and legitimacy. Such challenges to their legitimacy are especially likely when states deny basic rights of political expression, cultural autonomy, and access to economic resources to peoples that they govern. Ultimately, oppressed groups tend to rise up and demand fundamental rights, especially when the human rights abuses and deprivations they face are extreme. Thus, even though state sovereignty as a legal norm typically trumps self-determination, groups that foment civil conflict as a means of demanding self-determination can significantly frustrate the ability of states to fully enjoy their sovereignty. Nevertheless, the human rights ideal of self-determination for all peoples, where the term *peoples* does not merely refer to the state, remains an elusive goal.

Similarly, international human rights norms seeking to prohibit genocide have not had a dramatic impact on the reality of world politics. "Never again." These words became the common refrain uttered by victims, politicians, human rights activists, and average citizens responding to the horrors of the Holocaust. These simple words echoed the fervent belief that the world had learned its lesson, so great were the evils of Nazi Germany. Sadly, the Holocaust did not represent the first or the last case of genocide in history. As we know, the horrors of genocide have been perpetuated again and again in the twentieth century and beyond, beginning with the mass slaughter of Armenians in Turkey before the term *genocide* had been coined, through the genocide in Rwanda at the end of the century, and continuing with the current genocidal violence in the Sudan. Sadly, these cases are *not* isolated, and genocide has continued to occur across the globe despite the fact that international law prohibits state efforts to destroy particular communities. Thus, despite important developments in international human rights norms, a gap between these norms and state practice still exists. In the end, the international community typically does very little to try to prevent genocide, an indication that state sovereignty as a preeminent norm in world politics is alive and well.

DISCUSSION QUESTIONS

1. Is the idea of collective rights redundant? If states fully protected the basic political and economic rights of individuals, would this be sufficient for protecting the fundamental collective rights of groups? Why or why not?

2. Are collective rights and individual rights necessarily in tension? Are there times when the protection of collective rights would enhance individual rights? Can the provision of individual rights contribute to basic collective rights?

3. When conflicts between collective and individual rights exist, how should these conflicts be resolved? Should individual or collective rights take priority?

4. When conflicts between different sets of collective rights exist, how should these conflicts be resolved? What criteria should be used to determine which group's rights should be given a higher priority?

5. Should states exempt indigenous peoples from national laws in order to promote self-determination for these groups? Or do such policies involve an unacceptable infringement on the individual rights of other citizens in these states?

6. How should the term *peoples* be defined for the purposes of self-determination? What criteria should be used in determining which peoples are morally entitled to claim a right to self-determination?

7. Should peoples who have a right to self-determination also have a right to independence? Why or why not?

8. Was it necessary for the international community to adopt the concept of genocide as a way of highlighting the collective nature of state efforts to destroy particular groups? Or would international human rights norms that simply prohibit human rights abuses against individuals, such as the arbitrary deprivation of life, have been sufficient to condemn such mass violence?

9. Critics of the legal definition of genocide have argued that it is too limited in that it only protects national, ethnic, racial, or religious groups. Some of these critics argue that political groups should also be covered by the definition. Other critics contend that economic groups should be protected under the Genocide Convention. One might also argue that group identities based on biological sex, gender, or sexual orientation should also be protected. Should the legal definition of genocide be expanded to cover additional groups? Why or why not? If so, which additional groups should be added?

10. Are states ever justified in targeting members of particular groups with violence when some individuals in these groups engage in violence against the state? Why or why not?

11. Does the international community have an obligation to intervene in other countries in order to prevent genocide? Why or why not?

WEB RESOURCES

The Armenian Genocide (http://www.theforgotten.org/)

Foreign Policy in Focus: Self-Determination (http://www.selfdetermine.org/)

International Institute for Self-Determination (http://www.selfdetermination.net/)

Genocide Watch (http://www.genocidewatch.org/)

Prevent Genocide International (http://www.preventgenocide.org)

Convention Concerning Indigenous and Tribal Peoples in Independent Countries (http://www1.umn.edu/humanrts/instree/r1citp.htm)

Convention on the Prevention and Punishment of the Crime of Genocide (http://www.hrweb.org/legal/genocide.html)

Declaration on the Granting of Independence to Colonial Countries and Peoples (http://www1.umn.edu/humanrts/instree/c1dgiccp.htm)

International Convention on the Elimination of All Forms of Racial Discrimination (http://www.hri.org/docs/ICERD66.html)

International Covenant on Civil and Political Rights (http://www.unhchr.ch/html/menu3/b/a_ccpr.htm)

International Covenant on Economic, Social, and Cultural Rights (http://www.unhchr.ch/html/menu3/b/a_cescr.htm)

6

Economic and Social Rights in a World of Sovereign States

ECONOMIC AND SOCIAL RIGHTS AS HUMAN RIGHTS

The idea that all human beings are entitled to fundamental economic and social rights is grounded in the assumptions that human beings *cannot* live fully human lives unless their basic human needs are met and that the enjoyment of human rights in general depends upon the fulfillment of these basic human needs. For example, the right to life is perhaps the quintessential human right. In the classic formulation of human rights, the right to life is conceived as a civil and political right and is interpreted as a limitation that prohibits states from arbitrarily depriving their subjects of life. Conceived and interpreted in this way, proponents of human rights have used the right to life as a way of condemning and protesting against state policies that arbitrarily deprive individuals of life, including genocide, the killing of political dissidents, forced abortion, and the death penalty, especially when applied in a discriminatory manner or when due process protections are not in place.

While not denying the importance of these types of state violations of human rights, a perspective that emphasizes the importance of economic and social rights stresses that human life is also threatened when human beings do not have access to adequate food or nutrition, housing, or medical care. Indeed, more human lives are threatened by poverty and lack of access to food or health care on a daily basis than by intentional state killings. Precise comparisons are difficult to make because, for obvious reasons, states do not col-

lect data on intentional state killings. Nevertheless, R. J. Rummel has estimated that there were more than 169 million murders by states during the
twentieth century.[1] That translates into an average of more than 1.69 million
intentional state killings per year. In comparison, approximately 11 million
children alone die annually across the globe from preventable diseases and inadequate nutrition.[2] Although genocide and political repression justifiably receive high-profile media coverage, avoidable deaths resulting from poverty and
inequity represent no less of a moral crisis. As a result, proponents of economic and social rights frame these issues in terms of human rights as a way
of stressing that eliminating human deprivation is just as essential as prohibiting state violence if the idea of universal human rights is to represent a comprehensive and consistent moral perspective.

This chapter is based on the viewpoint that economic and social rights
represent a vital component of the larger struggle to promote universal human rights across the globe. Although the chapter will highlight the potential
tension between economic and social rights and civil and political rights, it is
premised on the notion that these two categories of rights are interconnected.
Ultimately, the attainment of civil and political rights will not be possible
without simultaneous efforts to promote and protect economic and social
rights. The chapter also examines the relationship between economic and social rights and state sovereignty, once again emphasizing the paradox that the
idea of human rights challenges state sovereignty at the same time that sovereign states must play a critical role in promoting human rights in all forms
across the globe. Finally, while stressing the importance of economic and social rights, the chapter also explores the obstacles that impede global efforts to
promote these rights through case studies of human development and poverty
and of health as a human right.

ECONOMIC AND SOCIAL RIGHTS
AND STATE SOVEREIGNTY IN TENSION

The relationship between economic and social rights and state sovereignty
mirrors in many respects the relationship between collective rights and sovereignty. Just as in the case of collective rights, the idea of economic and social
rights can either reinforce or challenge state sovereignty depending upon how
economic and social rights are applied and interpreted. On the one hand, states
have often relied on discourse stressing the importance of economic and social
rights as a way of reinforcing state sovereignty. To this end, states have depicted
economic rights as collective rights that states themselves are in the best
position to promote and defend. For example, states have highlighted the importance of economic development as a key component of the right to self-
determination. In turn, states have traditionally conceived of economic development in terms of *national* development; indeed, the right to development
was initially treated as a collective right.[3]

When states claim the right to development as a collective right, they articulate a defensible argument that states that are unable to develop economically will not be able to provide basic economic rights to their citizens.[4] States often claim to be acting on behalf of economic rights when they deny basic civil and political liberties on the grounds that doing so is necessary to serve the larger goal of national economic development. For example, Singapore's government often attributes its economic success as one of the "Asian tigers" to its authoritarian policies in the political sphere. According to this perspective, shared by many states, stability and order in the political sphere, provided by the repression of civil and political liberties if necessary, are essential for economic development and modernization. When conceived in this way, the idea of economic and social rights reinforces state sovereignty.

On the other hand, the idea of economic and social rights can challenge state sovereignty. Despite frequent cooption of human rights discourse by state elites, the idea of economic and social rights as collective rights that reinforce state sovereignty is not clearly supported by the evidence. In fact, aside from the right to self-determination for "all peoples" under Article 1, the International Covenant on Economic, Social, and Cultural Rights frames human rights in individual terms. The ICESCR uses the language "the right of everyone" to describe the actors that are eligible for the rights enumerated therein. In other words, "everyone" has a right to work, a right to form trade unions, and a right to adequate nutrition and health care. The word *everyone* suggests that all individuals have these rights—not groups or states. For example, the right to economic development, conceived in this manner, belongs to individuals and not states. As a reflection of this interpretation, the United Nations Development Programme measures *human* development rather than national development as a way of evaluating the performance of states in fulfilling their obligations to promote basic economic rights.[5] Interpreted in this way, economic and social rights are individual rights and, as such, can fundamentally challenge state sovereignty by suggesting that states have obligations to protect and provide these rights.

Even if economic and social rights are conceived of as individual rights that impose obligations on states, the form of these obligations is unclear. In some respects, international human rights law suggests that states have absolute obligations to protect and provide basic economic and social rights. Under Article 4 of the ICESCR, states are authorized to limit the rights defined therein only to the extent that such limitations are compatible with these rights and promote the general welfare. This language seems to limit a state's ability to deviate from the rights obligations identified in this covenant. Nevertheless, because states are the actors that ultimately define whether or not particular policies contribute to "the general welfare," this provision does not ultimately undermine state sovereignty.

Additionally, the ICESCR defines state obligations under the covenant in a vague manner that gives states a great deal of discretion. For example, Article 2 of the ICECSR says only that states that are a party to the treaty "must undertake to take steps . . . with a view to achieving progressively the full realization of the rights recognized in the present Covenant." This language does not specify what steps states must undertake to fulfill their obligations under the Covenant. Similarly, states' obligation to achieve the enumerated rights "progressively" gives states a great deal of leeway. It is important to remember that the ICESCR, like all international treaties, is a political as well as a legal document. As such, it should not be surprising that the state representatives who drafted the document included vague obligations that do not infringe upon state sovereignty to the extent that states would otherwise be reluctant to sign on to the treaty. Article 2 also requires a state to fulfill its obligations "to the maximum of its available resources," thereby suggesting that a lack of resources is a legitimate justification for failing to provide the rights enumerated in the covenant. Although such flexibility is necessary because states simply may not have the resources to provide all of the rights identified in the Charter, it also means that states to do not have immediate and concrete obligations under the Covenant.

In its comments on the nature of states' obligations under the ICESCR, the Office of the High Commissioner for Human Rights suggests that Article 2 requires parties to the treaty to take deliberate and concrete steps to fulfill their treaty obligations within a reasonable amount of time.[6] Even if this interpretation is correct, it is notable that the ICESCR does not create institutional machinery with the power to enforce these obligations effectively. Thus, in spite of the fact that the *idea* of economic and social rights theoretically challenges state sovereignty, international human rights law ultimately remains deferential to state sovereignty in practice.

In the end, the fact that international human rights law respects state sovereignty does *not* mean that economic and social rights do not matter. The absence of clear-cut obligations and enforcement machinery does not mean that states will not be influenced by norms suggesting that they have responsibilities to promote economic and social rights. Indeed, if economic and social rights are ever to become a reality, states will need to play a crucial role because of their ability to generate and administer financial and institutional resources to this end.[7] Moreover, an approach that allows for variation among states regarding *how* they seek to promote human rights reflects the cultural and ideological diversity that characterizes world politics and, as such, is more likely to encourage state cooperation in efforts to promote economic and social rights. For example, the ICESCR does *not* mandate that states must actively provide the rights enumerated in the document. Indeed, one scholar of human rights has suggested that a state's first obligation is not to interfere with individuals' efforts to seek their economic rights, followed by state obligations to prevent other actors such as powerful economic interests from violating the economic rights of other groups and individuals, and only as a "last resort" to actively provide economic rights or goods.[8] An approach asserting that states have obligations to promote and protect fundamental economic rights while respecting that sovereign states will do so in different ways is ultimately more likely to generate state cooperation than one rigidly insisting that states play an active role in providing these rights in all cases.

THE RELATIONSHIP BETWEEN ECONOMIC AND SOCIAL RIGHTS AND CIVIL AND POLITICAL RIGHTS

Critics of the idea that all human beings have fundamental human rights often assume that there is inherent tension between economic rights and political rights. Typically, these critics conceive of economic and social rights as "positive" rights requiring burdensome state expenditures that only large and powerful states can administer. In turn, they view civil and political rights as "negative" rights requiring inaction on the part of the state for their protection. Thus, these critics typically presume that it is inevitable that large, powerful states designed to promote basic economic and social rights will violate fundamental civil and political rights of individuals in the process. Because these critics believe fundamental civil and political rights should be inviolable, they thus reject the category of economic and social rights altogether.

However, as we saw in Chapter 1, it is a mistake to treat economic rights and political rights as rigidly dichotomous categories. For example, Article 8 of the International Covenant on Economic, Social and Cultural Rights recognizes the right of all human beings to form and join trade unions. This article embodies an economic right because trade unions provide human beings with an organizational vehicle for pursuing other basic economic rights, such as the rights to safe and healthy work conditions, to equal opportunities for promotion, and to reasonable work hours and paid holidays, as recognized in Article 7 of the ICESR. At the same time, the right to form and join trade unions represents a basic political right reflecting the broader right to freedom of association. Indeed, the right to form trade unions is also protected under Article 22 of the International Covenant on Civil and Political Rights. As this example illustrates, economic and political rights are *not* inherently in tension.

Indeed, economic and political rights are often interrelated in vital ways. Human rights that prohibit discrimination against ethnic or racial minorities provide an illustrative example. Discrimination against ethnic or racial minorities is typically conceived as a violation of basic civil and political rights. For instance, a state that denies the right to vote to ethnic or racial minorities is violating a fundamental political right. Similarly, when states sanction discriminatory treatment of minorities by the police or courts, they deny these minorities the equal protection of the law, a basic civil right. Notably, such political discrimination generally overlaps with economic discrimination. States that deny essential civil and political rights to minorities often represent societies that discriminate more generally against minorities in housing, employment, education, and health care. In this way, the denial of basic civil and political rights overlaps with and reinforces the fundamental economic and social deprivations suffered by minorities. As a result, any effort to eliminate discrimination and to promote basic rights for ethnic and racial minorities requires attention to civil and political as well as economic and social rights. As the case of discrimination against ethnic and racial minorities demonstrates, basic political and economic rights are often interrelated rather than being in tension.

Thus, at times, the only way to promote genuine economic and social rights may be to ensure that individuals and groups are able to exercise their fundamental civil and political rights, and vice versa. As Jack Donnelly has put it,

> civil and political rights, by providing accountability and transparency, can help to channel economic growth into national development rather than private enrichment. The redistributions required by economic and social rights similarly seek to assure that prosperity is diffused throughout society, rather than concentrated in a tiny elite. Conversely, those living on the economic edge or with no realistic prospect of a better life for their children are much less likely to be willing to accommodate the interests and rights of others.[9]

He goes on to note that interdependence between economic and social rights and civil and political rights is not inevitable. To be sure, conflicts between these categories of human rights are possible if not likely, and proponents of human rights need to make conscious efforts to link these categories in an effort to foster interdependence.[10] Still, the underlying point—that we cannot reject the legitimacy of economic and social rights on the grounds that they inevitably threaten civil and political rights—remains.

In a similar vein, it is incorrect to accept the rigid categorization of civil and political rights as negative rights and economic and social rights as positive rights. As we saw in Chapter 1, the state may have to take concrete actions to ensure that basic civil and political rights, such as the right to vote, are fulfilled. The right to vote typically requires significant financial resources and institutional support to ensure that everyone's right to vote freely and fairly without intimidation is protected. Whereas civil and political rights often require positive action on the part of the state, state inaction may be a more appropriate means for promoting basic economic rights in some cases. For instance, free market economists argue that state subsidies of certain national economic sectors, while justified as a way of promoting the economic interests of citizens who work in these sectors, actually undermine the well-being of citizens who do not benefit from these policies and who are taxed to fund these subsidies. Moreover, economists point out that subsidies limit the ability of individuals and groups in other countries to pursue their economic well-being. Agricultural subsidies are a classic example. Industrialized countries commonly provide agricultural subsidies to large corporate farms. Such subsidies often represent a transfer of wealth from individuals and groups who are less well-off to highly profitable corporate agricultural interests and give these large corporations an unfair advantage against small farmers both within and outside of these countries. In such cases, an economist might argue that basic economic rights would be better served if the state were to refrain from intervening.

The point of this discussion is not to delineate the appropriate role for the state in providing free and fair elections or to debate the costs versus the benefits of free trade. Rather, the bottom line is that the belief that all human beings deserve fundamental economic rights does *not* necessarily coincide with the presumption that the state must play an active role in providing these benefits, just as the view that all human beings have inviolable civil and political rights does not inevitably suggest that state inaction is required for their protection. In short, neither the presumption that economic rights inevitably lead to the violation of civil and political rights nor ideological resistance to large and powerful states provides a convincing rationale for dismissing the validity of economic and social rights. As Asbjorn Eide notes, asserting that states have obligations to ensure that basic economic and social rights are protected does not necessarily require "that the state actively fulfill the needs of individuals, by being a provider of material goods. It may well be that the state can avoid hunger better by being passive, by *not* interfering with the freedom of individuals and with their control over their own resources. Whether this is so depends on the concrete circumstances, the context, and cannot be answered in the abstract."[11] In the end, then, the acceptance of the principle that all human beings have fundamental economic and social rights need not be based on global consensus regarding the best means for fulfilling these rights.

CASE STUDY: HUMAN DEVELOPMENT AND POVERTY

As discussed earlier, states typically treat the concept of economic development as if it coincides naturally with the economic interests of the state. Accordingly, scholars and foreign policy practitioners involved in efforts to promote economic development continue to rely on national economic indicators, primarily per capita gross domestic product, as a measure of economic development.[12] A human rights perspective that depicts economic development as an individual human right challenges the idea that national economic indicators are an adequate measure for evaluating the economic well-being of human beings across the globe and for assessing states' performance in promoting fundamental economic and social rights. The United Nations Development Programme (UNDP) has adopted this broader perspective for measuring human development. To this end, the UNDP has created the Human Development Index (HDI), comprised of a combination of indicators that together provide a more complicated picture of the way in which economic development policies impact real human lives, not just the bottom line of national wealth. The HDI includes measures of life expectancy, educational attainment, and adjusted real income. In this way, the HDI serves as a better measure of equity and economic well-being for individuals than GDP, which primarily emphasizes national wealth and economic growth.

Conceptualized in this way, human development can be viewed as a corollary to human rights. According to the UNDP, both the concept of human development and the idea of human rights are fundamentally concerned with promoting human freedom. In its overview of the concept of human development, the UNDP suggests that human development is a fundamental component of a broader vision of universal human rights:

> Human development shares a common vision with human rights. The goal is human freedom. And in pursuing capabilities and realizing rights, this freedom is vital. People must be free to exercise their choices and to participate in decision-making that affects their lives. Human development and human rights are mutually reinforcing, helping to secure the well-being and dignity of all people.[13]

In this way, a human development perspective stresses the interdependence of economic and social rights and civil and political rights rather than the potential tension between these categories. The achievement of economic and social rights is necessary for the genuine enjoyment of civil and political rights, and vice versa.

Despite the rosy picture the UNDP paints of various human rights as interconnected in theory, the Human Development Index demonstrates a harsher global reality in which vast human deprivations continue to impede the achievement of basic economic and social rights across the globe. Consider the following statistics. More than 850 million adults in developing countries are illiterate, and roughly 15 percent of adults in developed countries are illiterate. More than 2 billion people in developing countries do not have access to basic sanitation, a fact that undoubtedly contributes to the preventable deaths of 11 million children throughout the developing world each year. More than 2 million people die from indoor air pollution in the developing world each year. Approximately 1.2 billion people living in developing countries survive on an income of less than $1 a day. Even accounting for differences in the cost of living, this extremely low income signals vast poverty across the globe. Poverty is also endemic throughout the developed world. For example, more than 130 million people in countries that are members of the Organization for Economic Cooperation and Development live in poverty.[14] According to UN estimates, roughly 27 million people are currently forced to work as slaves.[15] Millions of other people work under inhumane conditions in sweatshops across the globe.[16] This human suffering represents violations of numerous rights provided for under the International Covenant on Economic, Social, and Cultural Rights, including the right to an adequate standard of living, the right to adequate food, the right to the highest attainable standard of health, and the right to education.

The scale of human suffering represented by these human development statistics violates the basic idea of universal economic and social human rights, which suggests that available global resources should be marshaled to avert preventable deaths and human suffering. Additionally, these statistics suggest that civil and political rights cannot be fully enjoyed in a world in which vast numbers of human beings are unable to fulfill basic economic needs. Individuals who do not have enough to eat or who are ill as a result of their poverty will be unable to exercise civil and political rights in any meaningful sense. Similarly, poor, illiterate individuals are unable to engage in politics on a level playing field with individuals who have access to extensive financial and educational resources. Just as the denial of basic economic and social rights limits the ability of individuals to exercise their civil and political rights, violations of civil and political rights are an obstacle to the full enjoyment of economic and social rights. The effect of war on economic rights is an illustrative case. Violent conflict, which typically involves serious deprivations of civil and political rights, is a major cause of poverty across the globe. For example, the UNDP estimates that more than 14 million people currently suffer from hunger as a result of ongoing military conflicts.[17]

Notably, general indicators of poverty often reflect discrimination against specific groups—for example, religious, racial, or ethnic minorities, or women.[18] Discrimination against these groups reinforces their poverty when economic, social, and political institutions prevent the full and equal participation of their members. At the same time, the fact that these groups lack the same economic and educational opportunities means that they do not have the same capabilities to participate in civic or political institutions. Thus, economic and social deprivations create self-fulfilling prophecies that appear to support elite arguments that the poor, minorities, or women are incapable of participating as civic or political equals. In this way, the denial of basic economic and social rights and political repression commonly involve a vicious cycle that is difficult to break.

The fact that poverty and discrimination often coincide indicates that policies directed at eliminating poverty that fail to address discrimination based on race, ethnicity, gender, biological sex, or sexual orientation will be prone to failure. For example, improving women's access to education is one of the best methods for promoting the economic and social well-being not only of women but also of entire families.[19] Similarly, policies aimed at reducing discrimination that do not take equity issues into account are unlikely to succeed. Turning to women as an example again, Amartya Sen has found that when states promote greater equality for women in education, work opportunities, and property ownership, their general well-being improves.[20]

Despite the reality that human deprivation remains a widespread problem across the globe, the UNDP's human development report for 2003 notes that the situation is improving in relative terms. Life expectancy, literacy rates, access to basic sanitation, and general standards of living have generally been improving throughout the developing world.[21] At the same time, more than fifty countries have experienced declines in human development since the early 1990s.[22] Nevertheless, general improvements indicate that poverty is not an inevitable feature of the global political landscape. However, improvements in human development do not happen randomly. Rather, general increases in the HDI throughout the developing world came as a result of concerted efforts on the part of nongovernmental organizations, states, and international organizations to adopt policy solutions explicitly intended to improve the well-being of human beings across the globe. In poor countries, the challenge is to maximize human development for the large numbers of people who suffer economic deprivation. In rich countries, the challenge is to promote economic well-being for the smaller but still significant groups of people that have been left behind in the general progression toward national wealth.[23] Ultimately, states and international organizations will only implement and continue such policies if individuals and groups put forth a sustained political vision that stresses the ongoing importance of economic and social rights and the moral unacceptability of continued human suffering due to entrenched poverty.

Despite general improvements in human development, especially in the developing world, the statistics cited previously demonstrate that human death, deprivation, and suffering due to poverty are still widespread. Indeed, more people die and suffer each year as a result of poverty than of direct political violence or war. Making note of this reality does not undermine the moral or political significance of war and political repression as global problems. Rather, the vast numbers of people who suffer or die as a result of economic deprivations indicate that poverty also represents an unacceptable affront to human dignity and well-being across the globe. Accordingly, a human rights perspective suggests that we need to take economic and social rights seriously if we are genuinely committed to promoting universal principles in a world of sovereign states.

CASE STUDY:

HEALTH AND HUMAN RIGHTS

Think for a moment about the shock and sense of tragedy that rippled throughout much of the world, especially in the United States, in the aftermath of the September 11 terrorist attacks on U.S. soil in 2001. Nearly 3,000 human beings were killed in these airplane bombings on the two World Trade Center towers and the hijacking and subsequent crashing of two additional airplanes. Now, imagine that instead of two office towers and four airplanes being attacked with such devastating results, twelve office towers and twenty-four airplanes were attacked with the equivalent loss of human life. Further imagine that this tragedy occurred every day for a year. This scenario would translate into 30,000 deaths per day, and roughly 11 million deaths per year. Terrorism on this scale is almost unimaginable.

Yet that is how many children die every day across the globe from preventable causes. Approximately 11 million children under 5 die each year, or 30,000 children daily, from avoidable causes.[24] In Africa, one child dies from measles every minute.[25] One of the primary causes of preventable childhood deaths is diarrhea. According to the World Health Organization, more children died of complications from diarrhea in the 1990s "than all the people lost to armed conflict since the Second World War."[26] These figures represent only avoidable deaths among children. The number of preventable deaths each year due to health problems rises dramatically when adults are considered. The following figures from the United Nations Development Programme paint a grim picture:

> More than 500,000 women a year die in pregnancy and childbirth, with such deaths 100 times more likely in Sub-Saharan African than in high-income OECD countries. Around the world 42 million people are living with HIV/AIDS, 39 million of them in developing countries. Tuberculosis remains (along with AIDS) the leading infectious killer of adults, causing up to 2 million deaths a year. Malaria deaths, now 1 million a year, could double in the next 20 years.[27]

Notably, the individuals most likely to die from preventable causes are poor people, especially those living in rural areas and slums, who do not have access to affordable health care.[28] Deaths from preventable illness represent a violation of "the right of everyone to the enjoyment of the highest attainable standard of physical and mental health" under Article 12 of the International Covenant on Economic, Social, and Cultural Rights.

Although most deaths from preventable illness occur in the developing world, they also happen regularly in developed countries. In this case, avoidable deaths most frequently result when poor people, often ethnic minorities who experience discrimination as well as deep poverty, do not have access to affordable health care that would encourage and enable them to seek regular, preventive medical care. Moreover, the poor in developed countries often live in substandard housing that contributes to chronic illnesses such as asthma. In addition, the poor often cannot afford adequate nutritious food and, as a result, are more likely to experience chronic health problems such as hypertension and obesity. Poor people also commonly lack access to transportation, which makes it difficult for them to travel to health clinics often located far from their homes, a problem that is compounded when they have health problems that make travel painful or difficult.

The status of health care for the poor in the United States is an instructive example. Even though the United States spends more money on health care than any other country in the world, more than 43 million Americans, a majority of whom are gainfully employed, do not have health insurance. Despite high medical expenditures, the United States does not rank as highly as many other developed countries on numerous health indicators, including infant mortality, maternal mortality, and life expectancy. Bad outcomes are especially likely for ethnic minorities, who are less likely to have health insurance coverage. Because individuals without health insurance are less likely to seek preventive care, they are more likely to face serious health problems and complications when they ultimately seek medical care.[29] With pressure on state budgets, states across the United States are cutting spending on medical care, and the likely result will be that medical clinics serving the poor will be forced to close. According to the Institute of Medicine, "as many as 18,000 adults without insurance die prematurely each year [in the United States] because of their failure to get the kinds of tests and treatments people with good insurance take for granted. As states slash funding for their medical safety net, that number will almost certainly rise."[30]

If deaths from preventable illnesses were simply the result of fate or bad luck, they might not constitute a human rights issue. However, the international community could prevent most of these deaths simply by expanding the access of poor people to simple vaccinations, basic sanitation, adequate nutrition, and affordable health care and medications. For example, the World Health Organization, the United Nations Children's Fund, the American Red Cross, the U.S. Centers for Disease Control and Prevention, and the United Nations Foundation have partnered to initiate a campaign to make vaccinations available to children throughout Africa. As a result of this partnership, more than 72 million African children have already been vaccinated as of 2003. The World Health Organization estimates that these vaccinations will save an estimated 1.2 million lives in the next five years.[31] As this example illustrates, medical experts could mitigate the effects of preventable illnesses with relative ease if they had access to sufficient resources.

However, several obstacles hinder global efforts to reduce the number of deaths from preventable causes, including "a lack of resources for health systems (especially for basic health), a lack of equity in what systems provide and a lack of efficiency in how services are provided."[32] Many poor countries simply do not have adequate resources to improve basic medical care for their citizens. Wealthy countries typically are reluctant to provide sufficient amounts of aid to poor countries to address these problems, a reluctance that should not be surprising given that developed countries often resist expending sufficient resources to provide basic health care for all of their own citizens. As long as sovereign states continue to treat basic health care as a privilege and not a right, tragically large numbers of people across the globe will continue to suffer and die from preventable illness.

One of the reasons that critics resist treating health as a fundamental human right is that they prioritize other rights as more important. For example, one of the obstacles to reducing global deaths from AIDS is that the poor often cannot afford the lifesaving but highly expensive drugs for treating AIDS. For example, according to UN figures, some 25 million people in sub-Saharan Africa have AIDS or HIV but are unable to gain access to affordable generic AIDS drugs because of international patent agreements that prevent sales of cheaper generic drugs.[33] Pharmaceutical companies defend these patent agreements as a means of protecting intellectual property rights. According to this viewpoint, pharmaceutical companies would not have an economic incentive to expend the large amounts of economic resources necessary for drug research and innovation if they could not make profits from their discoveries. Without such incentives, lifesaving medicines might go undiscovered, to the detriment of the sick everywhere. Thus, this perspective suggests that protecting the right to intellectual property is essential to ensuring that researchers have an incentive to discover new, lifesaving medicines, even if it means that not everyone will have access to these medicines.[34]

Critics charge that pharmaceutical companies are being dishonest when they put forward this argument and that they are driven solely by a profit motive. Indeed, the pharmaceutical industry is highly profitable, prompting critics to charge that pharmaceutical companies abuse patent agreements by gaining monopoly power that allows them to charge exorbitantly high prices. Critics also point out that pharmaceutical companies routinely overstate the costs associated with research and development, which actually are quite small compared to the amount these companies spend on marketing. Moreover, critics note that using the concept of international property rights as a way of encouraging the discovery of new drugs is not necessarily effective because it actually gives pharmaceutical companies an economic incentive to spend money developing drugs to treat chronic but not life-threatening health problems, such as obesity, which generate massive revenues, as opposed to searching for cures to life-threatening but less lucrative illnesses, especially preventable diseases that threaten the lives of poor people in developing countries.[35] Notably, in many countries, taxpayers fund much of this profit-generating research and development through direct research and development subsidies as well as government health care programs that subsidize the purchase of prescription drugs. Even when governments do not provide direct subsidies, individuals fund research and development as consumers of these drugs and of health insurance in general.[36]

Before concluding this discussion, it should be noted that several pharmaceutical companies have recently agreed to provide AIDS medications to poor countries at discounted prices. However, the effectiveness of these agreements has been limited by chronic shortages of the covered drugs, the fact that the prices have not been lowered sufficiently to dramatically expand access, and the reluctance of companies to make drugs available to private suppliers and not just government programs in poor countries.[37] As one critic concludes, "many drugs are initially developed with government money with no risk to the transnational corporation (TNC). These huge pharmaceutical TNCs, after taking little or no financial risk, are then able to gouge AIDS patients for incredible profits. The sick in poor countries where these drugs are unaffordable are left to die."[38] More recently, the World Trade Organization has changed international trading rules, allowing developing countries to import generic versions of patented drugs, in order to make it easier for poor countries to gain access to lifesaving medicines.[39] It remains to be seen how effective these rule changes will be.

A similar dynamic involving conflicting rights claims is involved in debates over whether the poor in wealthy countries have a right to basic health care. The U.S. case is again illustrative. The Bush Administration has favored large tax cuts even when it means that the federal government will generate less revenue to contribute toward the provision of basic medical care and other services to its citizens. Defenders of these tax cuts tend to frame them in rhetoric suggesting that money is simply being returned to its rightful owners. In other words, the defense of tax cuts is often couched in a claim based on the right to property. Many proponents of the Bush Administration's tax policy have defended tax cuts that proportionally benefit the wealthy (by far the largest proportion of the tax cuts are targeted at a very small percentage of wealthy Americans) as an equity issue in which the wealthy and the middle class alike have an equal right to property and, as such, to having their taxes cut proportionally. Because wealthy individuals pay higher tax rates, the argument goes, they deserve the most "tax relief."

Moreover, conservative critics of high taxes often defend tax cuts on the grounds that high taxation rates lead to inefficient and wasteful government spending. They argue that government is ill positioned to provide basic rights, including health care, to its citizens. Conservatives believe that markets allocate resources more efficiently than government. As a result, conservatives do not trust government to spend tax dollars wisely. They believe that high taxes lead to bloated and wasteful government bureaucracies and that, even if proponents of government funding for health care have the right intentions, high taxes and "big government" do not necessarily lead to better health care outcomes for society.

Critics of the Bush Administration tax cuts favor progressive taxation, in which the wealthiest individuals are taxed at a higher rate in order to generate sufficient revenue to provide a social safety net, including basic medical care, for poor people. Accordingly, for proponents of a progressive taxation system, the most questionable tax cuts are those that are aimed primarily at a very small percentage of extremely wealth individuals. For conservative defenders of tax cuts in the United States, the right to property, embodied in opposition to progressive taxation, represents a higher priority than the right to health, especially because conservatives do not believe that government spending is the solution to the nation's health care problems. Conversely, proponents of health as a human right suggest that the right to property is not absolute and that progressive taxation is not only justifiable but morally imperative as a means of ensuring minimum standards of health and the right to life for all human beings.

This section has focused on health problems resulting from poverty and inequity. Health and human rights are also connected in other fundamental ways. The health of human beings across the globe is threatened when states violate the civil and political rights of their citizens. Torture is an obvious example. Torture is typically perceived as a violation of civil and political rights because it is a primary example of political repression. At the same time, torture results in obvious harm to the physical and psychological health of its victims and, as such, violates the right to health as well as political liberty. Slavery, racial discrimination, sexual violence, and other human rights abuses typically thought of first as violations of civil and political rights also involve the degradation of the right to health.[40] Regardless of whether the degradation of human health results from poverty and inequity or as a corollary of political repression, proponents of human rights believe that the resulting deaths and human suffering are preventable and, thus, represent an unacceptable human tragedy that creates moral obligations on the part of nation-states and the international community in general to act to promote health as a fundamental human right. In the words of Kofi Annan, "It is my aspiration that health will finally be seen not as a blessing to be wished for; but as a human right to be fought for."[41]

CONCLUSIONS

Criticisms of economic and social rights frequently involve the wholesale dismissal of the relevance of this category of human rights. Critics typically charge one of two things. Some critics contend that only unacceptably large and repressive states will be able to marshal the necessary resources to provide basic economic and social rights. Alternatively, other critics suggest that the idea of economic and social rights is too vague and creates obligations that states cannot realistically be expected to fulfill.[42] Because so many critics dismiss the validity of this category, this chapter has focused on providing both morally and politically compelling justifications for economic and social rights. As a means to this end, this chapter has sought to illustrate three basic truths: first, that economic and social rights are vitally important in their own right; second, that economic and social rights are also necessary for the genuine promotion of civil and political rights; and finally, that the moral justification for economic and social rights as human rights exists independently of global consensus regarding how best to achieve these rights.

In response to the criticism that only large, inefficient, and ultimately repressive states are capable of providing basic economic and social rights, this chapter has illustrated that the idea of economic and social rights does *not* necessarily require that states themselves directly provide human rights to all citizens. At a minimum, states certainly will have to tax their citizens in order to ensure that a social safety net exists that will protect the poorest and most vulnerable members of society if the idea of economic and social rights is to have real meaning across the globe. However, progressive taxation and social safety nets, to varying degrees, have been a standard feature of liberal democratic states that pride themselves on representing traditions that defend civil and political liberties. Thus, critics' fears of oppressive, totalitarian states as the only institutions capable of providing economic and social rights are unfounded. Similarly, this chapter challenges the notion that economic and social rights inevitably conflict with civil and political rights, thus refuting the facile idea that anyone genuinely committed to civil and political rights must reject economic and social rights as an inherent threat to liberty. Instead, economic and social rights and civil and political rights commonly reinforce one another, and for this reason, students of human rights need to take economic and social rights seriously.

Nevertheless, it remains important to note that the relationship between economic and social rights and civil and political rights is indeed fraught with potential tension. It is absolutely true that basic economic and social rights and civil and political rights may conflict and require certain trade-offs.[43] A classic example is the "liberty trade-off"—economic rights that stress equity as a social value may threaten liberty, a norm embodied in many civil and political rights.[44] Yet the fact that potential tension between these categories exists does not mean that the choice of which rights should take priority is obvious or that civil and political rights are always more important than economic and social rights, as critics of economic and social rights presume.

Tension exists not only between but within the various categories of human rights. Economic rights that stress equity as a social value may challenge other economic rights such as the right to property, at base an economic right. Civil and political rights claims of religious groups may conflict with the civil and political rights of other individuals and groups, including other religious groups, women, or gays. Ultimately, the fact that economic and social rights may conflict with civil and political rights is not sufficient grounds for dismissing the importance of this category. As in all cases involving competing human rights claims, difficult questions and trade-offs must be considered. What remains important for students and proponents of human rights is that considerations of principle—and not mere interests—frame efforts to answer these questions and to find just solutions.

DISCUSSION QUESTIONS

1. Are economic and social rights as important as civil and political rights? Why or why not?

2. The United States still has not ratified the International Covenant on Economic, Social, and Cultural Rights partly because it does not want to signal acceptance of the idea that it is obligated to play an active role in providing basic economic rights. Should the United States ratify this document? Why or why not?

3. Is it important for states to play an active role in *providing* basic economic and social rights? Why or why not? Are there times when economic and social rights will be better served through state inaction? What criteria should we use to determine whether state action or inaction will be more likely to promote economic and social rights?

4. Governing elites in states with scarce resources often argue that it is necessary to sacrifice certain basic civil and political rights in order to give priority to fundamental economic and social rights. Do you agree with this argument? Why or why not? If so, which civil and political rights can states validly repress in the name of economic and social rights?

5. Do you find the argument that health is a basic human right persuasive? Why or why not? If health is a human right, then violations of the right to health typically involve neglect and indifference on the part of states and the international community more than active repression. With this in

mind, is it more appropriate to reserve the label "human rights" for issues that involve direct political repression by the state? Why or why not?

6. When conflicts between the right to property and the right to health exist, how should they be resolved? Which right should be prioritized? What criteria should we use in making a decision about how to resolve potential trade-offs between these rights?

7. Cuba has had a policy of isolating AIDS patients and restricting their freedom of movement as a way of preventing the spread of the disease. From 1985 to 1994, AIDS patients were kept under forced, permanent quarantine. Today, AIDS patients are quarantined for a period of six to eight weeks. During this time, the Cuban government provides for the treatment and education of these patients as a method of preventing the spread of the disease. If AIDS patients engage in risky sexual behavior, they risk being placed under permanent quarantine.[45] Does this restriction of civil and political rights as a way of promoting the right to health represent a morally defensible trade-off? Why or why not?

WEB RESOURCES

International Covenant on Economic, Social, and Cultural Rights (http://www.unhchr.ch/html/menu3/b/a_cescr.htm)

Center for Economic and Social Rights (http://www.cesr.org)

Human Development Reports (http://hdr.undp.org)

Physicians for Human Rights (http://phrusa.org)

Global Lawyers and Physicians Working Together for Human Rights (http://www.glphr.org)

United Nations Web Resources on Human Rights (http://www.un.org/rights/index.html)

7

Sexual Equality
and Human Rights

SEXUAL EQUALITY AS A HUMAN RIGHT

Sexual equality for women and sexual minorities represents perhaps one of the last frontiers for advancing the idea that *all* human beings have fundamental rights. Sexual equality has been an especially controversial human rights issue because discrimination against women and sexual minorities is widely condoned by so many states and cultures. International organizations and even human rights organizations are not always cognizant of the ways in which they neglect or reinforce sexual inequality.[1] Disagreement is often manifested even among proponents of human rights on the question of whether states and cultures may legitimately sanction discrimination against women and sexual minorities in the name of state sovereignty or cultural relativism.

As we saw in Chapter 3, cultural relativism seems to resonate most strongly across cultures when it is used to justify discrimination against vulnerable groups such as women and sexual minorities. Even human rights advocates acknowledge that cultural relativism may justify deviation from an absolute adherence to universal interpretations of human rights with regard to rights that are viewed as less fundamental, a categorization commonly applied to the rights of women and sexual minorities. Similarly, proponents of human rights have been more likely to concede that sovereign states have a right to deviate from a rigid adherence to universal human rights norms when it comes to discriminatory treatment of women and homosexuals, so long as such discrimination does not involve grave violations of human rights such as genocide or torture.

The tendency to treat rights involving sexual equality as of lesser importance than other human rights rests in large part on what feminists refer to as the "public–private dichotomy."[2] Traditionally, human rights advocates have treated grave violations of human rights in the public sphere—those committed by the state and usually involving political violence and threats to human life—as the highest priority. Genocide, politically motivated killings, and torture are prime examples. Conversely, a human rights perspective historically has placed less emphasis on human rights abuses committed by non-state actors in the private sphere. Even though states have obligations to prevent the systematic abuse of human rights by non-state actors, proponents of human rights have tended to focus on violations of human rights *directly* perpetrated by the state.

However, feminists have pointed out that women are often most likely to suffer threats to their fundamental human rights in the private sphere. Many of the most serious threats to women's equal enjoyment of human rights, such as female genital mutilation, forced marriages, domestic violence, rape, and lack of access to education and employment, result from discrimination and violence in the private sphere. Sexual minorities are also highly vulnerable to discrimination and violence in the private as well as the public sphere. Notably, states often signal that they condone such violations of basic human rights when they fail to criminalize or prosecute violence or discrimination against women and sexual minorities.[3] Because the ideal of international human rights in both law and practice has downplayed the relative importance of human rights violations in the private sphere, the human rights of women and sexual minorities have received less attention than human rights in general.

As this discussion illustrates, it is appropriate to frame violence and discrimination against women and sexual minorities as violations of fundamental *human* rights regardless of whether abuses are perpetrated by state or non-state actors. To dismiss sexual inequality as irrelevant to the broader struggle for human rights simply because non-state actors are responsible for much of the violence and discrimination against women and sexual minorities undermines the ideal that human rights represent universal principles. In other words, many feminists contend that human rights abuses should be defined according to whether violent and discriminatory *actions* threaten fundamental human rights and not according to *who* has committed the violence or discrimination. From this perspective, relying on a human rights framework that encompasses human rights abuses by private actors as well as states is essential because much of the violence and discrimination perpetrated against women and sexual minorities occurs in the private sphere. Therefore, a human rights framework that does not deal with human rights abuses in the private sphere risks undermining support for human rights as an ideal to the extent that it signals indifference to many if not most of the violations of human rights experienced by women and sexual minorities.

This chapter highlights the need for prioritizing human rights abuses that threaten sexual equality. It examines sexual violence and inequality as violations of human rights that occur in the private sphere, as well as violations that are committed directly by the state, through case studies of violence against women and sexual orientation discrimination. Although this chapter focuses on issues that threaten the human rights of women and sexual minorities, it should be noted at the outset that a perspective emphasizing sexual equality could also enhance the basic human rights of men. The final case study examining sex-specific violence during war highlights this point. Ultimately, this chapter is based on the viewpoint that treating sexual equality as a fundamental human right is crucial to furthering the objective of promoting equal access to universal human rights for all human beings.

WOMEN AND SEXUAL MINORITIES: SPECIAL RIGHTS OR HUMAN RIGHTS?

Critics of the pursuit of sexual equality for women and sexual minorities as a human right often insist that "women's rights" and "gay rights" represent "special rights" that actually undermine the idea of universal human rights for all individuals as human beings. For example, in the United States, conservatives' condemnations of efforts by city or state governments to prohibit sexual orientation discrimination on the grounds that such policies represent "special rights" for gays reflect this perspective. To put the argument more positively, a critic might argue that violations of the rights of women or sexual minorities represent distinct problems that are applicable only to women and sexual minorities. As such, these problems should not be framed as human rights issues.

However, many feminists argue that treating violations of women's rights or the rights of sexual minorities as special categories is precisely the problem. As Hilary Charlesworth puts it in reference to women's rights:

> Because men generally are not the victims of sex discrimination, domestic violence, or sexual degradation and violence . . . these matters are often relegated to a specialized and marginalized sphere and are regulated, if at all, by weaker methods. Unless the experiences of women contribute directly to the mainstream international legal order . . . international human rights law loses its claim to universal applicability: it should be more accurately characterized as international *men's* rights law.[4]

This feminist perspective suggests that systematic violence and discrimination against women violates the basic *human* rights of women—rights to life, to political participation, to freedom from discrimination, to freedom from torture, to work, to education, and to a decent standard of living. The same logic can be applied to the case of sexual minorities who regularly face systematic violence and discrimination as a result of their sexual orientation or identity.

In this way, the objective of sexual equality for women and sexual minorities should be viewed as a means for ensuring their equal access to universal human rights, not special rights solely for their enjoyment. Indeed, it should be noted that men can be victims of sex discrimination, sexual violence, domestic violence, and sexual degradation by private actors, even if sexual inequality and violence do not affect men as frequently as they affect women. Thus, a human rights perspective that emphasizes sexual equality in the private as well as the public sphere does not necessarily constitute a case of pursuing "special rights" for women and sexual minorities. Rather, it frequently represents an effort to promote equal access to fundamental human rights for all individuals regardless of their biological sex or sexual orientation.

Having said that, there may indeed be times when women, men, or sexual minorities claim particular rights that are not applicable to other groups as a way of seeking to fulfill their general human rights. Differential treatment as a means of pursuing equal access to human rights is especially likely when real biological differences shape the ways in which men and women will be able to experience their human rights. For example, the biological reality that women bear children suggests that women may require special consideration for maternity leave in order to be able to fully enjoy the right to work. Many feminists defend such differential treatment of men and women as necessary to ensuring genuine equality in terms of other basic human rights, including the right to work, the right to equal economic opportunities, and the right to health. A critic of differential treatment might counter that a universal policy protecting *parental* leave, as opposed to just maternity leave, would provide a more equitable approach to promoting these rights for both men and women. Indeed, such an approach might actually advance feminist ideals—and the ability of women to enjoy the right to work and to equal economic opportunities—to the extent that it challenges traditional stereotypes that suggest only women are suited to playing the role of primary caregiver to young children. In any case, our objective here is not to resolve the debate over whether maternity leave represents an appropriate means for promoting basic political rights for women or unfair differential treatment. Rather, the point of this example is to illustrate that claims for sexual equality are often framed in terms of differential treatment rather than equal access.

An examination of the Convention on the Elimination of Discrimination Against Women (CEDAW) illustrates the complexities involved in debates over whether demands for sexual equality involve "special rights" for women and sexual minorities or merely represent an effort to ensure equal access to universal human rights norms for these groups. In the case of CEDAW, both demands for women's rights as human rights and for women's rights as particular rights are evident. Many of the articles in this treaty simply specify in explicit terms that women have a right to the equal enjoyment of human rights norms codified in other human rights treaties. For example, CEDAW asserts that women have equal rights to legal protection under the law, to political participation, to work and education, and to economic benefits. In this regard, one of CEDAW's primary objectives is to reaffirm that all of the rights enumerated in the International Bill of Rights apply equally to women.

At the same time, several articles in CEDAW claim that women have particular rights that are necessary in order for them to fully enjoy their human rights in general. For instance, Article 4 states that state policies "aimed at protecting maternity shall not be considered discriminatory." This provision suggests that state policies protecting maternity leave for women but not parental leave for men do not constitute discrimination and should be considered as consistent with other international human rights norms. Article 11, which generally calls for the elimination of discrimination against women in employment, elaborates on the right to maternity leave. Paragraph 2 of this article calls upon states that are party to the treaty to introduce maternity leave "with pay or with comparable social benefits" and to prohibit dismissal of employees because of pregnancy, maternity leave, or marital status. Article 11 also calls for states to support social services, including child care, to facilitate workers' ability to juggle family and work responsibilities. Notably, this provision is framed in gender-neutral language that applies to men as well as women. CEDAW includes additional provisions directed specifically at women, including language asserting rights to basic prenatal and postnatal care.

CEDAW tries to strike a fine balance between justifying differential treatment as an appropriate means for promoting genuine equality of opportunity and stressing that women's rights are human rights rather than special rights. This complicated effort to seek balance is evident in Article 4, which states:

> Adoption by State Parties of temporary special measures aimed at accelerating de facto equality between men and women shall not be considered discrimination as defined in the present Convention, but shall in no way entail as a consequence the maintenance of unequal or separate standards; these measures shall be discontinued when the objectives of equality of opportunity and treatment have been achieved.[5]

This language strives to balance two conceptions of equality that ultimately are difficult to reconcile—equality of opportunity defined by relatively equitable outcomes and equality of opportunity based on fair process. In the first conception of equality, *real* equality of opportunity is not possible when structural obstacles, such as historical discrimination, social and cultural norms that justify inequality, and gender stereotypes, limit the ability of women and girls to participate in economic and social life on a level playing field. Under this conception of equality, differential treatment—for example, affirmative action or maternity leave policies that treat women and men differently—are not only justifiable but necessary in order for women to gain equal access to human rights. Under the second conception of equality, creating a fair process under which men and women play by the same rules and in which nondiscrimination is the ultimate value is the most important objective. In this case, applying exactly the same rules to men and women in the present is the most appropriate method for guaranteeing equal opportunity, even if that means downplaying the importance of historical, social, and cultural obstacles to equal access to human rights. Tension between these two conceptions of equality remains one of the most formidable obstacles to generating consensus on the question of whether women's rights constitute human rights or "special rights."

One of the most significant ways in which CEDAW deviates from other international human rights treaties is in its assertion that states are obligated to challenge underlying social and cultural norms that reinforce sexual inequality. Article 5 requires state parties to the treaty "to modify the social and cultural patterns of conduct of men and women, with a view to achieving the elimination of prejudices and customary and all other practices which are based on the idea of the inferiority or the superiority of either of the sexes or on stereotyped roles for men and women."[6] This provision reflects the feminist argument that most of the human rights abuses experienced by women occur in the private sphere and reflect social and cultural norms that justify sexual inequality. In accordance with this argument, most feminists contend that entrenched social and cultural norms must be challenged if women are to have genuine opportunities to pursue their fundamental human rights. To this end, Article 5 highlights the importance of changing social and cultural patterns as a means of promoting equal access to human rights for women.

As this overview has illustrated, the pursuit of sexual equality for women and sexual minorities involves complex questions about how to frame these rights and whether or not differential treatment is a valid response to sexual inequality. On the one hand, claims for rights for women and sexual minorities simply involve efforts to ensure that these groups have equal access to existing international human rights norms. On the other hand, many proponents of sexual equality suggest that differential treatment is necessary to ensure that women and sexual minorities will be able to overcome structural barriers that have prevented their full enjoyment of basic human rights. Furthermore, many proponents of sexual equality contend that efforts to promote equal access to fundamental human rights for women and sexual minorities require dramatic challenges to entrenched discrimination in the private sphere. Notably, it is precisely the threat that sexual equality conceived in this way poses to state sovereignty and cultural relativism that makes so many state and cultural elites reluctant to embrace the cause of rights for women and sexual minorities as human rights.

CASE STUDY:

VIOLENCE AGAINST WOMEN

States across the globe directly perpetrate numerous forms of violence against women despite international human rights norms that call for states to respect fundamental human rights "without distinction of any kind," including biological sex. States commit violence against women when they sanction the rape of women by their military troops during war, as has happened regularly in wars throughout history. States also commit violence against women when they facilitate sexual slavery to "meet the needs" of their servicemen, as in the case of the Japanese government's creation and perpetuation of a sex-slave system in Asia during World War II. State violence against women is not limited to wartime. State police forces use sexual torture against female criminal suspects, and prison guards rape female prisoners.[7] States also sanction the use of cruel and inhumane punishments, such as flogging or death by stoning, for "crimes" committed by women, including adultery and premarital sex.[8] State policies that limit reproductive choices— for example, forced sterilization, coerced abortion, and policies that allow women to have only one child—contribute to violence against women and also lead to infanticide of baby girls in cultures where girl children are devalued. These forms of state violence represent violations of a wide range of basic human rights, including the right to life, the right to health, the right to be free from torture, the right to equal treatment under the law, and prohibitions against cruel and unusual punishment.

Non-state actors also perpetrate numerous forms of systematic violence against women, including dowry deaths (the killing of women by a husband or his family because of her family's failure to meet dowry expectations),[9] the practice of *sati* in India (the burning of the widow on her deceased husband's funeral pyre),[10] so-called honor killings (in which families and communities kill girls and women because they have been accused of engaging in premarital sex or committing adultery or even because they have been raped), forced prostitution, domestic violence, and female genital mutilation.[11] Once again, these forms of violence violate many fundamental human rights, including the right to life, the right to health, and the right to be free from torture. According to the World Health Organization, gender-based violence is a primary cause of injury and death for women. For example, WHO figures indicate "that domestic violence accounts for more deaths and disabling injuries among women aged 15–44 than cancer, malaria, traffic injuries, and war put together."[12] It is precisely because violence against women committed by non-state actors is so widespread that feminists argue that it is essential to frame such violence as a human rights issue. The idea of human rights will have little power or meaning for women if it does not apply to violence in the private sphere, where women are most likely to suffer from violations of their fundamental human rights.

Violence against women that occurs in the private sphere can be appropriately framed as a human rights issue when it represents a pattern of violence that the state has an obligation and the ability to prevent. The concept of state responsibility under international law "holds states accountable for the acts or omissions of their agents or organs."[13] Thus, the concept of state responsibility suggests that states are complicit in violence against women not only when they directly perpetrate such violence but also when they fail to take measures to prevent or punish it.[14] In accordance with this concept, when systematic violence against women occurs, states may be deemed responsible for human rights abuses if they actively condone violence committed by non-state actors or if they have failed to take measures designed to prevent and punish criminal violence against women. If states do not take violence against women seriously, women will not have legal recourse when they are victimized by violence because of their biological sex and, as a result, will not enjoy the equal protection of the law.

Domestic violence provides a compelling example of how states can be complicit in human rights abuses against women even when they do not actively commit these abuses. Domestic violence against women is a vast problem that occurs throughout the world's states and cultures. The perpetuation of domestic violence has been made possible by a rigid application of a distinction between the public and private spheres. Whereas states generally treat assault and murder as criminal behavior, the same behavior when perpetrated by a husband against a wife historically has been treated as a private, family matter by most states.[15] For example, in Brazil, wife killings by husbands were treated as noncriminal "honor killings" until 1991. Until 1980, it was legal for a man in Colombia to kill his wife because she had committed adultery. When men rape their wives, they commonly do not face the threat of legal consequences, even when rape within marriage is prohibited, because many states do not prosecute the crime seriously.[16] For instance, in England, a man could not be prosecuted for raping his wife until 1991. As these examples illustrate, the public–private distinction has resulted in states' failure to provide women with equal protection of the law in that murder and assault against men, which takes place primarily in the public sphere, is criminalized whereas murder and assault against women, which is more likely to occur in the home, is treated as a private matter.

This case study of violence against women demonstrates the critical ways in which different categories of human rights are interconnected. At a very basic level, violence against women involves the violation of basic civil and political rights, particularly the rights to life, to personal integrity, to be free from torture, and to equality under the law. Additionally, violence against women also prevents women from enjoying fundamental economic and social rights, perhaps most prominently the right to the highest standard of physical and mental health. At the same time, women's unequal access to basic economic and social rights also helps to explain the dynamics that drive the phenomenon of violence against women. Women who lack equal access to fundamental economic and social rights, including the rights to education, work, and decent housing, do not have genuine opportunities to flee personal circumstances and environments in which they are vulnerable to violence.[17] In sum, the case of violence against women illustrates that sexual equality, civil and political rights, and economic and social rights are connected in myriad ways. Ultimately, sexual equality needs to be taken seriously if women are to enjoy their basic human rights. To this end, states will need to give women equal access to economic and social rights as well as civil and political rights in order for sexual equality to be a real possibility.

CASE STUDY: SEX-SPECIFIC ABUSES
OF HUMAN RIGHTS DURING WAR

War provides the ultimate setting for human rights abuses. States facing threats to their security and sovereignty become increasingly likely to perpetrate or condone human rights abuses. Non-state actors that have embraced violence as a means of pursuing political and ideological objectives often justify their violations of basic human rights as a necessary means for achieving their ends. Throughout history, innocent civilians have been caught in the crossfire during war, and widespread human rights abuses have been the inevitable result. Interestingly, many violations of human rights during war are sex-specific—in other words, men and women experience distinct forms of wartime human rights abuses. Thus, an examination of sex-specific human rights abuses during war provides a lens through which we can consider larger questions related to sexual equality and human rights.

Sex-specific human rights abuses can be defined as the particular types of human rights abuses experienced by women and men because of their biological sex. The fact that men and women experience wartime violence in different ways does *not* mean that women and men can be placed in the dichotomous categories of "victim" and "perpetrator." Both men and women perpetrate violence during war. Some women as well as men commit rape, torture, and murder of "the enemy."[18] Some men and women engage in industrial work that supports the war effort; other men and women simply offer political and social support for war. Still other men and women oppose war, with varying degrees of activism and resistance. Bombs and bullets do not discriminate, and men and women alike are killed, maimed, and displaced during war.

Although many of the effects of war are neutral in terms of their impact on men and women, men and women experience distinct forms of human rights abuses during war. Women as a biological class are targeted with a wide variety of specific forms of violence during war, including mass rape, forced pregnancy, forced prostitution, and sexual slavery.[19] Rape in the context of war commonly involves multiple levels of violence as rapes committed against individual women are often committed in public and in front of family members and loved ones.[20] Sometimes sexual violence increases in the immediate aftermath of war as men seek to reassert control over women and to restore order after the chaos of war.[21] In the aftermath of war, women whose husbands have been killed often face extreme economic vulnerability in patriarchal societies in which women do not have basic economic rights.[22]

Men also experience distinct types of wartime human rights abuses. In particular, men are more likely to be killed during war as soldiers or potential soldiers. At first glance, it may appear that the killing of soldiers should not be framed as a human rights issue. The death of soldiers (usually male) in war is less frequently decried than the killing of "innocent civilians" (typically assumed to be women) because soldiers are commonly seen as legitimate targets of violence in wartime. However, the legitimacy of the killing of male soldiers can be called into question in contexts in which men face forced conscription, particularly when child soldiers constitute such a large number of fighters in many conflicts across the globe. Forced conscription threatens a variety of fundamental human rights, including the right to life, liberty, and security of person and the right to be free from slavery and forced labor.

In addition to the killing of male soldiers, many civilian men are killed because they are of fighting age and, thus, viewed as potential combatants.[23] Thus, many civilian men are likely to be killed as *potential* soldiers simply because they are males of "fighting age."[24] The killing of civilian men simply because of their age and biological sex constitutes an obvious threat to their right to life and, in this way, can be appropriately framed as a human rights issue. Additionally, men are victims of sexual violence during war, including rape and sexual torture.[25] These forms of sexual violence constitute clear violations of men's basic human rights. Furthermore, men are victimized when they are forced to rape or to watch their loved ones being raped. Thus, men suffer a variety of human rights abuses during war, perhaps most prominently when civilian men are targeted for killing as potential soldiers.

This case study of sex-specific human rights abuses during war illustrates the importance of paying attention to issues involving sexual equality in the study of human rights. Many critics of international human rights law have been feminists who focus on the ways in which it is biased against women. In their view, international human rights law does not focus adequately on rights that are of particular concern to women. By ignoring biological sex and gender, they contend, international human rights law fails to emphasize the extent and nature of abuses experienced by women. This case study supports this viewpoint. The sex-specific human rights abuses experienced by women during war historically have been ignored or downplayed by states and proponents of human rights. Feminist scholars have helped to highlight the enormous scale on which women suffer human rights abuses during war and, thus, have raised the profile of issues such as sexual slavery, rape during war, and forced pregnancy.

While acknowledging this reality, this case study goes beyond the argument that international human rights law is biased against women by demonstrating that international human rights law historically has not only failed to highlight the distinct forms of human rights abuses suffered by women but has also neglected the intentional ways in which men are targeted with specific violations of human rights. Although this case study has focused on sex-specific abuses faced by both women and men during war, it also needs to be noted that, like women, men face sex-specific violations of human rights during peacetime, including infant male circumcision, prison rape, and sexual orientation discrimination (discussed in the next section). By demonstrating the ways in which both women and men can be targeted with distinct forms of sex-specific violence, this case study demonstrates that paying attention to biological sex and gender can help to identify particular forms of human rights abuses that otherwise might be downplayed. The crucial point illustrated by this case study is that a focus on sexual equality and human rights can benefit men as well as women. Ultimately, identifying and examining sex-specific human rights abuses is the first step in fighting them as obstacles to fundamental human rights for *all* human beings regardless of their biological sex.

CASE STUDY:
SEXUAL ORIENTATION DISCRIMINATION

Sexual orientation discrimination is prevalent throughout the globe and is directed at a wide range of sexual minorities, including gay men, lesbians, bisexuals, and transgendered persons. Notably, sexual orientation discrimination is sanctioned in most cultures and religions and in developed as well as developing countries. Sexual orientation discrimination takes many forms. At an extreme, states have executed individuals for engaging in same-sex activities.[26] In other cases, states have failed to aggressively investigate and prosecute the murders of sexual minorities by private actors.[27] Many states across the globe still criminalize homosexuality. Even though numerous countries have decriminalized same-sex sexual activity in recent decades, very few states have adopted legislation prohibiting sexual orientation discrimination.[28] Moreover, many states repress sexual minorities' basic civil liberties, including freedom of speech and expression. Such restrictions are in place in democracies as well as non-democracies. For instance, it is illegal in both Great Britain and Austria "to publicly advocate, promote or encourage homosexuality."[29]

As this discussion illustrates, numerous human rights are threatened by sexual orientation discrimination. State policies that target gays, lesbians, bisexuals, or transgendered individuals for political repression or that condone or ignore violence committed against them by private actors threaten the right to life, liberty, and security of person of sexual minorities. State policies that prohibit private, consensual sexual activity violate the right to privacy. State policies that impinge upon an individual's right to openly express his or her sexual identity—for example, policies that allow openly gay people to be fired—violate the rights of freedom of thought, conscience, opinion, and expression. State-sanctioned job discrimination against sexual minorities also violates the right to work and equal pay. State policies that perpetrate or condone hate crimes and violence against sexual minorities, the repression of the open expression of sexual identity, and interference with private and family life serve as obstacles to the ability of sexual minorities to live physically and emotionally healthy lives and, as such, violate the right to physical and mental health.[30] State policies that deny gay men and lesbian women custody of children solely because of their sexual orientation represent a denial of equal treatment under the law.[31] Though not exhaustive, this list illustrates the numerous ways in which sexual orientation discrimination prevents individuals who are members of sexual minority groups from fully enjoying fundamental human rights.

Despite the threats that sexual orientation discrimination pose to the idea that *all* human beings deserve to enjoy fundamental rights, even human rights organizations have not aggressively sought to frame sexual orientation discrimination as a violation of human rights. For example, Amnesty International's mandate did not treat the political imprisonment of sexual minorities as a violation of fundamental human rights for decades. One of Amnesty International's most visible campaigns involves protests against the unfair imprisonment of "prisoners of conscience" in violation of basic human rights, including unfair trials and coerced confessions, or because of nonviolent exercise of the rights to freedom of association and expression. Amnesty International did not initially adopt individuals imprisoned solely because of their sexual orientation as prisoners of conscience. This policy changed in 1991 when the organization expanded its mandate to cover sexual orientation discrimination after nearly two decades of internal debate over this issue.[32] Today, Amnesty International takes a much stronger stance on sexual orientation discrimination and even has a special campaign, OUTfront, through which it advocates for human rights for gays, lesbians, bisexuals, and transgendered people. Nevertheless, the fact that a human rights organization had to struggle for so long before recognizing the political repression of sexual minorities as a violation of fundamental human rights indicates the extent to which sexual orientation discrimination is entrenched in political and social systems across the globe.

Unfortunately, most mainline human rights organizations and states still do not treat sexual orientation discrimination as a human rights priority. The failure of human rights organizations and states to protest repression and violence faced by gays in Palestine provides a stark example. Gay Palestinians, who often face harassment and violence from their own families and Islamic organizations, have alleged that they have been detained and tortured by the Palestinian Authority and that they have also received death threats. At least one allegation involves the death of a gay man who was deprived of food and water until he died. Increasingly, the Palestinian Authority is embracing Islamic law and, to this end, is openly criminalizing homosexuality.[33]

Despite growing repression against homosexuals in Palestine, international human rights groups have not paid significant attention to this issue. Many gay Palestinian men have risked their lives to flee to Israel where homosexuality is legal and where gays enjoy many basic rights, including prohibitions against workplace discrimination, despite the fact that Orthodox Judaism also opposes homosexuality. Unfortunately, as Palestinians residing unlawfully in Israel, these men do not have access to the protections accorded Israeli citizens.[34] Moreover, because of fears of terrorist attacks, Israeli government authorities are reluctant to allow Palestinian gays to live legally in Israeli territory and have sought to deport gay Palestinian men.[35] Thus, gay men who are living in Israel illegally escape the threat of repression by the Palestinian Authority but face constant fears of deportation and live on the edges of Israeli society in economic vulnerability. They are unable to seek refuge in other countries because most states do not recognize sexual orientation discrimination as grounds for granting political asylum.[36] In its annual report on human rights, the U.S. State Department merely said that homosexuals in Palestine "are socially marginalized, and occasionally receive physical threats."[37] As this case illustrates, even if they recognize sexual orientation discrimination as a violation of human rights, most human rights organizations and states do not treat this issue as a human rights priority.

The United Nations has demonstrated a similar reluctance to embrace the idea that sexual minorities deserve equal access to basic human rights. Up until it was renamed in 1999 as the Subcommission on the Promotion and Protection of Human Rights, the UN Subcommission on Prevention of Discrimination and Protection of Minorities rejected proposals to study discrimination on the basis of sexual orientation discrimination.[38] To date, the new Subcommission on the Promotion and Protection of Human Rights does not treat sexual orientation discrimination as a fundamental human rights abuse. After complaints from developing countries, the United Nations Development Programme modified its Human Development Report by replacing its "Human Freedom Index," which included "freedom for homosexual activity" as one of the criteria, with a narrower "Political Freedom Index," which excluded this criterion.[39] Similarly, the Human Development Report now includes a Gender-Related Development Index as a means of measuring equality of "all women and men" that notably excludes sexual orientation discrimination as one of its indicators.[40] The Platform of Action of the Fourth World Conference on Women in 1995 omitted references to sexual orientation because of opposition on the part of delegations from many countries, despite support from a majority of the delegations to the drafting committee.[41] Most recently, the United Nations Commission on Human Rights decided not to vote on a resolution that defined sexual orientation discrimination as a violation of human rights.[42] Because the UN is an international organization with nearly universal membership among nation-states, the United Nations resistance to the idea that sexual minorities deserve fundamental human rights reflects the widespread acceptance of sexual orientation discrimination by states across the globe.

As we saw in Chapter 2, international human rights law—a body of law that is, after all, created by states—currently sanctions sexual orientation discrimination. Although the main treaties that comprise the body of international human rights law specify that human beings are entitled to fundamental human rights "without distinction of any kind, such as race, colour, sex, language, religion, political or other opinion, national or social origin, property, birth or other status," they do not specifically identify sexual orientation as an inappropriate basis for discrimination. Although existing nondiscrimination clauses in these treaties could arguably be interpreted in a way that prohibits sexual orientation discrimination—for instance, by asserting that the categories of "sex" or "other status" cover gay, lesbian, and bisexual persons— the lack of specific language protecting sexual minorities from discrimination is indicative of the lack of intent on the part of signatories to the major human rights documents to extend protection on these grounds.

As this case study has shown, sexual orientation discrimination is one form of discrimination that is widely viewed as acceptable in most nation-states. Not only do nation-states generally sanction sexual orientation discrimination in varying degrees, but international organizations also have resisted the idea that sexual minorities deserve full access to fundamental human rights. Most surprisingly, human rights organizations generally have not endorsed the struggle against sexual orientation discrimination as a major human rights cause deserving of their full political attention and efforts. In this way, sexual orientation discrimination represents one of the last frontiers for advancing the idea that *all* human beings have fundamental rights. It is precisely because sexual minorities are so vulnerable and lack extensive political support that students and proponents of human rights need to take the issue of sexual orientation discrimination seriously.

CONCLUSIONS

Human rights abuses committed against individuals because of their biological sex or sexual orientation are pervasive in world politics. Although its forms vary, widespread violence against women takes place in all sorts of states, democratic and nondemocratic, developed and developing. Similarly, diverse cultures across the globe sanction violence against women and unequal treatment of women to varying degrees. The prevalence of discrimination against sexual minorities similarly transcends political and cultural boundaries. As the case of sex-specific violence during war demonstrates, men also may be victims of human rights abuses because of their biological sex. Such abuses are often treated with silence or skepticism in an international community all too willing to accept the killing of soldiers (without consideration of whether they are serving voluntarily) or "potential soldiers" as legitimate and resistant to the idea that men might be victims of rape or other forms of sexual violence during war.

If the claim that *all* human beings deserve equal access to human rights is to have genuine moral and political meaning, proponents of human rights will have to place greater emphasis on the importance of sexual equality in the pursuit of human rights. Sexual equality is a worthy moral objective in its own right. Additionally, sexual equality is necessary for the full enjoyment of other basic human rights. When human beings are discriminated against because of their biological sex or sexual orientation, they are unable to enjoy the full range of human rights, from civil and political rights to economic and social rights. Accordingly, efforts to promote sexual equality need to place greater emphasis on the violation of human rights by non-state actors in the private sphere because it is here that so much of the discrimination and violence targeted at individuals because of their biological sex or sexual orientation occurs.

Cultural relativism and state sovereignty pose formidable obstacles to sexual equality for all individuals as a universal human right. A wide array of states and cultures resists the notion that sexual equality is a fundamental human right. As this chapter has shown, even some human rights organizations have demonstrated resistance to treating sexual equality as a human rights priority. This resistance among even proponents of human rights only signals that it is crucial for individuals who are committed to fundamental human rights for *all* human beings to speak out on behalf of individuals and groups who are vulnerable as a result of their biological sex or sexual orientation. As we saw in Chapter 1, human rights as moral claims are especially important when the rights in question are not protected by law and when they do not have the backing of powerful political actors. If the language of human rights is the weapon of the weak and vulnerable, then framing sexual equality as a human rights issue represents an important tool for women and men who suffer human rights abuses because of their biological sex as well as sexual minorities in their quest for lives of equality and dignity.

DISCUSSION QUESTIONS

1. Feminists challenge the rigid separation of the private and public spheres in terms of responding to human rights abuses. Do you agree with this argument? Why or why not?

2. If the public and private spheres should not be rigidly separated, then how should public and private concerns be balanced? Are all private issues subject to public regulation? How should we decide which private issues should be subject to public regulation and which should not?

3. Is it appropriate to conceptualize sexual equality as a fundamental human right, or does it primarily involve "special rights" for women and sexual minorities?

4. Does the pursuit of sexual equality ever justify differential treatment of women, men, or sexual minorities? Why or why not? This chapter has explored the case of maternity leave in addressing this question. Can you think of other examples that might call for differential treatment as a way of advancing rights for women, men, or sexual minorities?

5. Feminists argue that it is essential to challenge discrimination, inequality, and violence in the private sphere as a means of promoting equal human rights for women and sexual minorities. Do you agree? Why or why not? How might such an approach advance human rights? Are there any ways in which such an approach might undermine other human rights?

6. The concept of state responsibility holds states responsible for violence against women when they directly perpetrate such violence and when they fail to take measures to prevent or punish it. Applying this concept, should a state be held responsible for isolated or random violence against

women in the private sphere? Under what circumstances, if any, should isolated or random violence against women be considered a human rights issue?

7. Can a human rights perspective emphasizing sexual equality improve men's access to human rights? Why or why not? This chapter has considered sex-specific violence during war as one example of when sexual inequality harms men. Can you think of other examples?

8. Should proponents of universal human rights take a stronger stance against sexual orientation discrimination as a violation of universal human rights? Why or why not?

WEB RESOURCES

Convention on the Elimination of Discrimination Against Women (http://www.un.org/womenwatch/daw/cedaw/econvention.htm)

Amnesty International OUTfront: Human Rights and Sexual Identity (http://www.amnestyusa.org/outfront)

Amnesty International Women's Human Rights (http://www.amnestyusa.org/women)

Human Rights Campaign: Working for Lesbian, Gay, Bisexual and Transgender Equal Rights (http://www.hrc.org)

Human Rights Watch Women's Rights (http://www.hrw.org/women/index.php)

International Gay and Lesbian Human Rights Commission (http://www.iglhrc.org)

International Law Guide IV: International Women's Human Rights and Humanitarian Law (http://www.law-lib.utoronto.ca/resguide/women2.htm)

International Women's Rights Action Watch (http://iwraw.igc.org)

The History of the Gay Male and Lesbian Experience during World War II (http://www.pink-triangle.org/)

Women's Human Rights Net (http://www.whrnet.org)

8

Promoting Human Rights from the Top Down

IMPLEMENTING HUMAN RIGHTS THROUGH INTERNATIONAL ORGANIZATIONS AND STATES

Efforts to promote human rights "from the top down" typically reflect a non-adversarial approach to human rights implementation. The United Nations and other international organizations concerned with the advancement of human rights seek to engage states in cooperative ways designed to further their voluntary embrace of human rights norms rather than imposing human rights from above. Regional organizations, to the extent that they have identified human rights as a priority, similarly employ cooperative strategies for promoting human rights. Such cooperative measures include creating human rights norms, raising awareness about human rights norms, and monitoring human rights performance. Beyond these measures, states have not willingly relinquished sovereignty in order to give international organizations the legal authority to enforce human rights norms.

In the rare cases in which international organizations or states have used forceful means to promote international human rights, such efforts have typically been used against relatively weak states that do not have the power to protect their right to sovereignty against the interests of the more powerful states that dominate international institutions. The fact that force has only been used against weak states in international efforts to promote universal human rights reflects the reality that some states have more sovereignty than others, despite the formal legal equality that sovereignty implies. When states unilaterally intervene in other countries on human rights grounds, it is typically difficult to determine whether they are genuinely motivated by human rights concerns or they are merely using human rights rhetoric to further narrow national interests. Thus, critics are skeptical about the validity of the use of force as a means of promoting human rights from the top down.

Ultimately, international efforts to promote human rights from the top down have been shaped by the interests of sovereign states, especially the most powerful states in world politics. This chapter explores this theme by providing an overview of the United Nations human rights system as well as regional human rights systems. Additionally, the chapter will consider the various foreign policy tools available to states as a means of promoting human rights. An examination of states, foreign policy, and human rights will consider not only how states have used foreign policy tools to promote human rights but also how states have appropriated the language of human rights to advance foreign policies that in reality have been designed to further more narrow national interests. Finally, the chapter provides a case study of humanitarian intervention in Kosovo to explore the promise as well as potential pitfalls of international efforts to promote human rights from the top down.

THE UNITED NATIONS
HUMAN RIGHTS SYSTEM

The United Nations has a number of institutional tools at its disposal for the promotion of global human rights. As we saw in Chapter 2, the United Nations has been the primary actor responsible for the creation of international human rights norms. In particular, the General Assembly has been the major incubator of international human rights treaties, which are typically crafted within this body before being submitted to states for signature and ratification. In addition to developing human rights norms, the General Assembly may vote on resolutions to condemn human rights abuses in particular cases. Notably, General Assembly resolutions are not binding legal decisions. As a result, the General Assembly's ability to respond to violations of human rights is limited to public condemnation of such abuses.

Moreover, because the General Assembly is a political body in which each member state has one vote and in which state interests obviously shape decision making, the General Assembly does not respond in a consistent manner to allegations of human rights abuses across the globe. For example, the General Assembly, dominated by developing states since the 1960s, limited its condemnations of human rights abuses during the 1970s primarily to the cases of South Africa, Israel, and Chile.[1] Although resolutions condemning human rights violations in these countries were valid, the General Assembly failed to apply consistent standards and did not condemn deplorable violations of human rights in other cases, including Cambodia in the 1970s when the ruling Khmer Rouge killed an estimated 2 to 3 million Cambodians in its drive for totalitarian domination.

The UN Charter gives the Security Council stronger powers for responding to human rights abuses. In particular, the Security Council can authorize enforcement action under Chapter 7 of the UN Charter *if* it determines that human rights abuses in a particular case constitute a threat to international peace and security. In theory, Chapter 7 enforcement action provides the Security Council with potentially strong and effective tools for preventing and punishing human rights violations, including economic sanctions, the creation of international criminal tribunals, and the use of military force. In practice, however, the Security Council's enforcement powers have been limited for a variety of reasons. Many states do not comply with Security Council resolutions calling for voluntary economic sanctions, and the Security Council has only called for mandatory sanctions once when it imposed economic sanctions on Iraq after it invaded Kuwait in 1990.[2] Moreover, economic sanctions often have a negative impact on civilian populations, especially when governments that are the target of sanctions refuse to utilize loopholes allowing for food and humanitarian aid as a way of generating internal support by pointing to economic sanctions, and external forces in general, as the cause of civilian suffering. The Security Council has only created a limited number of international criminal tribunals, which will be discussed in detail in Chapter 9. Even when they are created, ad hoc tribunals do not prevent human rights abuses but merely seek to punish those responsible after the fact.[3]

Moreover, the Security Council has applied its enforcement powers to human rights issues only in a limited and inconsistent manner. The Security Council's willingness to treat human rights violations as threats to international security peaked in the 1990s at the end of the Cold War, in part because the end of this ideological stalemate made Security Council agreement on such matters more likely. The Security Council authorized enforcement action in Bosnia, Haiti, Rwanda, and Somalia in the 1990s at least in part on the grounds that these violent "internal" conflicts involving widespread repression and human rights abuses threatened international peace and security. Nevertheless, the UN's reluctance to take stronger actions to end the war in Bosnia or to stop the genocide in Rwanda, and its inaction in the face of grave human rights abuses elsewhere, demonstrates that state sovereignty is alive and well. When the Security Council decides to invoke its enforcement powers in response to human rights abuses, it commonly does so because human rights norms converge with state interests in particular cases. In other cases, a lack of strategic concerns or conflicting political interests among member states helps to explain why the Security Council fails to act in response to most cases involving systematic violations of human rights. In short, the Security Council does not have a consistent policy of treating human rights abuses as threats to international peace and security, and the international community still does not sanction strong enforcement action to protect human rights.

Despite its status as the principal UN judicial organ, the International Court of Justice (ICJ) does not play a significant role in the UN human rights system. The fact that the ICJ has not been integrally involved in the promotion of international human rights norms does not result from a lack of authority, as the ICJ is competent to address state disputes involving any international legal norms. Rather, the ICJ's essential irrelevance to human rights processes within the United Nations results from the fact that only states can bring complaints to ICJ. Not surprisingly, states, preoccupied with protecting their own sovereignty, have been reluctant to bring human rights complaints before the courts. For example, Human Rights Watch, after finding that Iraq had committed genocide against the Kurds in the late 1980s, urged several states, including Canada, the Netherlands, and the Scandinavian countries, to bring genocide charges against Iraq at the ICJ. Eventually, two governments agreed confidentially that they would bring charges *if* a European government would join them in this case. To date, no such agreement has been forthcoming from any European government.[4] As this example illustrates, the International Court of Justice, as a judicial body primarily responsible for arbitrating interstate disputes, is not in a strong position to serve as a court for enforcing international human rights norms.

In addition to the powers of general UN institutions to respond to human rights issues, the UN human rights system involves a number of specific human rights bodies. The main human rights body within the United Nations system is the UN Commission on Human Rights, created by Economic and Social Council (ECOSOC) Resolution 5 (I) in 1946. Initially, the Commission on Human Rights did nothing with the plethora of complaints it received alleging violations of human rights. Indeed, in 1947, ECOSOC passed a resolution that prohibited the Commission from reviewing such complaints. Thus, in the early years of its existence, the Commission on Human Rights did not play an active role in monitoring human rights standards in member states. This situation changed in 1967 when ECOSOC adopted Resolution 1235, which authorizes the Commission on Human Rights to examine allegations of gross violations of human rights, particularly when human rights violations represent a consistent pattern of abuse.[5] The Commission has the authority to make recommendations and may conduct its examination in public, thus potentially embarrassing and applying political pressure to governments accused of abuses.

However, the complaint and monitoring procedure under Resolution 1235 is limited as a mechanism for implementing human rights in important respects. First, the UN Commission on Human Rights is a political body whose membership is comprised of fifty-three state representatives. Because it is a political body with membership representing UN member states, it should not be surprising that the Commission's human rights activities are shaped and constrained by state interests. As a result, the procedure is vulnerable to politicization, as states may only register complaints when they are driven by self-interested political motivations and may disregard systematic violations of human rights in other countries when they do not have any strategic interest in exposing them or when drawing attention to human rights abuses in friendly countries actually runs counter to national interests. Second, only states may register complaints under the 1235 procedure. Thus, individuals and nongovernmental organizations do not have legal standing under Resolution 1235 and may not submit complaints to the Commission under this procedure.

In 1970, ECOSOC passed Resolution 1503, which gives individuals and nongovernmental organizations the right to register complaints with the Commission on Human Rights. As in the case of the 1235 procedure, Resolution 1503 gives the Commission the authority to receive and review complaints involving a pattern of gross violations of human rights. In other words, the Commission does not have the authority to investigate allegations of isolated instances of human rights violations. The investigation procedure in cases involving individual complaints remains confidential until it is concluded. Despite this initial confidentiality, the UN Commission on Human Rights eventually publishes a list of countries that it has reviewed. However, it is important to note that the Commission does not provide details about human rights allegations against specific countries or its findings. Thus, typically the most that comes out of this procedure is negative publicity for states that appear on the list. The procedure does not lead to punishment or sanctions for the states in question, nor does it provide any recompense to the victims of human rights abuses. In this way, the mechanism primarily entails the monitoring and condemnation of human rights abuses but does not involve any real punishment or deterrent to continuing human rights abuses in countries on the list.

In addition to the Commission on Human Rights, the UN human rights system includes six treaty-monitoring bodies: the Human Rights Committee, which oversees the implementation of the International Covenant on Civil and Political Rights; the Economic, Cultural, and Social Rights Committee, which monitors state implementation of the International Covenant on Economic, Social, and Cultural Rights; and the Committee on the Rights of the Child, the Committee on the Elimination of Discrimination Against Women, the Committee on the Elimination of Racial Discrimination, and the Committee Against Torture, each of which is responsible for monitoring the implementation of the relevant treaty. Typically, the monitoring process involves committee review of reports submitted by parties to each treaty. Notably, the relationship between these committees and the states that they are monitoring is not adversarial. Rather, as noted by the United Nations High Commissioner for Human Rights, "the treaty bodies endeavour to establish a constructive dialogue with State parties to assist them in fulfilling their treaty obligations and to offer guidance for future action through suggestions and recommendations."[6]

An examination of the Human Rights Committee illustrates the way in which these treaty-monitoring bodies operate and also demonstrates the shortcomings inherent in monitoring as a mechanism for promoting human rights. The International Covenant on Civil and Political Rights called for the creation of the Human Rights Committee to oversee implementation of the treaty. Under the Covenant, states are required to submit reports every five years to the Human Rights Committee discussing progress and implementation, and the Human Rights Committee reviews these reports. Unlike the Commission on Human Rights, the membership of the Human Rights Committee consists of eighteen independent experts who may publicly question states. Nevertheless, this process does not involve a formal evaluation procedure but merely an exchange of information. Moreover, many states have failed to submit complete and timely reports.

Under the Optional Protocol to the International Covenant on Civil and Political Rights, the Human Rights Committee may consider individual complaints and has the authority to issue judgments as to whether state parties to the treaty are fulfilling their treaty obligations. The review process is confidential while investigations are ongoing, but the Human Rights Committee makes its decisions public at the end of the process. As a result, nongovernmental organizations, human rights activists, and states can use this information to exert political pressure on states to end their violations of human rights.[7] Approximately 100 states have signed on to the Optional Protocol, and it is notable that the Human Rights Committee has decided against states in nearly 100 cases.[8] More important, states sometimes respond with positive action to address the violation in question. For example, after the Human Rights Committee issued a decision against Finland brought by a military conscript who complained that he had not had an opportunity to challenge his military detention before a court, Finland responded by initiating legislation designed to give individuals the right to have judicial hearings on military confinement.[9] As in the case of the Commission on Human Rights, the Human Rights Committee can only render nonbinding judgments and make recommendations—its decisions do not have the force of law. Not surprisingly, many states do not comply with the committee's decisions.

The Economic, Social, and Cultural Rights Committee works in a similar manner. ECOSOC created this committee in 1985 to monitor the International Covenant on Economic, Social, and Cultural Rights. Like the Human Rights Committee, the Economic, Social, and Cultural Rights Committee has a membership consisting of eighteen independent experts. The committee's primary responsibility is to review the reports that state parties are required to submit, though, once again, many states fail to submit the "mandatory" reports. The committee engages in "constructive dialogue" with states about their human rights records rather than evaluating state progress in implementing human rights norms in a confrontational manner. After reviewing reports submitted by states, the Economic, Social, and Cultural Rights Committee issues "concluding observations," which include positive aspects of state performance, recommendations, an evaluation of obstacles to implementation, and an overview of major concerns about the state's performance in meeting its obligations under the International Covenant on Economic, Social, and Cultural Rights. The committee formulates its concluding observations in private but makes them public at the end of its session. When violations occur, the committee urges states to "desist from further infringements." As in the case of the Human Rights Committee, the recommendations of the Economic, Social, and Cultural Rights Committee are not legally binding.[10]

This overview of the Human Rights Committee and the Economic, Social, and Cultural Rights Committee illustrates the limitations of the treaty-monitoring bodies in the UN human rights system. Ultimately, these bodies have the authority to make recommendations to state parties to the relevant treaties, but their decisions are not binding. In this way, the treaty-monitoring bodies reflect the reality that international law and the UN system in general continue to prioritize state sovereignty as an organizing principle of world politics. Moreover, the treaty-monitoring bodies emphasize a cooperative rather than adversarial relationship with states. Such an approach is probably necessary given that states inevitably need to play a major role in implementation if international human rights norms are ever to become a reality. In general, the treaty-monitoring committees monitor state performance in fulfilling their international human rights obligations, but "the lack of mandatory and enforcement powers means the committees act as mere watchdogs, relying on publicity and pressure, as well as treaty obligations, to ensure compliance."[11]

In 1993, the General Assembly created the UN High Commissioner for Human Rights (UNHCHR). The High Commissioner's office has numerous responsibilities, including providing support to other human rights institutions, playing an advisory role, supporting and conducting research, and writing reports. The UNHCHR's mandate gives it the authority to address any human rights issue and to deal directly with governments in the process. The creation of this body represents an effort to bring greater coherence and coordination to the many monitoring and norm-creating functions of other bodies that are part of the UN human rights system. Finally, in addition to the general human rights bodies, the UN human rights system involves numerous specialized agencies with responsibilities for promoting specific human rights, including the UN International Children's Emergency Fund, the UN High Commissioner for Refugees, and the International Labour Organization. In some cases, for example, UNICEF and the UN High Commissioner for Refugees, these agencies can play a major role in coordinating aid and disseminating information on how to deal with serious human rights problems. Nevertheless, the mandates of these agencies are limited in that they often depend to a great extent on voluntary contributions from states and require state consent for their operations.[12]

At the end of the day, the UN human rights system emphasizes norm creation, information gathering, weak monitoring, and, sometimes, public condemnation as tools for promoting international human rights. In this way, the UN human rights instruments reflect the reality that the UN system prioritizes sovereignty as an international value. As such, the UN human rights system, as is the case with the UN in general, inevitably reflects the interests of the sovereign states that comprise its membership. In this regard, the limitations of the UN human rights system reflect the lack of political will on the part of states to engage in serious efforts to implement human rights norms rather than an inherent flaw in the UN system. As Nigel White concludes, "the problem is not the lack of human rights standards and mechanisms but the willingness of states to comply with obligations. The law is binding on states; the lack of enforcement is a combination of institutional deficiency and state unwillingness."[13]

REGIONAL HUMAN RIGHTS SYSTEMS

In addition to the UN human rights system, regional human rights systems provide various mechanisms for promoting and protecting international human rights. Because regional human rights systems, by definition, are applicable only within particular regions, they involve limited efforts to implement human rights as universal rights. The human rights norms in question may reflect universal principles, but regional human rights systems apply these norms only within particular areas and not on a global basis. Accordingly, various regional human rights regimes reflect divergent interpretations of universal human rights and challenge state sovereignty to varying degrees.

The European human rights system is the best developed and strongest among the various regional human rights regimes. Indeed, in many respects, the European human rights system poses a stronger challenge to the sovereignty of European states than the UN human rights system does to states in general. The European Convention for the Protection of Human Rights and Fundamental Freedoms, which emphasizes civil and political rights, and the European Social Charter, which delineates economic, social, and cultural rights, provide the overarching legal framework for the European human rights system.

Historically, the European Commission on Human Rights was the primary body in the European human rights system. The Commission consisted of one member from each state party to the European Convention. Commission members were elected by the Committee of Ministers of the Council of Europe. The European Commission on Human Rights was able to receive complaints both from states and from individuals or nongovernmental organizations. It had automatic jurisdiction in cases involving state complaints. It had the power to review cases involving complaints from individuals or nongovernmental organizations only if a state had accepted its optional jurisdiction in such cases. In dealing with complaints of human rights abuses, the European Commission on Human Rights had the authority to engage in fact finding, to attempt to negotiate "friendly settlements" to disputes, and to issue reports and make recommendations to the Committee of Ministers of the Council of Europe. Additionally, the Commission was able to refer the case to the European Court of Human Rights *if* the state party against which a complaint was lodged had recognized the compulsory jurisdiction of the court. As in the case of the UN Commission, the European Commission's recommendations were not binding. Nevertheless, it is notable that the Commission decided against states in the majority of cases it heard, and states typically followed the Commission's recommendations.[14]

At present, the European Court of Human Rights represents the heart of the European human rights system. In 1997, the Council of Europe adopted dramatic changes to the European human rights system that challenged state sovereignty to a greater extent by eliminating the Commission on Human Rights as mediator and authorizing individuals to file complaints directly with the European Court of Human Rights. Previously, individuals did not have direct standing before the court. Instead, individuals could appear before the court for a special hearing only if the Commission on Human Rights had ruled in their favor and if the involved state had recognized the right of private petition. As a result of Protocol 11 to the European Convention for the Protection of Human Rights and Fundamental Freedoms, which was adopted in 1997 and entered into force in 1998, individuals now have direct standing before the court. Of course, states also continue to have the right to bring complaints against other states before the court. Importantly, the Court has the authority to issue binding decisions. The Committee of Ministers of the Council of Europe has responsibility for overseeing the "execution of judgements" by states. Court decisions, as well as recommendations from the European Commission, have resulted in changes to member state human rights policies in numerous cases, on issues ranging from the treatment of immigrants to prisoner detention policies to policies involving privacy and freedom of the press.[15]

The European Court of Human Rights still retains some protections for state sovereignty. As in the case of the European Commission, each state party to the European Convention has a member on the court. The Consultative Assembly of the Council of Europe elects the court's membership. Thus, the court is not insulated from politics. Nevertheless, the legal authority of the European Court of Human Rights represents a significant challenge to absolute sovereignty and distinguishes the European human rights system from other regional human rights systems that remain more deferential to the principle of state sovereignty.

The European Social Charter calls for states to submit biennial progress reports to the Council of Europe's Secretary-General on their implementation of economic, social, and cultural rights. The Committee of Ministers of the Council of Europe nominates a Committee of Experts to review these reports. Eventually, the Committee of Ministers reviews the findings of the Committee of Experts and may subsequently make recommendations.[16] However, its recommendations are nonbinding, yet another sign that the European human rights system ultimately remains respectful of state sovereignty. In addition, the European Committee of Social Rights, the body responsible for overseeing the implementation of the European Social Charter, may receive and review complaints from individuals against states who have accepted an optional protocol to the Charter.[17] In general, the system for promoting economic and social rights is weaker than the system governing the implementation of civil and political rights.

In 1999, the Council of Europe added a new element to the European human rights system when it created the Office of the European Commissioner for Human Rights. The European Commissioner is elected by the Parliamentary Assembly of the Council of Europe for a nonrenewable six-year term. The Commissioner's primary responsibilities include raising awareness and promoting education about human rights in member states, monitoring member states' human rights records in order to identify shortcomings in their compliance with human rights obligations, and generally promoting and advancing human rights norms among member states. The Commissioner is not authorized to receive or evaluate individual complaints of human rights abuses. In general, the Commissioner's mandate is to cooperate with the governments of member states in promoting human rights norms.

One of the primary mechanisms by which the European human rights system has influenced state policies is by shaping the rulings of domestic courts within these states.[18] Domestic courts have drawn on the European Convention, European Commission recommendations, and European court rulings in issuing decisions that advance human rights norms within particular countries. Similarly, the existence of strong human rights norms in Europe has led states who wish to join European political and economic institutions to pay heed to these norms in constructing new constitutions or reforming existing governing structures in an effort to gain admission to these institutions. Such reforms happened when Greece, Portugal, and Spain sought to join Europe after the end of authoritarianism in these countries and when Central and Eastern European states sought to join Europe after the collapse of communism.[19] In this way, the European human rights system has contributed to the advancement of universal human rights in Europe without fundamentally challenging state sovereignty as a value. Ultimately, institutions within European states must take actions that incorporate human rights norms, so that these advances in human rights norms remain consistent with the norm of sovereignty.

One of the reasons that the European human rights regime has been relatively successful is that, generally speaking, European countries have relatively strong human rights records and share a basic commitment to the idea of universal human rights. As Jack Donnelly has noted, "A cynic might argue that the breadth and strength of the European human rights regime simply illustrate the paradox of international action on behalf of human rights: strong procedures exist where they are least needed. Because they require the permission of states, they are likely only where states have a high interest and good records."[20] However, Donnelly also points out that even in countries with relatively good human rights records, violations of human rights occur. Thus, effective human rights mechanisms remain necessary even in these cases.[21] Moreover, even when only a minority of victims of human rights abuses are helped as a result of regional human rights mechanisms, it is better than no protection at all.

In 1959, the Organization of American States (OAS) created the Inter-American Commission on Human Rights, the primary institution in the Inter-American human rights system. The Commission currently consists of eleven members, no two of whom may be from the same state, elected by the OAS General Assembly. The Inter-American Commission on Human Rights has several tools at its disposal for promoting human rights. It may seek to raise awareness about human rights norms, and it can request information on human rights issues from member states. The Commission can attempt to negotiate friendly settlements to disputes among state parties and reports to the OAS Secretary-General after such involvement. If a friendly settlement has been reached, the Secretary-General issues a public report. In the event that efforts at friendly settlement have failed, the Secretary-General can issue a confidential report or can make nonbinding recommendations to the parties involved. The Inter-American Commission also receives and reviews annual human rights reports from member states, though once again it can only make nonbinding recommendations. Finally, the Inter-American Commission can receive and review individual complaints, though it has done so rarely, and its decisions in these cases have not been widely accepted by member states.[22]

The Inter-American Court of Human Rights also consists, at present, of eleven members elected by states party to the 1969 American Convention on Human Rights. Individuals have no standing before the court. Instead, the Inter-American Commission on Human Rights files cases with the court. The Inter-American Court's decisions are binding, and the OAS General Assembly may impose sanctions on member states as a means of enforcing the court's decisions. However, the Inter-American Court has not been highly active and has decided only a few cases, and the OAS has not used its authority to enforce court decisions.[23]

The 1981 African Charter on Human and Peoples' Rights, which prioritizes collective rights and individual duties over individual rights, provides the legal framework for the African human rights system. The African Commission on Human and Peoples' Rights is the institution at the center of the African human rights system. It consists of eleven members elected by the heads of state of the Organization of African Unity and, as such, obviously reinforces the importance of state sovereignty. The African Commission has several implementation mechanisms at its disposal, including cooperative efforts to promote human rights through education and information exchange, the power to investigate alleged human rights abuses and issue nonbinding recommendations, private communications with states accused of violating human rights, and attempts to negotiate friendly settlements to disputes. Only states, and not individuals, may bring complaints before the African Commission. Indeed, the African Commission only has the power to investigate human rights "situations" and not individual cases.[24] Notably, the African human rights system does not have a court and emphasizes cooperative mechanisms rather than adversarial processes.

As this overview demonstrates, regional human rights systems typically remain deferential to state sovereignty in their efforts to promote human rights. The European human rights system, which challenges sovereignty more than any other regional system, provides a limited exception to this rule. Nonetheless, in general, states have not created regional human rights systems with strong enforcement powers but, rather, limit their human rights activities to monitoring, norm creation, and non-adversarial mediation roles. Notably, Asia and the Middle East do not have well-developed regional human rights systems. In Asia, the lack of a regional human rights system can be attributed to the size and diversity of the region coupled with strong resistance in Asian states to relinquishing any sovereignty to even a regional organization on the issue of human rights. In the Middle East, the reluctance to endorse or institutionalize regional or international human rights norms is even stronger.[25] Just as in the case of the UN human rights system, regional human rights systems are typically limited by the fact that states are unwilling to give up sovereignty in the name of universal human rights.

STATES, FOREIGN POLICY, AND HUMAN RIGHTS

Because states must play a central role in the implementation of international human rights norms if these norms are ever to become a reality in an international system organized around state sovereignty, state foreign policies represent an indispensable tool for the promotion of international human rights. Unfortunately, the historical record clearly demonstrates that states across the globe have, at best, imperfect records when it comes to promoting universal human rights through their foreign policies. At worst, state foreign policies undermine or actively violate human rights norms. As this section will show, foreign policy is an imperfect if necessary tool for promoting human rights because states inevitably balance an array of competing interests in formulating and implementing foreign policies. Human rights principles are only one priority—and typically a lesser priority at that—in a state's calculations of its national interests.

States have a wide range of foreign policy tools at their disposal for the promotion of international human rights norms. Analysts of foreign policy often categorize the foreign policy tools available to states as "carrots" or "sticks." "Carrots" refer to positive incentives that states may use in their efforts to shape the behavior of other states. States have used a variety of cooperative approaches and positive incentives in an effort to promote human rights norms in other countries, including quiet diplomacy, foreign aid, and development assistance. "Sticks" refer to the punishments or threats states make to induce states to engage in desired behavior or to adopt preferred policies. States have used a range of disincentives to promote human rights abroad, including public condemnation of human rights violations, economic sanctions, arms embargoes, the severing of diplomatic relations, and military intervention. Typically, states use various combinations of carrots and sticks in their foreign policies targeted at the promotion of international human rights.

A state's claim that its foreign policy is motivated by human rights concerns should not be accepted at face value. Typically, there is a gap between human rights rhetoric in foreign policy and the reality of this policy. Commonly, foreign policies framed primarily by human rights rhetoric are actually motivated by a state's narrower perception of its national interests. In such cases, states use human rights rhetoric because it is a powerful political tool. However, states typically are not motivated by human rights concerns alone. Moreover, careful analysis of the ways in which states spend resources and follow through in cases in which they claim to be acting in the name of human rights contradicts the notion that they are motivated primarily by human rights concerns. As the saying goes, actions speak louder than words. With this in mind, students of human rights should be cognizant of the ways in which the actual implementation and effects of foreign policy often differ from stated human rights motivations. The case study of American foreign policy that follows will demonstrate the ways in which a gap can exist between the rhetoric and the reality of human rights promotion through foreign policy mechanisms.

Although students should maintain a healthy skepticism about state claims to be acting on behalf of human rights, the point is not necessarily to dismiss the potential of foreign policy as a tool for promoting human rights. Even if states are only motivated to incorporate human rights principles into their foreign policies when these principles coincide with other national interests, this does not *inevitably* mean that such foreign policies are harmful to the cause of human rights. At times, it may be the case that foreign policies justified with human rights rhetoric actually undermine or threaten human rights norms. At other times, such policies may actually contribute to the advancement of human rights norms. Thus, it is important to keep in mind that the motivations underlying a foreign policy may be separate from the *effects* of this policy. As a result, particular cases need to be evaluated on their merits. In the end, state foreign policies will inevitably continue to reflect state efforts to balance competing interests and ideas. As we will see in Chapter 11, foreign policies that are genuinely consistent with the idea of human rights ultimately depend upon pressure exerted by domestic as well as transnational and international political actors that gives states an incentive to prioritize human rights principles relative to other concerns.

CASE STUDY: U.S. FOREIGN POLICY
AND AMERICAN EXCEPTIONALISM

U.S. foreign policy provides a useful lens for examining foreign policy as a tool for protecting and promoting fundamental human rights. A focus on U.S. foreign policy is particularly relevant for two reasons. First, the powerful position of the United States in contemporary world politics places it in an especially strong position of being able to influence, for good or ill, the status of human rights across the globe. Few other states have the power, resources, or will to affect human rights on a global scale to the same extent as the United States.

Second, U.S. foreign policy has been infused from the very beginning of the country's history with a sense of "American exceptionalism"—a belief that the United States is fundamentally different from other countries in its culture and politics. In general, American exceptionalism has been driven by a belief that American cultural and political values are not only different from but also superior to those of other countries. [26] This sense of American exceptionalism has contributed to a prominent American worldview that contends that it is not only appropriate but desirable for the United States to inject considerations of principle, and not just power, into its foreign policy.

American exceptionalism has been very influential in shaping the use of human rights rhetoric in U.S. foreign policy. Because the belief in "American exceptionalism" has usually meant that the United States views itself as superior to other countries, Americans often believe that they are in a better position than any other country to promote and protect human rights across the globe. According to this viewpoint, whereas skepticism about the humanitarian rhetoric of other governments might be warranted, the United States should be trusted by other countries and peoples when it claims to be acting on behalf of humanitarian principles. As discussed in the previous section, states often rely on human rights rhetoric to mobilize support for foreign policies that are ultimately derived from more narrow national interests. Although the United States is not alone in doing so, it has a particularly strong record of drawing on humanitarian rhetoric to advance its strategic objectives.

A case in point is the way in which the U.S. government developed its argument for war against Iraq in response to Iraq's invasion of Kuwait in 1990. In this case, the U.S. government used human rights rhetoric—for example, highlighting Amnesty International reports about political repression in Iraq—in order to build domestic and international support for war against Iraq. However, the Iraqi government did not suddenly become repressive when it invaded Kuwait in 1990. Rather, Amnesty International and other human rights organizations had long decried the violations of human rights in Iraq. Such condemnations typically fell on deaf ears in the United States and other powerful countries, which prioritized other foreign policy objectives and national interests, including regional stability and access to cheap oil, prior to the Iraqi invasion of Kuwait. Indeed, the United States considered Iraq an ally throughout the 1980s despite widespread evidence of government atrocities and human rights abuses. It was not until Iraq invaded Kuwait and, in doing so, challenged the U.S. government's conception of its national interests that the United States mobilized the language of human rights to justify its foreign policy toward Iraq. Notably, the U.S.-led war against Iraq, waged with the approval of the UN Security Council, ended once Iraq withdrew from Kuwait. The status of human rights *within* Iraq had never been the primary foreign policy concern, and the rhetoric of human rights became less important in U.S. policy toward Iraq after its withdrawal from Kuwait.

A similar pattern emerged after the September 11th terrorist attacks on U.S. soil. Prior to this time, governing elites in the United States did not prioritize women's rights in Afghanistan or the Middle East in foreign policy.

However, as the United States sought to bolster domestic and international support for its "war on terrorism," the Bush Administration began to highlight the plight of women living under Taliban rule in Afghanistan as a way of disarming critics of its foreign policy and mobilizing political support for a war in Afghanistan. As in the case of the 1990 Gulf War in Iraq, the U.S. government ceased to depict the status of human rights in general and women's rights in particular as major foreign policy concerns once the war in Afghanistan had been won. Instead, the U.S. foreign policy agenda began to focus on the next steps in the ongoing U.S. "war on terror." Once again, this case illustrates the way in which states use human rights language as a political tool in their formulation of foreign policies but do not necessarily prioritize human rights in the actual implementation of these policies.

Yet another example is provided by the more recent U.S. invasion of Iraq to topple the government of Saddam Hussein. The U.S. government offered many justifications for its invasion of Iraq in March 2003. Initially, the Bush Administration stressed that Iraq was a key component in its "war on terror." The view of Iraq as a security threat to the United States was based on two specific claims. First, the U.S. government argued that the Iraqi government had connections with Al Qaeda that contributed to terrorist threats to the United States. Second, the Bush Administration argued that Iraq possessed weapons of mass destruction that posed a direct threat to the United States. In its initial justifications of the war, humanitarian concerns were not as prominent in the government's rationale for the invasion of Iraq as the security justifications. However, over time, the government played up human rights rhetoric as the main rationale for war, especially when the U.S. military did not find evidence of weapons of mass destruction in Iraq and as critics of the war questioned the evidence of ties between Al Qaeda and Iraq.

It should be noted that one explanation for the shifting emphasis on humanitarian principles versus national security in the rationale for the recent U.S. invasion of Iraq is that different actors within the U.S. government disagreed about the reasons for going to war. For some, only real threats to U.S. national security provide a compelling justification for war, while for others concerns with democracy, freedom, and human rights are preeminent. Thus, bureaucratic politics, rather than crass self-interest on the part of the government, can help us understand why foreign policy rhetoric might shift over time. Moreover, it should be noted that supporters of the invasion argue that whatever initially motivated the U.S. government, proponents of human rights should celebrate the fact that the brutal regime of Saddam Hussein has been toppled. As discussed in the previous section, foreign policies may actually contribute to the advancement of human rights norms even if states are only motivated to incorporate human rights principles into their foreign policies when these principles coincide with other national interests. Because the U.S. invasion of Iraq is so recent, it is too early to tell whether democracy will take root in Iraq or to evaluate the ultimate consequences of the U.S. invasion in terms of human rights. For our purposes in this section, the important insight provided by this case is that, once again, human rights rhetoric is often a tool that governments do not employ unless they believe vital national interests are at stake.

A close examination of U.S. foreign policy is appropriate both because of the unparalleled power of the United States in contemporary world politics and because of the influence of American exceptionalism on the country's foreign policy, but it is important to stress that U.S. behavior is not altogether unique. Most states, especially powerful states, engage in similar foreign policy practices. In general, a gap between rhetoric and reality typically characterizes the relationship between foreign policy and human rights, not only in terms of the factors that shape foreign policy but also in terms of a state's rhetorical commitment to human rights and its actual human rights performance. States generally are more likely to embrace the cause of universal human rights as these norms apply to other countries but to resist the notion that they are constrained by universal norms in their own domestic policies. Moreover, a state's treatment of human rights within its foreign policy will inevitably reflect that state's particular conception of human rights and its understanding of its national interests.[27]

HUMANITARIAN INTERVENTION

Humanitarian intervention refers to military intervention for the purpose of protecting fundamental human rights. Humanitarian interventions can be either multilateral, involving the participation of many states, or unilateral, initiated and led by a single state. It is difficult to identify an accepted list of humanitarian interventions because there typically is not consensus in the international community regarding a state's claim that it has intervened in another country on humanitarian grounds. An example of a multilateral intervention is the UN's intervention in Somalia in the early 1990s, which was conducted with the approval of the UN Security Council. Examples of unilateral interventions that states have justified at least in part on humanitarian grounds include India's intervention in East Pakistan in 1971 to stop Pakistani atrocities against Bengalis; the Vietnamese invasion of Cambodia in 1978 to end the brutal rule of the Khmer Rouge; Tanzania's intervention in Uganda in 1979, which contributed to the demise of Idi Amin's reign; and the NATO intervention in Kosovo in 1999, discussed in a detailed case study later in this chapter. The United States has frequently used humanitarian language to justify its interventions in other countries, including the Dominican Republic, Grenada, and Panama.[28] The U.S. government also relied on humanitarian rhetoric as one of the justifications of its 2003 invasion of Iraq.

In the current international system, humanitarian intervention is consistent with international law under specific conditions—namely, if the UN Security Council authorizes it as a legitimate Chapter 7 enforcement action in response to a humanitarian crisis that poses a threat to international peace and security. For example, the UN-approved intervention in Bosnia was justified partially on the grounds that "ethnic cleansing" in the Balkans constituted both a humanitarian crisis and a threat to international peace and security.[29] By contrast, humanitarian interventions that do not have Security Council authorization violate the letter of international law. Nevertheless, defenders of humanitarian intervention contend that it is consistent with the spirit of international law, especially provisions calling for the promotion and protection of fundamental human rights.[30]

The primary argument against humanitarian intervention is that it represents an unacceptable challenge to the principle of state sovereignty. By challenging the concept of sovereignty, humanitarian intervention threatens to undermine global stability and generate disorder in the name of human rights. Some critics of humanitarian intervention are skeptical even of multilateral humanitarian interventions approved by the Security Council. In their view, the UN Charter only authorizes Chapter 7 enforcement action against threats to international peace and security. If the Security Council interprets threats to international peace and security too broadly, according to critics, it may undermine the system of state sovereignty on which global stability rests.[31] Unilateral humanitarian intervention without Security Council approval is especially problematic because, as we have seen, states often manipulate human rights rhetoric to justify the pursuit of narrower national interests. Thus, skeptics contend that state claims that they are intervening in another country for genuinely humanitarian purposes are dubious.

Despite the preponderance of evidence that international law does not sanction humanitarian intervention without UN approval, many proponents of human rights argue that humanitarian intervention is a legitimate tool for protecting fundamental human rights, especially in cases involving systematic threats to the lives of vulnerable individuals and groups. Indeed, states are often criticized for failing to take action in the face of gross violations of human rights. A case in point is the Rwandan genocide in 1994, when the United States and other powerful countries were condemned for not doing anything to prevent or stop the genocide. Writing of the U.S. failure to respond appropriately to the moral outrage represented by cases of genocide throughout the twentieth century, Samantha Power argues vehemently that a principled foreign policy calls for humanitarian intervention to stop genocide regardless of constraints imposed by international law. In her concluding words about genocide in the twentieth century, she asks, "How many of us do not believe that the presidents, senators, bureaucrats, journalists, and ordinary citizens who did nothing, choosing to look away rather than to face hard choices and wrenching moral dilemmas, were wrong? And how can something so clear in retrospect become so muddled at the time by rationalizations, institutional constraints, and a lack of imagination?"[32] For proponents of human rights, powerful states with the capability to stop systematic violations of human rights have not only the right but a moral duty to do so—regardless of whether or not international law formally sanctions humanitarian intervention.

Humanitarian intervention raises vexing questions of not only *whether* it is justified but also, for proponents of human rights who believe it is legitimate, *when* and *under what conditions.* Just war theory, which is consistent with the idea that humanitarian intervention can be legitimate under the right circumstances, sets out specific criteria that can be applied to determine whether humanitarian intervention is justified in particular cases. Under just war theory, the most basic condition that must be met for a war to be considered just is just cause. In addition, a state must publicly declare its objectives in advance for it to conduct a war in accordance with the requirements of just war theory. Next, war must be a last resort under just war theory. The final criterion is that the harm caused by a war must be proportional to the harm it is seeking to prevent. Under this condition, a war fought for the noblest of purposes is unjust if it inflicts more harm than it prevents.[33]

An application of just war theory to humanitarian intervention suggests that a state's declaration that it is acting on behalf of humanitarian principles is not enough to legitimize the intervention. Instead, the state must actually be motivated by the right intent for a humanitarian intervention to fulfill the criteria of just war theory. States must have exhausted other remedies before resorting to humanitarian intervention for it to be considered legitimate under just war theory. Finally, good intentions are not enough. Even interventions genuinely motivated by humanitarian concerns will not be judged kindly by the international community or by history if they cause more harm than they prevent.

Problems associated with the conditions under which humanitarian intervention is justified are not entirely settled by just war theory. Even if every real-world example of humanitarian intervention fulfilled just war criteria, the fact that states do not consistently intervene to stop gross violations of human rights remains a problem. Critics of humanitarian intervention often point to inconsistency in state practices toward humanitarian intervention as evidence that the "humanitarian" motives of states cannot be trusted. Why did NATO intervene in Kosovo (a case that will be discussed in detail in the next section) on humanitarian grounds, but not in Chechnya or Rwanda? A short answer is that NATO countries were motivated by an interest in regional stability in the case of Kosovo. The failure of the international community to intervene in Rwanda can be explained by a lack of national interest on the part of powerful countries that might have had the capability to stop the genocide. As discussed in Chapter 5, the United States and European countries have downplayed human rights abuses committed by Russia in Chechnya for a variety of political reasons. Certainly, Russian political power and nuclear capabilities provide a compelling explanation for why the international community has not been more critical about Russian atrocities in Chechnya. Furthermore, the "war on terror" in the United States in the aftermath of September 11 helps to explain why the United States has been relatively deferential toward Russia's Chechnya policy, which the Russian government frames as a response to terrorism.

Students of human rights are left with a basic question: Does the inconsistency of the international community in practice undermine the legitimacy of humanitarian intervention as a response to human rights crises? Critics answer this question in the affirmative. However, any expectation of perfect consistency in state responses to humanitarian crises is not politically realistic. States have limited economic, political, and human resources. It is difficult enough for states to marshal sufficient political will for humanitarian intervention when such a policy coincides with underlying national interests. It would be that much more difficult for states to generate political support domestically and abroad for humanitarian interventions everywhere that human rights abuses occur. Proponents of humanitarian intervention might counter that even if states cannot respond to each and every case of human rights abuses across the globe, doing so in cases of egregious human rights abuses might serve as a deterrent to governing elites, who might be more likely to refrain from adopting repressive political tactics if they feared that the international community would respond with force to grave violations of human rights.

This discussion of humanitarian intervention has raised more questions than it has answered. While international law is clear that humanitarian intervention is not legal unless it has the sanction of the United Nations Security Council, state practice suggests less consensus on this point. Moreover, neither scholars nor human rights activists agree on whether unilateral humanitarian intervention is justified in cases of genocide and other egregious threats to fundamental human rights. The following case study of the NATO intervention in Kosovo in 1999 on humanitarian grounds demonstrates the way in which some of these issues play out in practice and details the complexities of humanitarian intervention in the real world.

CASE STUDY: HUMANITARIAN INTERVENTION IN KOSOVO

The NATO intervention in Kosovo in 1999 demonstrates the tensions surrounding humanitarian intervention in contemporary world politics. Prior to its disintegration in the mid-1990s, the Federal Republic of Yugoslavia was made up of six constituent republics: Bosnia-Herzegovina, Croatia, Macedonia, Montenegro, Serbia, and Slovenia. In 1989, Kosovo, which has a large Muslim ethnic Albanian majority (approximately 90 percent of the population), was an autonomous province located within Serbian territory. Other ethnic groups living in Kosovo include Christian Orthodox Serbs and Montenegrins.

Prior to 1989, nationalism among both Albanians and Serbians in Kosovo was on the rise as the Cold War was coming to an end. Nationalist tensions between the two groups erupted when Yugoslavia revoked the autonomous status of Kosovo in 1989 and instituted police rule in the province. Serbian police rule was accompanied by torture, arbitrary arrests, killings, and the firing of ethnic Albanians from state jobs.[34] Given the growing movements for self-determination in Bosnia and elsewhere in Yugoslavia, the Serbian government's effort to crack down on Albanian nationalism in Kosovo is not surprising. However, rather than mitigating this Albanian nationalism in Kosovo,

Serbian repression contributed to the growth of a pro-independence move-ment in the province. When pro-independence forces conducted an un-sanctioned "underground" referendum in 1991, 99 percent of those voting favored independence for Kosovo. The Democratic League of Kosovo (LDK), the ruling ethnic Albanian party at the time, represented the majority of Kosovo's population and practiced peaceful resistance. However, the Kosovo Liberation Army (KLA), created in the mid-1990s, embraced violent tactics in its demands for Kosovo's independence.[35]

As violence by the KLA escalated, the Yugoslav government labeled the KLA a "terrorist" group and used the threat of terrorism as justification for further repression. Indeed, after several KLA attacks on Yugoslav authorities in Kosovo, Yugoslavia initiated a military crackdown in Kosovo in which Yugo-slav forces killed Albanian civilians as well as suspected members of the KLA. A cycle of governmental repression by the Yugoslav government and anti-government violence by the Kosovo Liberation Army began to spiral in the 1990s.[36]

In the face of escalating violence, the Contact Group on the former Yugo-slavia, consisting of ministers from Britain, France, Italy, Germany, Russia, and the United States, began to work on forging a consensus on how to respond to the crisis in Kosovo. Early in March of 1998, the Clinton Administration warned that the United States would intervene if the Serbs used "massive force" in Kosovo. Nevertheless, the Yugoslav government escalated its military campaign in Kosovo. Ultimately, in the face of growing refugee flows out of Kosovo and reports of Yugoslav atrocities in the province, the North Atlantic Treaty Organization (NATO) initiated a military intervention in Kosovo for the purpose of stopping Yugoslav aggression in Kosovo.

The NATO military campaign targeted both Yugoslav forces in Kosovo and state targets within Yugoslavia proper. This case is striking for several rea-sons. First, Kosovo was not a republic within the former Yugoslavia but a province located within Serbia. The international community had not recog-nized it as an independent political entity; it was unquestionably a part of Serbian territory. Thus, the NATO intervention represented a crucial chal-lenge to the sovereignty of Yugoslavia. NATO did not insist on independence for Kosovo and, indeed, continued to recognize Kosovo as part of Serbian ter-ritory. Still, it is precisely because NATO recognized Kosovo as part of Serbia that the intervention represents such a striking challenge to Yugoslavia's sover-eignty. Second, the UN Security Council did not approve of the NATO bombing campaign. Thus, the NATO intervention in Kosovo violated inter-national legal principles against intervention in the internal affairs of other states. Finally, this case is notable because NATO countries were motivated primarily by a genuine concern with humanitarian principles. Although the United States and Europe did point to their interests in regional stability,[37] they did not have base economic interests, such as oil, at stake in Kosovo.

The aftermath of the NATO military campaign in Kosovo continues to reflect global disagreement about the moral legitimacy of humanitarian inter-vention. Critics charge that the NATO bombing actually unleashed Serbian violence and repression in the region by giving the Yugoslav government a justification for responding with overwhelming force. Indeed, Serb forces killed thousands of Kosovar Albanians after the NATO bombing campaign began. Yugoslav forces tortured and raped countless additional Albanians.[38] Additionally, the Serbian military forced almost 800,000 Albanians out of the country and displaced an additional half-million Albanians within Kosovo.[39] Moreover, the NATO bombing itself resulted in the deaths of approximately 500 Serbian and Albanian civilians.[40] In addition, critics point out that Kosovar Albanians have gone on to repress Serbs living in Kosovo in the aftermath of the war. Thus, critics contend that the NATO campaign caused more deaths and suffering than it prevented.

However, defenders of the NATO bombing point out that the Yugoslav government had already killed thousands of Kosovar Albanians prior to the NATO intervention. Furthermore, they argue that the Yugoslav government had plans to perpetrate "ethnic cleansing" against Kosovar Albanians and merely used the NATO bombing campaign as a convenient justification for putting their genocidal plan into motion.[41] For proponents of humanitarian intervention, the NATO campaign represented a success in that it enabled more than a million Kosovar Albanians to return to their homes and ended Serbian killing and repression in the province. While outsiders decry the NATO campaign as an example of unlawful and ineffective military violence, Kosovar Albanians typically view the violence they suffered during the war as an acceptable price for their freedom from oppression.[42]

CONCLUSIONS

"Top-down" efforts to promote international human rights norms reflect the reality that state sovereignty is alive and well in world politics. International and regional organizations typically adopt non-adversarial approaches toward human rights implementation. The UN human rights system emphasizes norm creation, information gathering, weak monitoring, and, less commonly, public condemnation as tools for promoting international human rights. Ultimately, the UN system prioritizes state sovereignty as a higher value than fundamental human rights. Similarly, regional human rights systems remain deferential to state sovereignty. Rather than creating human rights institutions with strong enforcement powers, existing regional human rights systems emphasize monitoring, norm creation, and non-adversarial mediation roles. The European human rights system is a limited exception to this rule. However, the European human rights system remains highly respectful of state sovereignty. The European system has been relatively successful primarily because the European states that participate in the system represent political cultures that are highly supportive of the idea of human rights and, thus, have been willing to uphold and implement regional human rights norms. In general, the limited enforcement powers available to the United Nations and regional human rights institutions reflect the reality that states have ultimately been unwilling to give up sovereignty to allow for the active promotion of universal human rights.

The place of human rights in the foreign policies of most states also illustrates that states have generally been reluctant to relinquish sovereignty to further the goal of universal human rights. It would be too cynical to conclude that considerations of principle never shape foreign policy. Nevertheless, foreign policy is rarely if ever a reflection of pure principle. Rather, it is inevitable that states' perceptions of their national interests fundamentally drive foreign policy. When a state pursues foreign policies directed at furthering human rights norms, it is usually the case that human rights norms coincide with the state's perception of its national interests. Moreover, it is too often the case that states merely adopt the rhetoric of human rights to advance narrow national interests. Although proponents of human rights might prefer that states always be motivated by pure principle in their foreign policies, such an outcome is unlikely. In an imperfect world in which politics inevitably shape state behavior, the best a proponent of human rights might hope for is that states increasingly define their national interests in ways that encompass human rights norms and that their foreign policies do more good than harm to universal principles of human rights.

Humanitarian intervention is an exception to the rule that state sovereignty generally trumps universal human rights. However, it is notable that foreign policy practitioners and scholars of human rights widely dispute the legitimacy of humanitarian intervention as a means for promoting human rights. Not only do critics of humanitarian intervention charge that it is a violation of international law unless it has been approved by the United Nations, but they also contend that the concept of humanitarian intervention is often exploited by states seeking cover for military actions that they are actually pursuing for self-interested reasons. Furthermore, many critics argue that humanitarian intervention is an oxymoron. According to this perspective, humanitarian intervention actually violates human rights in the ostensible drive to promote human rights by causing more death and suffering than it prevents. In contrast, proponents of humanitarian intervention typically view it as the last resort for saving lives and preventing human suffering in the face of gross violations of human rights such as genocide. In such cases, advocates of humanitarian intervention argue that states may have a moral duty to intervene in order to protect vulnerable individuals and groups, regardless of whether or not humanitarian intervention has the legal sanction of the international community, precisely because an international legal system grounded in state sovereignty devalues humanitarian principles in favor of global stability and the status quo.

In a world of sovereign states, it is inevitable that states and the international organizations in which they participate must play an important role in the implementation of international human rights. The necessity of implementing universal human rights through sovereign states involves an important paradox. Because states typically are the actors most responsible for perpetrating human rights abuses, it is difficult to imagine that they will voluntarily agree to promote and protect universal values that pose an inherent challenge to their sovereignty. Yet that is precisely the reality that proponents of human rights face. In the absence of an effective international organization with the authority and power to implement human rights, sovereign states will need to play a crucial role if human rights are to be protected. Furthermore, states typically will not consent to join international organizations and to embrace international legal norms unless international organizations and international law contain protections that affirm the principle of sovereignty. Efforts to promote human rights from the top down necessarily reflect and are limited by this reality.

DISCUSSION QUESTIONS

1. Why do international organizations generally rely on a non-adversarial approach to promoting international human rights? What are the strengths and weaknesses of non-adversarial methods for promoting international human rights?

2. Does the UN human rights system represent an effective approach for promoting international human rights? Why or why not?

3. Do existing regional human rights systems represent effective approaches for promoting international human rights? Why or why not?

4. Does the fact that states typically prioritize human rights in their foreign policies only when human rights norms coincide with national interests undermine the legitimacy of these policies? Why or why not?

5. What criteria can we use to evaluate foreign policies directed at the promotion of international human rights? How can we assess whether such policies represent a genuine commitment to human rights or whether states are merely using human rights rhetoric to advance narrow national interests?

6. Does humanitarian intervention represent a morally appropriate response to grave violations of human rights? Why or why not? Is it ever valid for a state or a group of states to engage in humanitarian intervention without the approval of the UN Security Council? Why or why not?

7. Consider the case of NATO's humanitarian intervention in Kosovo. From Serbia's perspective, the Kosovo Liberation Army was a terrorist organization. As such, the Serbian government sought to justify political repression in Kosovo on the grounds that it was fighting terrorism. Was Serbia justified in its failure to respect certain human rights norms in its efforts to suppress what it viewed as an insurrection? Why or why not? Does your perspective change if you compare this case to U.S. restrictions on basic civil liberties in the aftermath of September 11? Why or why not?

WEB RESOURCES

UN Charter (http://www.un.org/aboutun/charter/)

International Covenant on Civil and Political Rights (http://www.unhchr.ch/html/menu3/b/a_ccpr.htm)

International Covenant on Economic, Social, and Cultural Rights (http://www.unhchr.ch/html/menu3/b/a_cescr.htm)

United Nations High Commissioner for Human Rights (http://www.ohchr.org/english/)

United Nations Commission on Human Rights (http://www.unhchr.ch/html/menu2/2/chr.htm)

United Nations Human Rights Treaty-Monitoring Bodies (http://www.unhchr.ch/html/menu2/convmech.htm)

European Convention for the Protection of Human Rights and Fundamental Freedoms (http://conventions.coe.int/treaty/Commun/QueVoulezVous.asp?NT=005&CL=ENG)

European Social Charter (http://www.coe.int/T/E/Human_Rights/Esc/)

European Commissioner for Human Rights (http://www.coe.int/T/E/Commissioner_H.R/Communication_Unit)

European Court of Human Rights (http://www.echr.coe.int/)

Inter-American Commission on Human Rights (http://www.cidh.org)

Inter-American Court of Human Rights [official Web site in Spanish] (http://heiwww.unige.ch/humanrts/iachr/iachr.html)

Overview of Inter-American Court of Human Rights (http://www1.umn.edu/humanrts/iachr/general.html)

African Commission on Human and People's Rights (http://www.achpr.org)

9

Punitive Justice
and Human Rights

PUNITIVE JUSTICE AS A RESPONSE
TO HUMAN RIGHTS ABUSES

In the satirical play *The Firebugs*, by Max Frisch, the protagonists allow two py-romaniacs to live in their attic. These "firebugs" subsequently destroy the city with firebombs. Although the main characters are not directly guilty of any crime, they are morally complicit because they knowingly allowed these pyro-maniacs in their home out of both moral cowardice and fear. As a result, in the second act they end up in hell, where Satan (one of the "firebugs" from the first act) declares hell "on strike" because only mundane sinners are being ban-ished to hell for punishment while the rich, the nobility, and other elites have been able to "buy" their way into heaven. Satan protests that if hell cannot rightly lay claim to everyone who deserves to be there, then it should just be shut down altogether. The play was written by Frisch at the end of World War II and serves as an allegory for the pursuit of justice in the aftermath of the Holocaust. Frisch pokes fun at the average citizen, who he clearly holds ac-countable for moral cowardice and for looking the other way in the face of evil. Yet he also raises questions about the legitimacy of punishment that does not bring accountability to all who are guilty, especially those individuals most directly responsible for the orchestration of evil.

Questions of guilt and accountability are central to punitive models of jus-tice. Punitive justice emphasizes the punishment of perpetrators of war crimes and human rights abuses in post-conflict societies. In most cases, punitive justice stresses the punishment of *specific* individuals guilty of perpetrating war crimes and human rights abuses, though in some cases punitive justice may involve a punishment imposed on a society at large (for example, taxpayers whose government funds reparations to a victimized group). Because of its focus on individual perpetrators, a punitive approach to pursuing justice in the aftermath of human rights abuses and war crimes has as one of its essential elements the identification of "the guilty."

Several additional questions follow. Who is guilty? Who shall be held responsible for the violation of human rights abuses and war crimes? How shall the guilty be punished? The moral dilemma raised by Frisch in *The Firebugs* is that it may not seem just to hold low-level officials who directly committed violence accountable for their actions if higher-level officials who orchestrated or instigated the violence are not punished. At the same time, the standards of justice in liberal democracies typically hold that there must be proof that an individual directly committed a crime for him or her to be found guilty of that crime. In this case, the dilemma is that it may be difficult to prove that high-level officials were directly responsible for human rights abuses unless elites have left a clear record of their complicity. Consideration of questions of guilt, accountability, and appropriate punishment are key themes of this chapter, which provides an overview of judicial efforts to punish war crimes and human rights abuses. This chapter focuses on trials; the following chapter will examine truth commissions and other restorative justice practices.

TRIALS AND PUNITIVE JUSTICE

Advocates of punitive justice tend to favor trials as the mechanism most likely to produce genuine justice and lasting reconciliation in the aftermath of human rights abuses or war crimes. Judicial efforts to punish war crimes and human rights abuses are grounded on the idea that "neutral" institutions designed to apply the rule of law are the most appropriate types of institutions for evaluating guilt and innocence and for determining punishments in the case of crime. The punishment of perpetrators of crimes, rather than an emphasis on reconciliation or peace building, is a fundamental feature of judicial mechanisms as a path to justice.

In a domestic model of law and judicial punishment, the law itself provides for the creation of judicial institutions and delineates the rules under which judicial institutions will operate. In liberal democracies, provisions for basic civil rights protect the accused, and judicial institutions operate with a degree of independence from other political organs of the state. In this way, judicial institutions are seen to have political legitimacy. Because societies coming out of a violent conflict often have no tradition of the democratic rule of law and rarely have the financial or social resources to create effective judicial mechanisms, domestic efforts to pursue justice in the face of war crimes or human rights abuses commonly lack this political legitimacy. As a result, victims often seek to turn to international judicial mechanisms as an alternative.

Unfortunately, the domestic model of judicial justice does not translate readily to the international sphere. In the case of international war crimes and human rights abuses, the relevant body of law involves the laws of war and the emerging body of international human rights law. Prior to the end of World War II, the relevant body of law was limited essentially to basic laws of war that required that even during wartime, civilians and unarmed or wounded soldiers be immune from intentional violence and treated humanely. Up until that time, there were only a limited number of laws for any judicial body, had one existed, to interpret, adjudicate, or enforce. Moreover, the laws of war deal only with the treatment of soldiers and civilians during wartime and do not protect the basic human rights of individuals in general. As discussed in Chapter 2, the end of World War II saw a surge in the development of international human rights law. Although the development of international human rights law represents an important step in the creation of international norms that provide human beings with certain basic rights, which governments are under a moral obligation to respect, international law does not have the force of domestic law.

Simply put, no "world government" exists that parallels even remotely the government of established nation-states. The General Assembly of the United Nations serves in some respects as a legislative body that establishes norms for global governance. However, the United Nations does not have effective institutions for the enforcement of these norms. The UN Security Council does serve in some respects as an enforcement body. Nevertheless, its authority is essentially limited to cases involving threats to international peace and security. The scope of its authority does not extend to enforcing international human rights norms unless the Security Council determines that violations of human rights threaten international peace and security.

In addition, there are to date no judicial institutions that parallel the role of judicial institutions in most nation-states, especially liberal democracies. Although Article 98 of the UN Charter makes all UN member states parties to the Statute of the International Court of Justice (ICJ), this court does not have the level of authority of judicial institutions in most countries. The ICJ has jurisdiction only under certain circumstances: (1) in cases in which both parties voluntarily agree to submit a particular case to the ICJ's jurisdiction; and (2) in cases that fall within a category over which the relevant parties have agreed to accept the ICJ's compulsory jurisdiction (in essence, "compulsory jurisdiction" means a state recognizes the jurisdiction of the court for all relevant cases in advance). The ICJ may give "advisory opinions" even when state parties to a conflict have not recognized the ICJ's jurisdiction, but, of course, such advisory opinions do not have the force of law. The extent to which the recently created International Criminal Court (ICC) will develop into an effective mechanism for the pursuit of justice in the aftermath of human rights abuses and war crimes remains to be seen. In short, although the body of international human rights law has grown significantly, there still are no effective institutions for interpreting, adjudicating, or enforcing it. An absence of effective judicial institutions at either the domestic or the international level has limited, to date, trials as punitive mechanisms for bringing justice to the perpetrators of war crimes and human rights abuses and their victims.

TRIALS IN HISTORICAL PERSPECTIVE:
THE DEVELOPMENT
OF AD HOC TRIBUNALS

In the absence of standing judicial bodies, ad hoc tribunals have emerged as an alternative mechanism for pursuing justice through the prosecution of war crimes and gross violations of human rights. Contrary to widespread perceptions, the idea of holding trials for war criminals is not a new one and did not begin with the notorious Nuremberg Tribunal. At the turn of the twentieth century, the United States held war crimes trials in the aftermath of the Spanish-American War, and Great Britain similarly prosecuted war crimes after the Boer War. Victorious states have also considered pursuing trials for "war criminals" in the aftermath of other high-profile conflicts, including the Napoleonic wars, the Armenian genocide, and World War I. In each of these cases, trials ultimately failed.[1] Nevertheless, the debate over the question of whether or not to pursue punitive justice through trials in each of these cases provides insight into the limitations of ad hoc tribunals as well as the political obstacles faced by proponents of trials as mechanisms for pursuing justice. Although trials have been considered as an option for punishing defeated powers in the aftermath of war, it is telling that foreign policy elites historically have placed considerations of stability and national interest above a legalist and punitive approach to justice.

At the end of the Napoleonic wars in 1815, the Allies decided to banish Napoleon to St. Helena. Prussia proposed simply shooting Napoleon, but Great Britain opposed this extrajudicial solution. Instead, Britain initially favored having the restored Bourbon monarchy in France try Napoleon and the Bonapartists. Because the Bourbon monarchy feared it would not be able to withstand political backlash if it held trials, the Allies settled on banishment as the option least likely to upset stability, both internationally and within the Allied states.[2]

During World War I, a number of politicians in the Allied countries argued that authorities from the Central Powers should be tried for war crimes and for waging a war of aggression. Among the Allies, France and Belgium pushed the hardest to create a war crimes tribunal, primarily because these countries had suffered enormous death tolls during the war. Great Britain and the United States were less inclined to make the creation of a war crimes tribunal an issue in peace negotiations. Indeed, the Wilson Administration actually raised objections to war crimes trials. For many officials in the Wilson Administration, the proposed war crimes trials represented a form of "victor's justice" contrary to the spirit and letter of international law.[3]

Ultimately, because Germany and other defeated countries were not occupied, war crimes trials were doomed to fail in this case. Germany refused to turn over its leaders and soldiers to an international tribunal to face prosecution. Instead, the Allies and Germany agreed to allow a small number of cases to be tried in a German court. However, the outcome of these trials did not create faith in the ability of a state's courts to try its own citizens for war crimes in the aftermath of violent conflict. Ruling that the accused had been following superior orders, the German court gave light sentences to a few of the accused and acquitted the rest.[4] Because the Allies were unwilling to take military action to capture accused war criminals, the prospect of pursuing justice through judicial means in the aftermath of World War I was dead. Indeed, Gary Jonathan Bass argues that the only impact of demands for war trials in this case was to "galvanize the nationalist right" in Germany, thus contributing to the political climate in Germany that ultimately led to World War II.[5] In this case, by initially elevating principle over national interest only to back down in the end, the international community may have undermined both the pursuit of justice and stability.

In a similar case, the British pressured the Ottoman government to create a court to try officials in the wartime Ottoman government for war crimes against the Armenians in 1915, when approximately 1 million Armenians were targeted for slaughter in what we would now call genocide.[6] The Ottomans subsequently held a series of trials for individuals responsible for planning and carrying out Armenian massacres and deportations. In contrast to the German court responsible for trying German soldiers after World War I, the Ottoman tribunal initially issued two guilty verdicts carrying strong punishments. In its first ruling, the Ottoman court found Kemal Bey, the lieutenant governor of the Yozgat district, guilty of ordering the deportation and murder of Armenians and sentenced him to death. Major Tevfik Bey, a police commander, was also found guilty of the same crime and was sentenced to fifteen years in prison.[7] However, after these rulings, the Ottoman tribunal began to fall apart. After Kemal's sentence, death by hanging, was carried out, a nationalist backlash ensued. Rather than convincing the Turks that the slaughter of the Armenians had been wrong, Kemal's death sentence led Turks to view him as a hero and a martyr.[8]

The trials of the Turkish leadership that followed were ineffective. After Great Britain began to withdraw troops from the Ottoman Empire, it was no longer in a strong position to pressure the Ottoman government to carry out effective and serious trials. A number of the accused escaped to Germany, and the Ottoman tribunal simply released twenty-six accused wartime government officials saying that it had no case against them. The tribunal also released other prisoners to appease nationalists, and Great Britain basically gave up on the tribunal. The Ottoman tribunal subsequently issued two additional death sentences, though notably the sentenced individuals were not actually in custody. The tribunal also sentenced several other accused individuals to prison, only one of whom was in custody. British diplomats argued that the tribunal had been manipulated to give the appearance of doing justice by producing convictions but ensuring that those convicted, especially with death sentences, were not actually in custody.[9]

AD HOC TRIBUNALS AFTER WORLD WAR II:
NUREMBERG AND TOKYO

Despite the failures of earlier tribunals, support for the idea of war crimes trials grew in the ensuing years, and the horrors of World War II led to a consensus among the victorious powers for the creation of war crimes tribunals for both German and Japanese leaders. Unlike previous tribunals, the Nuremberg and Tokyo tribunals carried out serious trials against high-level German and Japanese officials and meted out strong penalties in each case. The International Military Tribunal at Nuremberg tried twenty-two high-level German officials. Three of the accused were acquitted. Of the nineteen defendants found guilty, eleven received the death penalty, though only nine were executed. (Hermann Goring committed suicide just hours prior to his scheduled execution, and Martin Bormann had been tried in absentia.) The tribunal sentenced the remaining officials to long prison terms.[10] The International Military Tribunal for the Far East, commonly known as the Tokyo Tribunal, tried twenty-eight Japanese leaders. Twenty-five of these accused leaders were found guilty, seven of whom were sentenced to death by hanging. Sixteen Japanese war criminals were given life sentences, though several later received early parole, and the other two Japanese leaders found guilty of war crimes received shorter sentences. (In addition to the twenty-five senior defendants found guilty, two defendants died of natural causes during the trials, and another defendant was institutionalized after a mental breakdown, though he was later released.)[11] Numerous additional trials were carried out in European and Asian states that had fought against or been occupied by Germany or Japan. In the end, more than 3,000 Germans and approximately 2,800 Japanese faced war crimes trials, and hundreds were executed.[12]

The charters for both the Nuremberg and Tokyo tribunals established that individuals could be indicted for three types of crimes: crimes against peace, war crimes, and crimes against humanity. Interestingly, the Nuremberg war crimes trials focused primarily on the first category, crimes against peace, even though they are commonly recalled as trials prosecuting Nazis for the Holocaust.[13] The Tokyo Tribunal similarly emphasized crimes of aggression. The emphasis on crimes against peace over crimes against humanity was evident in the Roosevelt Administration's interpretation of the Nuremberg Tribunal's purpose: "In a rare explicit statement on war criminals, Roosevelt had called for indicting the top Nazis for waging war. He mentioned aggression, not the Holocaust, atrocities against civilians, or war crimes. At Nuremberg's conclusion, Truman echoed Roosevelt: 'The principles established and the results achieved place International Law on the side of peace as against aggressive war.'"[14] Nevertheless, defenders of the post–World War II war crimes tribunals point out that they produced a detailed record of crimes against humanity even if this objective was not the primary motivation behind the trials.[15]

The post–World War II trials signaled a landmark moment in international human rights law in which prohibitions against war crimes became widely accepted. Although the creation of these tribunals reflected a sea change in international human rights law, the post–World War II war crimes trials also reflected the limitations of ad hoc tribunals as mechanisms for pursuing justice in the aftermath of violent conflict. In particular, critics have challenged the legitimacy of the Nuremberg and Tokyo tribunals on the grounds that they did not fulfill liberal requirements of due process by relying on an *ex post facto* application of the law and by blurring the lines between individual and collective guilt. Critics also contend that the post–World War II trials represent an illegitimate form of "victor's justice" in which similar crimes by the Allies were ignored.

Although the Nuremberg and Tokyo tribunals represented a legalist approach to pursuing justice in the aftermath of World War II, it was not at all clear that a well-established body of laws made the actions in question official crimes. For instance, the waging of aggressive war was categorized as a crime against peace, but no formal law had clearly made the waging of aggressive war illegal. The 1928 Treaty of Paris called for the peaceful settlement of disputes and renounced war as an instrument of policy but did not clearly state that the waging of aggressive war was illegal. Similarly, no international laws existed prior to World War II that clearly delineated crimes against humanity. Although war crimes dealt with violations of the laws of war, such as those set out in the Hague Convention, no formal treaties setting out basic human rights existed prior to the end of World War II. Although many might argue that the slaughtering and inhumane treatment of civilians obviously violate moral laws of humanity, the absence of formal laws meant that these tribunals fell short of the standards of law and justice that we typically expect for domestic judicial models, at least in liberal democracies. Hence, critics have argued that these tribunals resulted in the *ex post facto* application of the law and, as such, fell short of standards of justice for the accused. Critics would pose the following question: How can an individual be found guilty of a "crime" for an action that he or she did not know was criminal?

In addition, critics have argued that the post–World War II tribunals blurred the lines between individual and collective guilt. For instance, both the Nuremberg and Tokyo tribunals used the "conspiracy" doctrine to indict and punish accused war criminals. Under the conspiracy doctrine, mere membership in a "criminal organization" confers guilt on an individual. The conspiracy doctrine relies on a notion of *implied* guilt rather than proving that a specific individual is guilty of committing a specific crime. If an organization is guilty of a crime, then the guilt of a member of that organization, in essence, is assumed.

The blurring of individual and collective guilt was particularly acute in the Tokyo trials because the "conspiracy" doctrine was central to the indictments of and judgments against major Japanese war criminals, whereas the Nuremberg Tribunal limited the application of the conspiracy charge.[16] The case of Hirota Koki provides a telling example. Hirota, who had served as Japanese foreign minister and, briefly, as prime minister between 1933 and 1938, was sentenced to death by the Tokyo Tribunal on the grounds that he had participated in a conspiracy to wage aggressive war because the Japanese Cabinet had adopted an expansionist and aggressive foreign policy during that time period. In issuing this verdict, the tribunal ignored evidence that Hirota personally had opposed military action. Moreover, the tribunal disregarded evidence that the Japanese military, and not the Japanese Cabinet, was responsible for initiating military aggression.[17]

Conspiracy indictments are problematic under a liberal system of law because they presume guilt for individuals who may not have been voluntary members of an organization or who may not have been aware of the organization's criminal policies. At the same time, war crimes and human rights abuses of the scope perpetrated by the Nazi regime are, by nature, collective in that they require the force and organization of a complex bureaucracy. Thus, traditional notions of individual criminal culpability are problematic as well. As David Cohen puts it, "How, then, is individual responsibility to be located, limited, and defined within the vast bureaucratic apparatuses that make possible the pulling of a trigger or the dropping of a gas canister in some far-flung place?"[18] Unfortunately, the post–World War II trials do not suggest an easy response to the dilemma of determining individual culpability in the context of war crimes and human rights abuses, which, by their very nature, have a collective dimension.

Moreover, critics have held that such ad hoc tribunals represent "victor's justice" in that only the "losers" in a war are held accountable for their actions. For example, in the case of World War II, tribunals were established only for Germany and Japan. In contrast, the Allies were not held accountable for the firebombing of Dresden that inflicted widespread death and destruction on the civilian population in Germany. Similarly, the Soviet Union was not held accountable for war crimes and crimes against humanity in Soviet-occupied territory, such as the Katyn Forest massacre of Polish officers.[19]

Finally, the post–World War II trials can be criticized for having a sexual and ethnic bias, as illustrated by the case of victims of Japan's sex-slave system in Asia during World War II, euphemistically termed "comfort women." At the end of the war, a military tribunal was created in Indonesia to prosecute high-ranking Japanese officers for the sexual internment and abuse of Dutch women. The tribunal convicted several officials, and one was sentenced to death. Notably, however, the tribunal only tried cases involving Dutch women who were victims of the sex-slave system. The tribunal did not prosecute alleged perpetrators for their victimization of Asian women, despite the fact that Asians, especially Korean women, may have comprised 70 percent of all comfort women.[20] Although the work of this tribunal was important, it is significant that the prosecution of sexual crimes received much less attention and fewer resources than the prosecution of other crimes against humanity or peace in the post–World War II trials.

Defenders of the tribunals have pointed out that "victor's justice" could have been taken to an even greater extreme; Stalin and Churchill advocated the summary execution of all accused German war criminals. When viewed against this alternative, the war crimes tribunals at least represented an effort to introduce the rule of the law into the pursuit of justice at the end of World War II. Moreover, whereas most critics of the Nuremberg and Tokyo tribunals argue that they went too far in prosecuting alleged war criminals, other critics argue that they did not go far enough. Raphael Lemkin, the man who coined the term *genocide* and the driving force behind the adoption of the Genocide Convention, criticized the Nuremberg Tribunal because it only prosecuted "crimes against humanity" committed by Germany outside of internationally recognized German territory. It did not prosecute alleged war criminals for atrocities committed within Germany proper. As Samantha Power writes, "Nazi defendants were thus tried for atrocities they committed during but not before World War II. By inference, if the Nazis had exterminated the entire German Jewish population but never invaded Poland, they would not have been liable at Nuremberg."[21] Ultimately, despite the shortcomings of these tribunals, the creation of the Nuremberg and Tokyo tribunals at the end of World War II is recognized as a milestone in the evolution of international efforts to punish and prosecute war crimes internationally.[22]

THE INTERNATIONAL TRIBUNAL FOR THE FORMER YUGOSLAVIA

In the aftermath of the Nuremberg and Tokyo tribunals, the international community proceeded with efforts to create a permanent International Criminal Court. Coupled with the further codification of the laws of war in the Geneva Conventions of 1949 and the Genocide Convention of 1951, as well as the treaties on human rights established after World War II, the creation of a permanent International Criminal Court would have gone a long way toward addressing the flaws of the Nuremberg and Tokyo precedents. However, until quite recently, efforts to create a permanent International Criminal Court have faltered. During the Cold War, balance-of-power politics and ideological conflict prevented the consensus building necessary to forge support for a permanent International Criminal Court.

Thus, when the international community was faced with the question of how to pursue justice in the aftermath of violent conflict at the end of the Cold War, it returned to the Nuremberg precedent. In spite of the fact that international human rights law had developed significantly since the end of

World War II, there still were not established judicial institutions for applying this law by punishing perpetrators of war crimes and human rights abuses. As a result, the UN Security Council has created two ad hoc war crimes tribunals since the end of the Cold War: the International Criminal Tribunal for the Former Yugoslavia (ICTY) and the International Criminal Tribunal for Rwanda (ICTR).

In response to war crimes and "ethnic cleansing" in Bosnia, the UN Security Council created the International Criminal Tribunal for the Former Yugoslavia (ICTY) in 1993. The work of the ICTY, which is ongoing, has avoided some of the problems of the post–World War II tribunals while at the same time demonstrating new problems with the pursuit of punitive justice through trials. Because international human rights law has been codified to a much greater extent, there are fewer problems with the *ex post facto* application of international humanitarian law in this case. Moreover, the problem of "victor's justice" is less applicable. The Tribunal was established by the UN Security Council. Although the UN was involved in trying to enforce international peace and security in the region and in fostering peace negotiations, the members of the Security Council were not direct protagonists in this conflict. The Tribunal has tried individuals from all three of the major ethnic groups involved in this conflict, and the convicted individuals include Croats, Muslims, and Serbs. Indeed, according to Richard Goldstone, the first chief prosecutor of the Tribunal, despite the fact that Bosnia "had the least to account for," it was Bosnia that first carried out a Hague warrant by arresting two indicted Bosnian Muslims who had been accused of murder and torture of Bosnian Serbs.[23]

Although the International Criminal Tribunal for the Former Yugoslavia has avoided some of the problems that marred the Nuremberg and Tokyo tribunals, it has been faced with new dilemmas. Unlike the post–World War II setting, which involved the defeat of Germany and Japan by other major world powers, the nature of the conflict and the post-conflict setting in the former Yugoslavia are quite different. This ethnic conflict ended in a negotiated political settlement rather than in the outright defeat of any of the parties. Notably, the settlement was contested by major segments of each ethnic group, particularly the Bosnian Serbs. The "outside parties" were involved not as direct protagonists but as representatives of the international community acting in the region at the behest of the UN Security Council, which deemed the Balkan conflict a threat to international peace and security. The post-conflict situation in Bosnia involved a tenuous peace settlement. As a result, political leaders who had been key in instigating the war crimes and genocide in Bosnia were also key participants in the establishment and implementation of the peace agreement. Thus, this situation put representatives of the international community in a delicate position. Diplomats responsible for negotiating the peace agreement were concerned primarily with maintaining a tenuous peace, even if this meant "looking the other way" when it came to indictments for war crimes abuses, and NATO forces did not take certain indicted war criminals into custody because of diplomatic concerns that doing so would undermine the peace process.

This dilemma is well documented by Richard Holbrooke, the chief American negotiator in the Bosnian conflict.[24] Initially, Holbrooke made clear to President Slobodan Milosevic of Serbia that the indicted Bosnian Serb leaders Ratko Mladic and Radovan Karadzic could not participate in an international conference on the Balkan crisis, even though in previous negotiations Karadzic and Mladic had met with Cyrus Vance, Lord David Owen, Jimmy Carter, Lord Carrington, and other Western negotiators. In the end, Holbrooke also decided to negotiate with the indicted war criminals. In justifying this decision, Holbrooke writes:

> I was deeply influenced by the stories of Raoul Wallenberg and Folke Bernadotte, two legendary Swedes . . . who had negotiated, respectively, with Adolf Eichmann and Heinrich Himmler in 1944–1945. Each man had decided to deal with a mass murderer to save lives. History had shown the correctness of their decisions, which had resulted in the rescue of tens of thousands of Jews.[25]

As this statement indicates, diplomats like Holbrooke ultimately put a higher premium on forging a peace agreement than in bringing indicted war criminals to justice.

This situation left indicted war criminals free to continue to operate in Bosnia after the war. For example, after the war, Karadzic technically followed the requirements of the Dayton Peace Accords by disbanding Bosnian Serb military forces. However, these forces were simply reorganized into "special police" units that continued to intimidate Bosnian Muslims and to undermine stability. The International Force in Bosnia did nothing to stop these police units. In addition to negotiating with indicted war criminals, peace negotiators also had to work closely with Slobodan Milosevic, the Serbian head of state. In spite of the fact that the international community was aware of Milosevic's role in fanning the flame of ethnic hatred in Serbia in the 1980s and that many scholars of the Balkans held Milosevic responsible for inciting genocide, Western diplomats found that they had to work closely with Milosevic in pursuing a peace agreement. Initially, Milosevic was not indicted for war crimes, and, indeed, his position as head of state was reinforced by his place in peace negotiations. Instead of being isolated as a pariah, Milosevic emerged from negotiations for the Dayton Peace Accords with the status of other world leaders.[26]

However, Milosevic was ultimately indicted for war crimes, and he lost his protected status as head of the Yugoslav state when he was defeated in the fall 2000 Yugoslav presidential elections. Subsequently, the international community negotiated with the new Yugoslav government to turn over Milosevic, who was taken into custody in Serbia, to the International Criminal Tribunal for the Former Yugoslavia. As part of the negotiations, the international community, with strong pressure from the United States, made aid to Yugoslavia conditional on Milosevic's being turned over to the Tribunal. An interesting turn of events took place at the end of June 2001. The Serbian government, acting against the wishes of the Yugoslav government, turned Milosevic over to the ICTY. Milosevic's trial began in February 2002. He has elected to defend himself and has turned his defense into an indictment of the international community and the ICTY. Drawing on the historical critique of Nuremberg, Milosevic has argued that the ICTY represents a form of "victor's justice." According to Milosevic, NATO bombing during the war violated Yugoslavia's sovereignty. Milosevic also contends that the manner of the bombing, resulting in the indiscriminate killing of civilians, constituted war crimes that should be prosecuted. Milosevic's trial is ongoing and, as of November 2004, the ICTY has not yet issued a judgment in this case.

The work of the International Criminal Tribunal for the Former Yugoslavia continues. As of November 2004, the Tribunal has rendered forty-six guilty verdicts and has acquitted four indicted individuals. Appeals are pending in eighteen cases. Several indictees died before coming to trial, and the Tribunal withdrew charges in several cases. Cases involving more than thirty-five indictees are at the pretrial or trial stage, and twenty-one indictees remain at large.[27] The Tribunal's staff has been increased over time to more than 1,000 individuals, and the budget for 2004–2005 is more than $271 million.[28] Hopefully, this increase in staff and funding will help to streamline the judicial process, as lengthy trials and the drawn out process have undermined the Tribunal's legitimacy in the eyes of critics.[29]

THE INTERNATIONAL CRIMINAL TRIBUNAL FOR RWANDA

The International Criminal Tribunal for Rwanda (ICTR) was established by the UN Security Council in 1994 in response to the slaughter of an estimated 800,000 Tutsi and moderate Hutus by the majority Hutu ethnic group in Rwanda in a matter of just 100 days. The ICTR has received less funding than the Tribunal for the Former Yugoslavia, with a budget of just over $258 million for 2004–2005. Although this budget represents an increase from previous years, critics charge that the ICTR has inadequate facilities and staff. The ICTR has indicted more than seventy individuals, and more than sixty of the indictees are in custody. To date, the ICTR has completed thirteen trials, resulting in twelve convictions and one acquittal. The Appeals Chamber confirmed eight of these convictions as well as the one acquittal; four appeals are pending. More than twenty indictees are currently on trial. Fifteen indictees are at large.[30] The ICTR has tried a handful of high-profile indictees, notably including Jean Kambanda, the former prime minister of Rwanda during the genocide, who was found guilty of genocide. The Rwandan tribunal has also become renowned as a result of its landmark decision in the Akayesu case, in which it ruled that rape during internal armed conflict constitutes genocide.

Despite the high-profile conviction of the former prime minister and important contributions to the developments of international humanitarian law, the relatively small number of trials that have been completed by the Rwandan tribunal has left many Rwandan victims with the impression that the international community is more interested in symbolic action against war crimes than in real justice for the majority of perpetrators of war crimes in Rwanda. As of November 2004, the tribunal for Rwanda had completed only thirteen trials, with twelve convictions and one acquittal.[31]

Like the ICTY, the Rwandan tribunal has avoided the Nuremberg problems of *ex post facto* prosecution and "victor's justice." Again, well-established international human rights laws and the fact that the UN was not a direct protagonist may enhance the legitimacy of ad hoc tribunals in the post–Cold War world. However, the Rwandan case also poses new dilemmas for the pursuit of punitive justice through trials. The fact that the UN was not a direct protagonist in the conflict is viewed by critics as telling evidence of the insincerity of the international community's efforts to pursue universal principles in world politics. The UN had been warned of the increasingly hostile climate on the ground in Rwanda by its own peacekeepers in the region. Hutu extremists had been using state media to whip up anti-Tutsi sentiment in Rwanda, and evidence of imminent violence was mounting just before the genocide. Yet the UN did not intervene to prevent the genocide because of insufficient political will among the UN Security Council powers that would have had the authority to authorize enforcement action in the region.

Samantha Power writes the following indictment of Western leaders in their response to the Rwandan genocide:

> Western leaders had vowed that they would 'never again' stand idly by in the face of genocide. And when the televised slaughter commenced, they wanted to appear to be 'doing something.' Yet they were unprepared to do anything much, and so they responded to public calls for action by pledging to punish perpetrators after the fact. And now they have deprived the tribunals of the enforcement authority and funding necessary (but not necessarily sufficient) for success.[32]

According to critics, then, the creation of war crimes tribunals after the fact rather than the adoption of preventive policies before genocide happens represents an effort to soothe the moral conscience of individuals in Western societies rather than a sincere desire to promote global morality and justice.[33]

Additionally, the Rwandan case poses special problems because of the overwhelming number of citizens who participated in the genocide. Approximately 125,000 genocide suspects have been taken into custody. Remarkably, this number represents only a small fraction of individuals involved in slaughtering Tutsi. Many of the indicted criminals in custody are held by Rwandan courts rather than the international tribunal, and as of January 2002, the Rwandan courts had tried only approximately 5,000 suspects.[34] As Elizabeth Neuffer has noted, it would take 150 years for the Rwandan courts, working at the current pace, to try all of the accused genocide suspects.[35]

Approximately 120,000 genocide cases remain to be tried in Rwandan courts. Obviously, it is infeasible for this overwhelming number of cases to be tried in a regular judicial system, especially one that has been decimated by a genocide that killed many of Rwanda's judges and lawyers. In addition, those trials that have been conducted have not provided basic due process rights to defendants. Many accused individuals were not informed of their right to a lawyer under the Rwandan genocide law. Moreover, most of the few practicing lawyers that remain in Rwanda have refused to defend accused genocide suspects. Among those cases that have been tried, only small numbers of the accused have been acquitted. Among the convicted, almost one-third have been sentenced to death and another one-third sentenced to life in prison. Approximately 100 of those convicted have been executed to date. Most of the remaining genocide suspects continue to be detained in prison without having been tried several years after they were imprisoned.[36]

Complicating matters, there has been no coordination between the International Criminal Tribunal for Rwanda and Rwandan national courts. Indeed, Rwanda allows for the death penalty while the UN mandate for the International Criminal Tribunal for Rwanda forbids the use of the death penalty. This difference poses a moral dilemma in that perpetrators found guilty of genocide would be subject to different punishments depending on where they were tried. This dilemma is particularly problematic because high-level officials responsible for planning and instigating the genocide were more likely to be tried by the international tribunal. In contrast, low-level officials and ordinary Rwandans who participated in implementing the genocide are likely to be tried in Rwandan courts where they are subject to the death penalty. This moral dilemma is compounded by the fact that individuals convicted in Rwanda will serve time in Rwandan prisons, which do not meet internationally recognized minimum standards, whereas individuals convicted by the International Criminal Tribunal for Rwanda will serve time in states designated by the Tribunal or in the special detention facility in Arusha, Tanzania, built and managed by the United Nations. As Professor Tom Farer has noted, the outcome could be that "those convicted of masterminding the genocide will serve their sentences in country club settings, while those convicted by Rwandan courts will serve their time in appalling prison conditions."[37] In any event, many high officials responsible for instigating the genocide were in exile and out of reach of both the Rwandan national courts and the International Criminal Tribunal for Rwanda.

Not surprisingly, many Rwandans have grown frustrated with the slow process of justice. As a result, the Rwandan government has turned to a traditional justice system called *gacaca,* in which local representatives at different administrative levels, rather than official government courts, try the accused. Early in 2002, the Rwandan government began to train 260,000 *gacaca* judges in legal principles, conflict resolution, and judicial ethics. The goal is to deal with the nearly 1 million suspects charged with genocide, or lesser crimes committed during the genocide, languishing in Rwandan jails with no realistic prospects of a trial in the immediate future. The Rwandan government has created four administrative levels to try different types of crimes, as ranked by the Rwandan government. Under *gacaca,* representatives at the local village level will try those accused of what the government has classified as lesser offenses, such as arson or looting. The next category of crimes, such as wounding with intent to kill, will be tried at a higher administrative level, and murder will be tried at the level of commune and district. The crimes classified as the worst offenses by the government, including orchestrating genocide and participating in sexual torture, will be tried by the regular courts at the national level. In these cases, the courts can impose the death penalty, whereas the greatest penalty under the *gacaca* system is life imprisonment.[38]

Critics have many concerns about the *gacaca* system. Although the principle behind *gacaca* is that local tribunals will represent the moral force of local communities "to shame perpetrators into admitting the truth," the problem is that Hutus were the majority before the genocide. The surviving Tutsi victims are certainly outnumbered after the genocide decimated the already minority Tutsi population. So, survivors argue that the *gacaca* process will hide rather than discover the truth and that perpetrators will escape justice for their crimes. Another potential problem is that these informal tribunals do not provide effective due process safeguards for the accused, and there are no lawyers representing the accused or the victims.[39]

Yet, the impetus to turn toward these types of remedies is reinforced by the limitations of judicial efforts to pursue justice in response to war crimes in the Rwandan case. Proponents of *gacaca* acknowledge that the process will not result in punitive justice for most perpetrators. According to Protais Musoni, the Rwandan local government ministry's top official, "The central issue here is truth more than punishment . . . It is a cleansing mechanism. We will move the genocide from our subconscious to the conscious, and hopefully, at the end we will allow bygones to be bygones."[40] Even some survivors reluctantly accept what they see as the imperfect justice of *gacaca* as better than nothing. One director of a survivors group says, "Gacaca is a compromise political solution, but at this point, it is all we have to look forward to."[41]

THE INTERNATIONAL CRIMINAL COURT

The shortcomings of ad hoc war crimes tribunals reinforced calls for a permanent International Criminal Court (ICC). The international effort to create a permanent International Criminal Court is not a new development. Indeed, advocates of a permanent International Criminal Court can be traced back to the unsuccessful efforts to create a war crimes tribunal after World War I. Building on both the successes and failures of the Nuremberg and Tokyo tribunals, efforts to create a permanent ICC began more in earnest after World War II. However, such efforts were soon stymied by the Cold War political climate. It was not until the end of the Cold War, when a sufficient number of major powers began to support the idea, that discussions of creating a permanent ICC again became feasible.

On July 17, 1998, in Rome, 120 nation-states[42] signed a treaty creating the International Criminal Court (ICC). The Rome Statute of the International Criminal Court was approved by 120 nation-states; another 21 states abstained during the vote; only 7 states voted against the Rome Treaty, including the United States, China, India, and Russia. The treaty entered into force on April 11, 2002, after 60 nation-states had ratified the treaty, and the ICC formally opened in March 2003. The Rome Treaty gives the ICC jurisdiction in cases of genocide, crimes against humanity, and war crimes in both internal and international conflicts where national courts have failed to prosecute these crimes. Previously, crimes against humanity only covered crimes committed in international conflicts, and even some war crimes committed during internal conflicts were not governed by international humanitarian law. The Rome Treaty also clarifies prohibitions against sexual crimes in international humanitarian law. Thus, the Rome Treaty contributes to the advancement of international human rights norms in very important ways.

The treaty provides that the ICC has jurisdiction under the following circumstances: (1) when the Security Council refers a case; (2) when the state in which the crime was committed (state of territory) has signed and ratified the treaty or, in the absence of ratification, voluntarily accepts the jurisdiction of the court; or (3) when the state in which an alleged criminal has citizenship (state of nationality) has signed and ratified the treaty or, in the absence of such ratification, voluntarily accepts the jurisdiction of the court. Cases may be referred to the ICC for prosecution by the Security Council, by a member state of the ICC, or by the ICC's prosecutor. In cases referred by member states of the court or by the prosecutor, only individuals who are citizens of consenting states or who commit a crime in a consenting state are subject to the ICC's jurisdiction.[43] Under the principle of complementarity, the ICC may exercise its jurisdiction only in the event that the state of primary jurisdiction proves itself unwilling or unable to investigate and, if necessary, prosecute a case.[44]

The ICC will consist of eighteen judges from countries that have become members of the court. Three judges will preside over any particular trial, and although the Rome Treaty calls for efforts to achieve unanimity, decisions shall be made by majority. Other judges will serve in a pre-trial chamber and in the appeals chamber. Nation-states that have signed and ratified the Rome Treaty will send ambassadors to an annual meeting, where the members of the court will be chosen for nine-year terms.

In order to gain political support for the Rome Treaty, jurisdictional principles were watered down so that the court only has jurisdiction when the state of territory or nationality has ratified the treaty or voluntarily accepts its jurisdiction. As Amnesty International pointed out in a news release immediately following the Rome conference, this jurisdictional requirement means that tyrannical heads of state would have to give their prior consent in order to be tried under the ICC. Obviously, such consent would not be forthcoming. Thus, many human rights advocates suggest that the nation-states most likely to ratify the treaty are those states that are least likely to have their nationals tried as war criminals before the ICC.

Moreover, the United States voted against the creation of the ICC at Rome and, in doing so, undermined the international consensus that could have given greater moral force to the ICC. Although the Clinton Administration later signed the treaty at the end of 2000, American opposition to the ICC remains strong. Indeed, President Clinton stressed continuing U.S. objections at the time that he signed the treaty, and in May 2002, the Bush Administration in essence "withdrew" the U.S. signature when it submitted a letter to the UN Secretary-General stating that it does not intend to become a party to the Rome Treaty and that the United States has no legal obligations resulting from the Clinton Administration's signature in December 2000.[45] Subsequently, Congress passed the American Service Members' Protection Act of 2002, which was signed into law by President Bush. This law prohibits the United States from participating in peacekeeping missions in countries that have ratified the Rome Treaty, makes most countries that are members of the court ineligible for military aid unless they guarantee that they will not hand over U.S. citizens to the ICC, and gives the president the authority to use force to liberate U.S. military personnel in the ICC's custody.[46] This legislation has significant human rights implications not only because of the way in which it weakens the ICC but also because it "makes the world's worst human rights abusers, which for obvious reasons have declined to join the Court, preferred recipients of the United States' huge military assistance program."[47]

U.S. opposition to the court is based primarily on the argument that the ICC might be used for politically motivated prosecutions of U.S. citizens. U.S. officials involved in the Rome negotiations were particularly concerned that the chief prosecutor for the ICC would have too much discretion in pursuing cases. (The domestic political context at the time needs to be noted. Independent Prosecutor Ken Starr's investigation of President Clinton was ongoing at the time, underscoring critics' fears of prosecutorial abuse in the ICC.) However, proponents of the ICC argue that the potential for prosecutorial abuse will be limited because a three-member panel of judges must approve investigations by the prosecutor and state members of the ICC can remove the prosecutor through a simple majority vote.[48]

In addition to basic jurisdictional concerns, many U.S. foreign policy elites fear that the ICC would treat unilateral U.S. military operations as crimes of aggression. Thus, critics contend, the United States might be less likely to pursue international justice through humanitarian intervention, such as the U.S.-led NATO intervention in Kosovo. Many U.S. foreign policy elites also fear that membership in the ICC would hamstring the United States in its pursuit of unilateral military actions deemed by them to be crucial to securing the national interest. This concern has been heightened with the Bush Administration's unilateral military campaign in Iraq on the grounds that it has a right to engage in "preemptive self-defense." Both the U.S. intervention in Iraq and the Bush Administration's doctrine of preemption have generated widespread and energetic public opposition across the globe, even among many U.S. allies. It is precisely this sort of widely unpopular unilateral action that critics of the ICC fear would make U.S. soldiers especially vulnerable to politically motivated charges.

Critics' fears about potentially subjecting U.S. soldiers to ICC jurisdiction have been exacerbated by revelations about the prison abuse scandal at Abu Ghraib and allegations of torture by U.S. forces elsewhere in Iraq and Afghanistan. These abuses, as discussed in the case study of Abu Ghraib and torture in Chapter 4, are exactly the types of violations that might fall under the jurisdiction of the ICC if the United States were to ratify the Rome Treaty. Proponents of human rights argue that this is precisely the point: U.S. soldiers should not be above the law, and if the United States does not pursue serious prosecution and punishment of these crimes, they should be subject to ICC jurisdiction. In contrast, opponents of the ICC believe that the United States can be trusted to deal fairly with allegations of war crimes violations and do not believe that the United States should relinquish any of its sovereignty on this point.

Interestingly, U.S. reluctance to join the ICC underscores a tension in the development of effective international human rights laws and institutions. Human rights advocates typically view the watering down of checks on state sovereignty in international human rights law as detrimental to the advancement of universal norms, but such loopholes are required to gain the necessary state consent. Unfortunately, there appears to be an inherent trade-off built into the development of international legal norms. Such norms must acknowledge the ongoing importance of state sovereignty if states are to acquiesce to them. Yet to the extent that it continues to recognize sovereignty as an ordering principle, international law limits the expansion of universal humanitarian principles as governing norms in world politics.

Although it is important to underscore the limitations of the ICC in its current form, the fact that 120 nation-states were able to agree on the creation of a permanent ICC clearly represents a milestone in the development of international human rights law. Fifty years ago, international consensus on an ICC simply would not have been politically feasible, even in the aftermath of the Holocaust. Currently, the ICC is poised to consider its first two cases. Uganda has referred a case seeking investigation and prosecution of atrocities committed by the Lords Resistance Army in northern Uganda. The Democratic Republic of Congo has asked the ICC to investigate and prosecute crimes against humanity and war crimes that have been committed since July 2002.[49] (The ICC can only investigate crimes that have been committed since it opened on July 1, 2002.) The extent to which the ICC may develop into an effective mechanism for the pursuit of international justice remains to be seen.[50]

PROSECUTING INTERNATIONAL CRIMES
IN DOMESTIC COURTS

A final avenue for the judicial punishment of war crimes and human rights abuses involves the prosecution of international war crimes and human rights abuses in domestic courts. The case of Augusto Pinochet represents a high-profile example of such an effort.[51] Augusto Pinochet was the head of state in Chile during the military rule of that country between 1973 and 1990. The military government during the Pinochet dictatorship was responsible for widespread human rights abuses, including the systematic use of torture, disappearances, and a general campaign of terror. In 1978, Pinochet imposed an amnesty law that prohibited the prosecution of "political crimes." Although a democratic government was elected in Chile in 1990, this amnesty law is still on the books and has prevented the prosecution of most of the former military leaders.

In 1998, Pinochet was arrested in England as a result of a Spanish request to extradite him to Spain to face criminal charges of genocide, terrorism, torture, and forced disappearances. Spanish victims of human rights abuses under Pinochet and Spanish human rights organizations initiated the effort to bring Pinochet to trial in Spain, and charges were filed by a group of Spanish prosecutors acting in their private capacity. Although the Pinochet case has received the most press coverage, these prosecutors also brought charges against former military leaders of Argentina as well as other Chilean military leaders. Interestingly, the Spanish public prosecutor's office, asserting that Spain did not have jurisdiction, tried to block these prosecutions. However, the Audiencia Nacional upheld Spanish jurisdiction on the grounds that Spanish courts had universal jurisdiction to try crimes of torture, terrorism, and genocide.

The prosecution of Pinochet faced new hurdles in England. Although the British Law Lords denied Pinochet's claim of immunity as a former head of state, they narrowed the consideration of extradition offenses to torture and conspiracy, then to torture, and further narrowed the scope of the case to those charges committed after December 8, 1988, the date on which England ratified the Torture Convention. In January 2000, the British government announced its intention to return the elderly and ailing Pinochet, who several medical doctors had said was unfit to stand trial, to Chile on "humanitarian grounds" rather than extraditing him to Spain.

At a fundamental level, then, this case represents a failure of the strategy to pursue prosecution of international war crimes and human rights abuses in domestic courts. At another level, this strategy has nonetheless been important in maintaining attention on the abuses of the Pinochet regime in Chile. Emboldened by the international attention, human rights lawyers in Chile sought to prosecute Pinochet and other military leaders in Chilean courts.[52] Early in August 2000, Chile's Supreme Court stripped General Pinochet of his immunity, which meant that he could stand trial in Chile for human rights abuses committed during his dictatorship. In December 2000, Judge Juan Guzman Tapia charged Pinochet in disappearances committed by his regime after the 1973 coup against the Allende government. The judge was able to circumvent the Chilean amnesty law by arguing that the missing individuals might, in fact, be alive and, as a result, ruled that the alleged crimes are not covered by the amnesty law. However, the case against Pinochet ran into a variety of obstacles. In March 2001, the charges against Pinochet were reduced to covering up the crimes committed by his government rather than orchestrating death squads and disappearances. Finally, in July 2002, the Chilean Supreme Court terminated the prosecution of Pinochet on the grounds that he was not mentally fit to stand trial. Nonetheless, the international and domestic political pressure generated by the Pinochet case generated important public debate in Chile about human rights violations under the Pinochet regime. Under the pressure of public scrutiny and aggressive tactics by human rights lawyers, numerous military officers confessed their crimes during Pinochet's rule.[53] These confessions represent a major advancement in terms of establishing a truthful record about political repression under Pinochet, even if most of the individuals responsible for the violence escaped punishment.

An earlier U.S. court case also illustrates the ways in which domestic courts might be used to prosecute war crimes and human rights abuses. The case of *Filartiga v. Pena-Irala* involved the kidnapping, torture, and killing of Joelito Filartiga in Paraguay. Joelito Filartiga was the son of Joel Filartiga, a doctor who ran a health clinic for the poor in Paraguay. Because of Dr. Filartiga's work on behalf of the poor, both father and son were presumed by the military government to have leftist political sympathies. Pena-Irala was one of the police officials accused of participating in the torture and killing of Joelito in 1976.

Pena-Irala came to New York on a visitor's visa in 1978. Dolly Filartiga, Joelito's sister, learned that Pena-Irala was in the United States, and Dolly and her father brought wrongful death charges against him. The district court initially sought to dismiss the case on the grounds that it lacked jurisdiction because the crime occurred outside of the United States and because neither the victim nor the alleged perpetrator was a U.S. citizen. However, the U.S. Court of Appeals (Second Circuit) asserted that it had jurisdiction under the Judiciary Act of 1789 (Alien Tort Claims Act), which provides that district courts have original jurisdiction in civil actions by aliens for torts (personal wrongs) committed in violation of the law of nations. The relevant "law of nations" in this case involved the Universal Declaration of Human Rights, the UN Declaration Against Torture, and other elements of customary international human rights law. After the Court of Appeals decided that the case could be tried in the United States, it was returned to the trial court, which decided in favor of the plaintiffs in 1984 and awarded a judgment of more than $10 million. By that time, Pena-Irala had been deported to Paraguay and did not appear before the court. As a result, the United States was no longer in a position to enforce the court decision. Thus, although the Filartigas "won" the court case, their victory was merely symbolic.

The Alien Tort Claims Act also has been invoked in two lawsuits against Bosnian Serb leader Radovan Karadzic. In February 1993, the Center for Constitutional Rights, the City University of New York (CUNY) Law School, the CUNY International Women's Human Rights Clinic, and the International League for Human Rights filed a claim on behalf of victims of Bosnian Serb atrocities committed during the war in Bosnia. Although this suit was filed on the immediate behalf of two women, Jane Doe I and Jane Doe II, who were Bosnian refugees living in Croatia at the time the suit was filed, the lawyers sought to represent all women and men who had been victimized by the Bosnian Serb forces under the command and control of Karadzic. This lawsuit, *Doe v. Karadzic,* alleged that forces under Karadzic's command and control were responsible for rape, genocide, summary execution, torture, and other inhumane acts committed during the Bosnian war.

In March 1993, feminist law professor Catharine MacKinnon and the National Organization for Women's Legal Defense and Education Fund filed a similar suit against Karadzic. This complaint, *Kadic v. Karadzic,* focused specifically on crimes against women, including mass rape and forced pregnancy. Eventually, the *Kadic v. Karadzic* complaint was incorporated into the *Doe v. Karadzic* case. The U.S. District Court for the Southern District of New York initially dismissed the case for lack of subject matter jurisdiction, but the Court of Appeals remanded the case back to the district court, arguing that the United States did have jurisdiction under the Alien Tort Claims Act. Karadzic was served with the lawsuits when he was temporarily in the United States on diplomatic business. The *Doe v. Karadzic* trial concluded in August 2000 with a $745 million judgment against Karadzic. Even though the court decided in favor of the plaintiffs, they will not be able to collect damages unless the court is able to locate Karadzic's assets. Nevertheless, a guilty verdict makes it more difficult for Karadzic to visit or invest money in the United States. Still, victory in this case likely will provide merely symbolic justice rather than direct punishment of the perpetrator or reparations to the victims.

Although the *Filartiga v. Pena-Irala* and *Doe v. Karadzic* cases have received the most attention, the Alien Tort Claims Act has also been used successfully in other cases. A former Guatemalan defense minister, Hector Gramajo, was ordered to pay $47 million to nine Guatemalans and an American nun as a result of human rights abuses perpetrated under military rule in Guatemala. Similarly, a U.S. court issued a $41 million judgment against Prosper Avril, a general in Haiti's former military government. In another case, an Argentine citizen was awarded $21.1 million in a successful suit against a former Argentinean military general, Carlos Suarez Mason. In 1989, a U.S. court awarded approximately 10,000 Philippine citizens a $1.9 billion judgment against the estate of Ferdinand Marcos, the former dictator of the Philippines. Unfortunately, only the Marcos case has made progress toward the actual transfer of financial compensation to the victims of human rights abuses. In 1999, representatives of the Marcos family and representatives of the victims negotiated a $161 million settlement, though to date no money has changed hands because a court in the Philippines has issued a judgment saying that frozen assets in Swiss bank accounts cannot be used to fulfill the settlement. More recently, in August 2000, the Center for Constitutional Rights served papers on the former Chinese premier, Li Peng, for a lawsuit filed against him by a group of Chinese students for his role in the Chinese government's actions in the 1989 Tiananmen Square incident. Similarly, Kosovar Albanians have filed a civil action in U.S. courts.

Congress strengthened the ability of U.S. courts to try cases involving human rights abuses abroad when it passed the Torture Victim Protection Act in

1992. This legislation explicitly provides that both U.S. citizens and foreign citizens may bring suit in U.S. courts for cases of alleged torture abroad. Victims of human rights abuses have also initiated lawsuits against various corporations in pursuit of justice through the U.S. court system. For example, a 1999 California law allows victims to sue companies who allegedly benefited from slave labor in the past in California state courts. In a recent case brought under this law, a group of Chinese men who worked as forced laborers for Japanese companies during World War II have filed a class action lawsuit against the Mitsubishi and Mitsui companies. The plaintiffs are seeking an apology and compensation. Other groups of Chinese victims, including women who were forced into prostitution during the war and victims of the Japanese use of biological weapons, are also pursuing lawsuits against the Japanese in U.S. courts. Such lawsuits are modeled after the successful class action suits brought by victims of the Holocaust against Swiss banks and German corporations who used forced labor during World War II.[54]

Another interesting example of the pursuit of justice through domestic courts involves Korean victims of Japan's World War II sex-slave system. As mentioned in the previous discussion of the post–World War II trials, the Indonesian tribunal that prosecuted high-ranking Japanese officers for sexual abuse of the euphemistically termed "comfort women" did not deal with crimes against Korean women, who comprised the majority of the victims. As a result of campaigns by Korean women's groups beginning in the 1970s, the issue of "comfort women" achieved a high profile by the 1990s. In 1991, Kim Hak San, a former "comfort woman," agreed to go public and brought suit in Japan along with two other anonymous victims. Throughout the postwar period, the Japanese government had maintained that the brothels frequented by the Japanese military during the war were privately operated and were not maintained by the government. During the litigation process, official documents demonstrated that, in fact, the operation of a sexual enslavement system was official government policy. These revelations led Japanese Prime Minister Miyazawa to issue an apology in 1992, but he did not provide compensation to victims. Ultimately, thirty lawsuits were filed by former victims and women's groups. In an April 1998 ruling in one of the trials, the court ordered Japan to compensate three Korean women $2,300. Unfortunately, Kim Hak Sun died in 1997, so the decision was too late for her. Nevertheless, the ruling does provide hope of at least some justice for surviving victims.[55]

In general, the cases discussed here illustrate the limitations of efforts to pursue prosecutions for war crimes and human rights abuses in domestic courts. To date, this strategy remains undeveloped and has not been highly successful in bringing individuals who perpetrate war crimes or human rights abuses to justice. Additionally, critics contend that prosecuting human rights crimes in national courts risks a reaction of politically motivated prosecutions in other countries, a particular danger given that many national courts fail to provide basic due process rights.[56]

Despite its limitations, the prosecution of violations of international humanitarian law in domestic courts may afford some hope for the victims of these crimes. Domestic prosecutions in national courts may provide at least symbolic justice to victims of war crimes and human rights abuses by publicly acknowledging the validity of their claims and proclaiming the guilt of the individuals who perpetrated violence against them. Certainly, mere symbolic justice is not a satisfactory outcome for victims of war crimes or human rights abuses, but, sadly, such small "victories" may be the most that proponents of human rights can hope for in the current international legal order.

CONCLUSIONS

Chapter 9 has focused on trials as the primary mechanism for pursuing punitive justice because trials represent a form of punitive justice that is consistent with the rule of law and, as such, compatible with more general human rights norms. Despite their limitations, trials represent a legalist approach to pursuing punitive justice that is not necessarily the instinctive response of nation-states in the context of war and violence. Historically, new governments in states confronting a recent history of violence have often chosen to respond with one of two extremes, amnesia or purges.

Countries emerging from conflict may simply choose to forget the past in an effort to move forward beyond violence. In his book, *Justice and Reconciliation: After the Violence*, Andrew Rigby describes what he calls "amnesty and amnesia" in the case of the Spanish transition to democracy after Franco's death in 1975. The Franco regime was renowned for its violation of basic human rights, and yet, as Spain made its transition to democracy, the new government did not seek to punish or purge former members of the Franco government. Rather, Rigby writes, "There was an unwritten, if not unspoken, agreement that the Francoist past should be forgotten, at least in public. There was a generally accepted exercise in collective amnesia. Everything was subordinated to the need to ensure the peaceful transition to parliamentary democracy."[57] Even in countries that pursue prosecution against high-level officials, there may be efforts to extend amnesty to large segments of a population. For example, in post–World War II Germany, the new West German government faced widespread political pressure to give amnesty to former Nazis, even many who had already been convicted as war criminals. Accordingly, in the years immediately following the war, the West German government pursued policies that annulled the punishments of many former Nazis, with the exception of a small group of high-level Nazis, and sought to reintegrate them into German society.[58]

In stark contrast to amnesia as a response to mass violence, societies in transition from a recent history of violent conflict may choose purges as a form of punitive justice. Purges involve the punishment of individuals who collaborated with repressive governments by imprisoning them, dismissing them from public jobs, depriving them of citizenship rights, or, in extreme cases, executing traitors. Such purges may result from some form of judicial trial, but more commonly they are legislatively mandated by a new government. Even purges resulting from trials can be viewed as an extrajudicial form of punitive justice in that trials leading to purges typically have not taken place in regular courts and have not been hindered by due process considerations.

Purges were common in post–World War II European countries that had been occupied during the war and that sought ways to respond to collaborators. One of the dilemmas involved in purges is that it is difficult to establish degrees of culpability. Life in occupied territories is obviously difficult, and individuals collaborate to different degrees. Moreover, because so many individuals in occupied countries during World War II were implicated in collaboration, it was difficult to establish fair trials for all of them. Most European countries responded by setting up special tribunals or courts for collaboration. By the 1950s, most European governments granted amnesty to individuals who had been found guilty of collaborating in an effort to promote societal reconciliation. Purges were also commonly used by Eastern European countries at the end of the Cold War as many of these countries made the transition to democracy after the fall of the Soviet Union. Once again, purges in these countries were flawed in that it was difficult to evaluate the degree of culpability when a majority of a society was arguably complicit in repression. Moreover, purges typically were not hindered by due process considerations.[59] For example, Czechoslovakia adopted a lustration law that provided for the dismissal of state workers who had formerly worked for or collaborated with the state security agencies. The law also barred former Communist Party members from high public office. Critics have pointed out that such lustration laws fail to make a presumption of innocence and assume guilt based on mere membership in a group rather than on individual culpability.

In the case of external actors confronted with human rights abuses or war crimes in other states, nation-states most frequently respond to violence with inaction, in the case of violence that does not concern their own interests or citizens, or revenge, when the violence is directed at their national interests or citizens. By far the most common response of nation-states to violence that does not directly affect their own nationals or interests is inaction. Such inaction in the face of human atrocity is neither punitive nor just (at least from the victims' point of view), though it is an understandable response of nation-states operating in a chaotic global system. Although numerous historical examples of "humanitarian intervention" exist, nation-states are most likely to act on a humanitarian impulse when it coincides with other national interests. To the extent that universal principles have power in world politics, it is because they overlap at some level with fundamental political interests.

For precisely this reason, nation-states are most likely to respond to war crimes and human rights abuses when their own interests or citizens have been harmed. In the case of harm to their national interests, nation-states have commonly been motivated by the impulse to simply kill the enemy—an impulse that certainly is punitive and may even fulfill certain criteria of justice. Because revenge killings through extralegal means will certainly result in the deaths of some individuals who truly are innocent, this non-legalist approach represents a perversion of a basic axiom of the U.S. justice system—that it is better for many guilty individuals to go free than for an innocent individual to be wrongly convicted and punished. A punitive justice pursued through extrajudicial killings assumes that it is better for some innocent individuals to be killed than for the truly guilty to go unpunished.

For example, U.S. officials seriously discussed killing Nazis at the end of World War II as a way of pursuing a punitive justice. Henry Morgenthau, Secretary of the Treasury in the Roosevelt Administration, "once suggested eliminating all Nazi Party members," even after being informed that they numbered in the millions. Another Administration official had suggested executing 2,500 Nazis. Interestingly, when discussing this option, American military officials worried that U.S. soldiers would not carry out summary executions and wanted there to be a clear policy so soldiers would have the "excuse of following superior orders."[60] (In the end, fewer than 300 Germans were executed by the Allies after the post–World War II trials.[61]) Morgenthau's proposal to execute all members of the Nazi Party was based on a sense of collective justice in which individuals are complicit in crimes to the extent that they embrace an ideology and support institutions that lead to the commission of specific crimes. In this regard, the guilty are not only those individuals who pull the trigger of the gun that kills but also those who buy, pay for, and endorse (explicitly or implicitly) the use of these guns for criminal purposes.

Although this conception of collective justice is more likely to punish individuals who are guilty in various forms, it will surely lead to the wrongful punishment of individuals who are innocent or, perhaps, guilty of nothing more than ignorance. Proponents of legalism contend that trials provide a form of individualized justice that is more likely to punish *specific* individuals guilty of *specific* crimes than simply assuming collective guilt. Moreover, the impulse to seek vengeance violates legal norms, both international and domestic in many cases, and may be seen to perpetuate a cycle of violence that ensures more carnage and atrocities in the future. Madeleine Albright, a proponent of legalism, expressed this belief after the war in Kosovo when she said, "The wounds opened by this war will heal much faster if collective guilt for atrocities is expunged and individual responsibility is assigned."[62]

In addition to assigning individual guilt, trials, by producing an authoritative record of atrocities, may serve the goals of educating the public about human rights abuses so that violent history does not repeat itself. In this sense, the international community's gradual but incomplete development of a legalistic approach to punitive justice since the end of World War II represents tentative progress toward solidifying the status of universal principles in world politics that may serve as the foundation of global order and peace. Again, in Madeleine Albright's words, "We believe that justice is a parent to peace."[63]

Despite the ideal of individualized justice, this form of justice also has its own limitations in practice. Unfortunately, there is not always a clear, bright line dividing the innocent and the guilty. Although they stress individual as opposed to collective guilt, trials do not perfectly attain individualized guilt in that numerous guilty individuals often escape punishment and accountability. According to Daniel Jonah Goldhagen, author of *Hitler's Willing Executioners: Ordinary Germans and the Holocaust*, at least 100,000 individuals should be considered perpetrators of the Holocaust, and the number of guilty might be as high as 500,000.[64] Yet only 3,000 Germans were ultimately tried for crimes committed during the Holocaust. As the discrepancy between these figures indicates, trials may only place guilt on a very small number of those who are actually guilty of the crimes in question. As Gary Bass concludes, trials do *not* typically fulfill the ideal of individualized, punitive justice. Instead, trials may fulfill a far more limited, and political, objective: "Tribunal justice is inevitably symbolic: a few war criminals stand for a much larger group of guilty individuals. Thus, what is billed as individual justice actually becomes a de facto way of exonerating many of the guilty."[65]

In response to the claim that "justice is the parent of peace," critics contend that putting justice before peace is a luxury. In an ideal world, justice would never be sacrificed in the name of peace. The principled, legalistic response to every case of war crimes and atrocity might be to hold the responsible individuals accountable for their crimes. However, in the real word, principled legalism might simply contribute to an ongoing cycle of violence, as guilty individuals choose to continue to perpetrate violence to cling to power rather than face the possibility of punishment for past crimes. At times, it may be necessary to give amnesty to the perpetrators of human rights abuses in order to convince them to relinquish their hold on power or to renounce the continued use of violence. Again, in Gary Bass's words, "a moralistic insistence on punishing war crimes may make it impossible to do business with bloodstained leaders who, however repulsive, might end a war."[66] Sadly, when human rights abuses, war crimes, and genocide are perpetrated, vast numbers of people are typically implicated. Some individuals directly perpetrate violence. Other individuals might be seen as political, economic, social, or military collaborators with various motivations, including power, fear, or the desire to protect oneself, one's family, and one's friends.[67] Recognizing the widespread nature of complicity and the variety of motivations driving collaboration with repugnant regimes gives one pause about putting too great an emphasis on punitive justice in a political context in which peace, stability, and reconciliation are also important goals.

As we will see in the next chapter, critics of punitive justice argue that trials and other mechanisms emphasizing punishment are adversarial and divisive. Critics believe that trials, and punitive justice in general, foster ongoing mistrust and animosity among groups in conflict rather than promoting peace and reconciliation. In their view, the goal of long-term peace may be better served by foregoing trials in favor of other mechanisms, such as truth commissions, which they believe are more likely to foster reconciliation. Proponents of trials reject this view of punitive justice. In their view, there can be no peace without justice, and there can be no justice if the guilty go unpunished.

DISCUSSION QUESTIONS

1. Does a punitive approach to justice represent an appropriate response to human rights abuses or war crimes? Why or why not?

2. Do purges represent a just response to human rights abuses or war crimes in countries emerging from conflict? Why or why not?

3. Should "collective amnesia" ever be considered an appropriate response to human rights abuses or war crimes in countries emerging from conflict? Why or why not?

4. Do ad hoc war crimes tribunals contribute to the pursuit of punitive justice for the perpetrators of human rights abuses? Why or why not?

5. Will a permanent ICC be an improvement on ad hoc war crimes tribunals? Why or why not?

6. What are the limitations of trials as a mechanism for pursuing justice in response to human rights abuses or war crimes? What are the strengths of trials?

7. Who should be held primarily responsible for war crimes and gross violations of human rights—those individuals responsible for orchestrating and instigating these crimes or the individuals who directly perpetrate the violence?

8. If high officials responsible for orchestrating human rights abuses and war crimes are not held accountable, is it just to prosecute the lower-level officials and citizens who directly perpetrated these crimes?

9. How should individual and collective guilt for human rights abuses and war crimes be balanced? Should individuals who support repressive regimes be punished in some way, or should punishment be limited to individuals who directly commit crimes?

10. Legalist models of punitive justice emphasize individual over collective guilt. Is an emphasis on individual as opposed to collective guilt always appropriate? Consider the situation in Rwanda, where many ordinary Hutus participated in killing an estimated 800,000 Tutsi in a matter of just 100 days. Proponents of legalism assume that it would be better to let many guilty go free than for an innocent person to be wrongly punished. Does this assumption hold in a situation like the Rwandan genocide? Why or why not?

WEB RESOURCES

The United Nations Web site on the International Criminal Tribunal for the former Yugoslavia (http://www.un.org/icty/)

The United Nations Web site on the International Criminal Tribunal for Rwanda (http://www.un.org/ictr/)

The United Nations Web site on the International Criminal Court (http://www.un.org/law/icc/index.html)

10

Restorative Justice
and Human Rights

RESTORATIVE JUSTICE AS A RESPONSE
TO HUMAN RIGHTS ABUSES

In *The House of the Spirits*, Isabel Allende, the niece of Chile's assassinated President Salvador Allende, ends this tale of love and violence spanning three different generations as well different economic classes and cultures with a message of reconciliation. The primary narrator is a woman against whom political violence has been perpetrated and whose loved ones have also been victimized by political violence in the novel's unnamed Latin American country. While she and her loved ones have been victims of violence, her ancestors have also been guilty of perpetrating violence in this war-torn society. Allende's female narrator, traumatized but strong, writes the following words at the end of the story:

> And now I seek my hatred but cannot seem to find it. I feel its flame going out. . . . It would be very difficult for me to avenge all those who should be avenged, because my revenge would be just another part of the same inexorable rite. I have to break that terrible chain. I want to think that my task is life and that my mission is not to prolong hatred but simply to fill these pages while I wait for Miguel, while I bury my grandfather, whose body lies beside me in this room, while I wait for better times to come, while I carry this child in my womb, the daughter of so many rapes or perhaps of Miguel, but above all, my own daughter.[1]

In the end, Allende's narrator chooses the affirmation of life over the perpetuation of death and violence. In doing so, she articulates a message of reconciliation and forgiveness, rather than a message of revenge and retribution, as an
appropriate response to unspeakable violence.

Allende's novel raises important questions about the place of forgiveness
and reconciliation in establishing justice and peace in societies that have been
riven by conflict and violence. One of the primary themes in *The House of the
Spirits* is that violence can only be properly understood when placed in context. Those characters who commit violent acts in the novel are often driven
by a complicated set of historical, social, and psychological factors. As the
novel starkly illustrates, violence begets violence. Allende does not believe that
recognition of the context in which violence is committed justifies it. Nevertheless, she does suggest that recognizing the context that perpetuates violence may help its victims and perpetrators understand it. In seeking such understanding, individuals caught up in violent conflict may seek to take steps
to end the cycle of violence, as Allende's narrator ultimately does.

As we saw in the previous chapter, critics of punitive justice argue that trials and other mechanisms emphasizing punishment for war crimes and human
rights abuses are adversarial and divisive. Like Allende's narrator, these critics
believe that responding to violence with retribution fosters ongoing mistrust
and animosity among groups in conflict rather than promoting peace and reconciliation. Critics of punitive justice often favor a restorative approach to justice. Rather than emphasizing the punishment of the guilty, restorative justice
emphasizes the restoration of social relationships as the most important goal
for societies emerging from violent conflict. Proponents of restorative justice
believe that genuine justice is more likely to be produced by processes that
seek to repair social relationships among groups that have been in conflict
than by processes emphasizing retribution.[2] In turn, they believe that justice
mechanisms based on the desire to foster reconciliation and social repair are
more likely to contribute to sustainable peace in the long run. In its emphasis
on reconciliation and social repair, restorative justice calls for processes that
encourage societies scarred by human rights abuses to wrestle with collective
guilt and responsibility for violence rather than mechanisms that single out
specific individuals for punishment.

Many scholars and human rights activists prefer restorative justice to punitive justice on pragmatic grounds. Although they favor the judicial prosecution of guilty individuals in theory, a variety of factors can inhibit the effectiveness of judicial mechanisms for pursuing justice in post–conflict situations.
Societies emerging from war and civil conflict are often entering into a transition to democracy, and such transitions are typically tenuous. In these cases,
unconsolidated democratic governments commonly wish to avoid the instability that would be engendered by prosecuting officials of the former regime.
In such cases, the military is often hovering in the wings ready to overthrow
any new government if it seeks to punish military officials who have been
complicit in human rights abuses. As a result, new governments may favor
restorative justice processes as a less inflammatory way to seek justice and to

promote reconciliation. Similarly, trials might be inappropriate when peace negotiations are still ongoing; parties to a conflict may be more likely to compromise if they do not fear that they will be subject to prosecution for war crimes or human rights abuses. Moreover, the demands of judicial justice commonly outweigh the financial and human resources of governments in societies emerging from violent conflict.

Other scholars and human rights activists favor restorative justice on principle. Whereas punitive justice emphasizes the punishment of individual perpetrators and justice for individual victims, restorative justice stresses the importance of collective healing and peace at the societal level. Proponents of restorative justice place a premium on the restoration of social relationships rather than the punishment of perpetrators. They contend that restorative mechanisms may be the preferred means of pursuing justice and reconciliation in societies in which relationships among groups have been badly damaged by violence.[3]

According to its proponents, not only does restorative justice emphasize social repair, but it may also do a better job than punitive justice of assessing the guilt of perpetrators and responding appropriately. Whereas judicial trials stress individual guilt, institutional mechanisms emphasizing restorative justice may do a better job of forcing communities at large to wrestle with their collective guilt. Proponents of trials contend that in the absence of individual accountability an entire group may be deemed collectively guilty, but the reverse may also be true: By focusing on individual accountability, trials may inappropriately remove the burden of collective guilt from relevant groups. As noted by Laurel E. Fletcher and Harvey M. Weinstein, "The proposition that if everyone is guilty then no one is guilty, ignores the possibility that holding everyone responsible for past atrocities may force a nation to come to terms with its past as well as to lay the groundwork for true reconciliation."[4]

Proponents of restorative justice assert that truth commissions and other processes emphasizing social repair may be better suited than punitive mechanisms to fostering an examination of collective guilt and responsibility and the structural and institutional context in which mass violence occurs. Hence, they favor restorative justice on principled rather than just pragmatic grounds. An exploration of restorative justice as an approach to pursuing justice and peace in the aftermath of human rights abuses is the central theme of this chapter. The chapter will explore this theme as it provides an overview of truth commissions, reparations, and apologies as mechanisms for responding to human rights abuses.

TRUTH COMMISSIONS

Truth commissions, or commissions of inquiry, involve efforts to establish a record of truth about the incidence of war crimes or human rights abuses in a particular country. Sometimes these commissions offer amnesty to perpetrators of war crimes or human rights abuses in exchange for their testimony about these crimes. Such testimony is used to build a record of the truth, which then establishes the legitimacy of victims' claims and an historical record for future generations. Ideally, truth commissions will contribute to the creation of an authoritative record of past atrocities that will help to prevent the recurrence of violence. Robert I. Rotberg underscores the importance of uncovering the truth about human rights abuses and war crimes as a preventive measure:

> If societies are to prevent recurrences of past atrocities and to cleanse themselves of the corrosive enduring effects of massive injuries to individuals and whole groups, societies must understand—at the deepest possible levels—what occurred and why. In order to come fully to terms with their brutal pasts, they must uncover, in precise detail, who did what to whom, and why, and under whose orders. They must seek, at least, thus to uncover the truth—insofar as this aim is humanly and situationally possible after the fact.[5]

In addition, proponents of truth commissions believe that truth-telling processes can contribute to social reconciliation and individual healing. Ultimately, truth commissions stress social repair and peace as higher priorities than punishment in the pursuit of justice.

At least seventeen truth commissions have been established since 1974.[6] Successor governments to authoritarian regimes have created most of these commissions. These governments seek to maintain a delicate balance between the demands of the victims of authoritarianism who have supported the transition to democratic governance and the perpetrators of violence, many of whom remain in positions of authority or can threaten the stability of the new regime in some manner. Although most of these commissions have been established by successor governments, truth commissions for El Salvador and Haiti were established by UN Security Council resolutions. One of the most recent truth commissions, the Serbian Commission for Truth and Reconciliation, was opened in February 2002.

Some commissions of inquiry offer amnesty to individuals who testify truthfully before the commission; others do not. The truth commission in Argentina granted amnesty to former military leaders. The South African Truth and Reconciliation Commission (TRC) offered amnesty to individuals who testified truthfully before it, but such amnesty was not automatic. In order for applicants to receive amnesty, they had to fully confess and to show political motivations for their actions. Indeed, the TRC denied amnesty in cases when it was determined that the individual in question was lying. For instance, the Amnesty Committee of the TRC denied amnesty to four ex-police officers who the commission determined had lied when they testified that their 1977 killing of anti-apartheid activist Steven Biko was accidental. It is important to stress that amnesty and truth commissions are not inevitably linked. The case of the commission of inquiry in El Salvador provides an interesting example. In this case, the Salvadoran government granted unconditional amnesty to leaders of the former regime despite the fact that amnesty was *not* recommended by the

UN-created Commission on the Truth for El Salvador. Thus, in this case, amnesty and the final report of the truth commission were separate. Indeed, critics argue that the government-granted amnesty may have undermined the full power of the commission's report in generating reconciliation.[7]

Commissions of inquiry differ in other regards as well. Truth commissions have been created through quite different processes. A few truth commissions have been established through democratic processes. For example, South Africa's Truth and Reconciliation Commission was created by South Africa's newly elected democratic Parliament in 1995. Other truth commissions, such as the one in Argentina, were established by executive orders. As noted previously, the truth commissions for El Salvador and Haiti were authorized by UN Security Council resolutions.[8] Testimony before a truth commission may or may not be anonymous. Chile's truth commission was built on anonymous testimony, whereas South Africa's Truth and Reconciliation Commission named the individuals testifying. Finally, commissions of inquiry differ on the question of whether they are considered replacements for or complements to trials. Some truth commissions serve as replacements for trials, but others function simultaneously with trials. For instance, the TRC in South Africa threatened judicial prosecution of those individuals who did not come before the commission to testify.[9]

Juan E. Mendez outlines a number of potential flaws with truth commissions as mechanisms for pursuing justice.[10] Mendez points out that the "truth telling" embodied in these commissions does not necessarily promote reconciliation or social repair better than trials, as proponents of commissions of inquiry have argued. Rather, he suggests that truth without punitive justice for perpetrators may lead to lasting bitterness in the hearts of victims of atrocities and, in this way, may hinder lasting peace or reconciliation. In his view, one cannot assume that social reconciliation will automatically follow a truth commission. He writes:

> In the first place, true reconciliation cannot be imposed by decree; it has to be built in the hearts and minds of all members of society through a process that recognizes every human being's worth and dignity. Second, reconciliation requires knowledge of the facts. Forgiveness cannot be demanded (or even expected) unless the person who is asked to forgive knows exactly what it is that he or she is forgiving. Third, reconciliation can only come after atonement. It seems to add a new unfairness to the crimes of the past to demand forgiveness from the victims without any gesture of contrition or any acknowledgement of wrongdoing from those who will benefit from that forgiveness.[11]

Mendez believes that trials, in which testimony is subject to cross-examination and the testing of evidence, may actually do a better job of establishing a record of truth than commissions of inquiry. According to Mendez, another problem with truth commissions is that governments may use them for cynical purposes. For instance, Zimbabwe has not released the final report of its truth commission and instead used the process more as a method of gaining legitimacy than fostering genuine reconciliation. Similarly, the Haiti Truth Commission delayed the release of its final report for months and then did not distribute it widely, undermining its effectiveness.[12]

Critics of trials often say they should not be pursued because justice in international war crimes trials will inevitably be selective, but Mendez points out that truth commissions result in selective justice as well. Mendez does not argue that truth commissions are inevitably unfair or ineffective, but he contends that proponents of truth commissions should not be quick to dismiss the importance of trials when they are politically feasible. In his view, one of the most important moral justifications for trials is that they "are the most effective means of separating collective guilt from individual guilt, and thus to remove the stigma of historic misdeeds from innocent members of communities that are collectively blamed for the atrocities committed on other communities."[13]

In general, critics of truth commissions are skeptical of the claim that commissions of inquiry will necessarily contribute to reconciliation. Individuals might "tell the truth" before a commission of inquiry in order to receive amnesty if it is available, rather than out of a genuine sense of remorse. In this case, critics question whether "truth telling" can represent a genuine step toward reconciliation. Problems faced by the South African TRC are illustrative in this regard. Many African victims of apartheid have expressed resentment at the amnesty process that was part of the TRC. For example, the family of Steven Biko, the prominent anti-apartheid activist, tried unsuccessfully to fight the establishment of the TRC. Although Biko's killers were ultimately denied amnesty, the family remained firmly opposed to a process that might have granted his killers amnesty. Other victims expressed concern that the TRC would generate only "empty apologies and hollow reconciliation."[14] Although the Final Report of the TRC acknowledges that reconciliation involves a long process requiring participation from both victims and perpetrators, few white South Africans attended or participated in the hearings of the Commission.[15]

Even proponents of truth commissions recognize their limitations in providing a comprehensive version of "the truth." As Anne Hayner notes, commissions of inquiry typically have limited mandates that prevent a detailed exploration of the truth as it relates to repression by governments and violent conflicts. Moreover, truth commissions often operate with limited resources and under time constraints that limit the extent to which the full truth can be explored and disclosed. For example, the Serbian Commission for Truth and Reconciliation had received an annual budget of only $20,000 as of 2002.[16] Hayner also points out that truth commissions typically fail to explore the role of foreign governments in aiding repressive regimes. Finally, she notes that abuses against women often go under-examined. In part, the failure to deal adequately with violence against women results from mandates that prioritize "politically motivated crimes" and an interpretation of these mandates that treats much wartime violence against women—in particular, rape and other forms of sexual torture—as nonpolitical crimes.[17]

In terms of truth commissions and gender inequity, the limitations of the South African Truth and Reconciliation Commission (TRC) are illustrative.

Initially, the TRC did not plan any hearings focused on the victimization of women. However, after nongovernmental organizations began to pressure the TRC, it instituted three special hearings for women. Yet critics have charged that many women were reluctant to testify in these hearings. As Beth Goldblatt has noted, "many women felt uncomfortable about exposing experiences of violence, particularly sexual violation, in public forums; some women felt that they had dealt with the past and did not want to open old wounds; others confronted a sense that submitting the violations they had experienced at the hands of comrades felt like a political betrayal."[18] In general, evidence suggests that women were hesitant to discuss sexual victimization before the TRC.[19] In large part, this reluctance was due to social constructions of gender identities that led women to believe that they would be socially stigmatized if they admitted that they had been raped.[20] Although scholars have focused on the reluctance of women to testify about rape, it should also be noted that men who have experienced rape and other forms of sexual torture during war or other social conflicts likely experience the same reluctance to testify about this victimization in public forums.

Not only did gender norms serve as an obstacle to truth-telling about sexual violence before the TRC, but they also limited the willingness of women to testify about themselves as victims. Social constructions of femininity that idealize women as selfless caregivers who put their families before their own individual needs shaped the truth that was produced by the TRC. Notably, although a majority of the individuals who testified before the TRC were women, they testified almost exclusively about violence committed against their husbands, children, and loved ones. As a general rule, women simply did not testify about their own victimization and often perceived themselves as "lesser victims" than the men in their lives.[21] Because of these limitations, the TRC has been criticized for perpetuating gender inequity even as it played a crucial role in dismantling the racial inequity of apartheid. The failure of the TRC to address gender equity in an adequate manner is problematic not only in terms of justice but also because this failure renders the truth that was produced by the TRC incomplete.

The belief that commissions of inquiry necessarily promote healing for victims also needs to be evaluated carefully. Although some proponents of truth commissions genuinely believe that unburdening one's pain before a truth commission may be a step toward healing, it is a mistake to assume that truth commissions effectively promote long-term individual healing. Truth commissions are not the same thing as therapy. Although they may be useful in promoting societal reconciliation, we cannot assume that societal reconciliation is the same thing as individual healing. Typically, trauma therapy is a long and grueling process that unfolds over a period of many years. Truth commissions, with limited mandates and resources, are not structurally designed to facilitate this process.[22] Thus, the widely held assumption that truth commissions are designed to foster *individual* healing cannot be sustained by existing evidence.

While critics charge that truth commissions do not necessarily lead to restorative justice or social repair, proponents counter that they have the potential to be powerful mechanisms for promoting reconciliation among groups in conflict. In the South African case, numerous South African victims expressed their belief that the truth commission enabled them to meet their transgressors in a spirit of forgiveness. In a speech at the University of Iowa in the spring of 1999, Archbishop Desmond Tutu, the chairman of South Africa's Truth and Reconciliation Commission, exemplified this spirit of forgiveness. He spoke of countless victims, both black and white, who were able to forgive the individuals who violated their human rights and of perpetrators of human rights abuses who expressed genuine remorse. He has called the commission "the only alternative to Nuremberg on the one hand and amnesia on the other."[23]

In the end, although truth commissions may represent an imperfect mechanism for pursuing justice in societies scarred by violence, they at least offer the opportunity to publicly condemn war crimes and human rights abuses. Ideally, they help to break the cycle of violence by creating an authoritative record of past atrocities that vindicates the stories of victims and forces a society to reckon with collective responsibility. When they work, truth commissions can highlight the responsibility of institutions and society at large for violence and human rights abuses rather than just punishing individuals who directly committed these acts.[24] Thus, the collective focus of truth commissions may better serve the goal of promoting the larger social reforms necessary to achieve comprehensive justice. Truth commissions may not bring justice to all *individuals,* either victims or perpetrators of war crimes and human rights abuses. However, the hope is that these mechanisms will foster *collective* reconciliation, justice, and peace over time.

REPARATIONS

Reparations, which involve compensation by the nation-state responsible for committing human rights abuses or war crimes to victims or their survivors, represent a rather straightforward effort to bring justice directly to the victims of these atrocities. Most commonly, reparations refer to material compensation provided to victims, such as cash payments, the restoration of confiscated property, the provision of medical and psychological treatment, and employment or educational opportunities. Indemnity, the making of cash payments, is the most common form of reparations. Reparations also sometimes refer to "nonmaterial" compensation to victims, such as affirmative action or the provision of medical or educational services to victimized groups.[25] Nonmaterial reparations have also included special policies and considerations for indigenous populations—for example, casino licenses and exclusive fishing rights in certain areas for Native American tribes in the United States.[26]

Reparations do not inherently represent a form of restorative justice. Indeed, reparations can be consistent with a punitive model of justice, and, historically, punitive reparations have been imposed by victorious powers after war. A prime example of externally imposed punitive reparations is the case of the reparations imposed upon Germany by the Allied Powers at the end of

World War I in the Treaty of Versailles.[27] The harsh nature of these reparations has been identified as a major contributing factor to World War II. In this way, externally imposed punitive reparations are not consistent with the idea of restorative justice. Thus, the focus of this section is not on externally imposed reparations but rather on the reparations that states, or more recently corporations, voluntarily provide to victims of mass violence.

World War II generated the most prominent examples of the use of reparations as a means of promoting justice for the victims of gross violations of human rights. The best-known World War II case involves German reparations to victims of the Holocaust. Soon after the war ended, the Federal Republic of Germany passed a series of laws, stemming from a 1952 agreement between the German and Israeli governments, designed to compensate the victims of Nazi persecution. Under these laws, Germany paid restitution to victims of Nazi persecution for loss of life, physical harm, deprivation of liberty, and professional or economic harm. The initial German–Israeli agreement provided for the payment of $1 billion, but the reparations legislation adopted by the German government provided for several billion dollars of additional reparations in subsequent years.[28]

Holocaust survivors have also sought reparations from German corporations that profited from the use of slave labor during World War II. Recently, the movement for corporate reparations in Germany has had some success. In 1999, a number of German companies, including Volkswagen, Siemens, Deutshe Bank, and DaimlerChrysler, agreed to pay reparations of more than $4 billion to former slave laborers. The statute of limitations makes it unlikely that corporations can be compelled to pay restitution, but reparations proponents hope that companies will feel morally compelled to make financial restitution.[29]

Despite widespread accolades for Germany's reparations policy, it has been criticized as an insufficient effort to compensate the victims of Nazi persecution. Critics have charged that some survivors have received too little compensation and, in other cases, that survivors have received nothing. Eastern European Jews were only recently given reparations, at levels much lower than prior recipients of reparations and at a time when many of these elderly survivors have already died. In addition, Gypsies (Roma) and homosexuals have been left out of Germany's reparations scheme. Critics have also charged that the pensions given as part of Germany's reparations are inadequate to provide a decent standard of living for survivors. The inadequacy of reparations seems especially stark when it is noted that thousands of former SS and Gestapo veterans have received lifelong pensions from the German government.[30]

At the same time, some victims of the Holocaust have rejected reparations in principle. Many of these survivors suggest that reparations are an inadequate response to the Holocaust and criticize the fact that Germany did not pursue a more punitive response in the aftermath of World War II—for example, by pursuing a rigorous "denazification" policy that would have removed significant numbers of Nazis from official positions.[31] Because of Germany's failure to fully accept responsibility for its crimes during the Holocaust in this way, some Holocaust survivors have rejected reparations as an unprincipled effort to buy off the victims rather than a sincere effort to initiate social repair.[32]

In addition to Germany, a number of other countries adopted reparations policies as a response to discriminatory practices during World War II, though often not for decades. One prominent case involves U.S. reparations to Japanese Americans and other Japanese residents in the United States who were interned by the government during World War II. Under the Civil Liberties Act of 1988, the U.S. Congress apologized for the U.S. government's internment of Japanese Americans during World War II and appropriated funds for a special foundation to sponsor research and public education on this case. Congress also appropriated funds for a $20,000 reparation payment to each survivor of internment who was still living.[33] This policy has led to the payment of reparations to approximately 80,000 survivors of the World War II internment at a cost of more than $1.6 billion.[34]

Another reparations case stemming from World War II is the Japanese government's response to its involvement in perpetrating a sex-slave system in Asia during the war. As discussed in Chapter 9, the "comfort women" who were victims of this sex-slave system brought a number of suits in Japanese courts during the 1990s. In addition to these trials, victims of this sex-slave system have also demanded restitution. For example, in South Korea, the Comfort Women Problem Resolution Council demanded reparations for victims. In 1992, a Japanese legislative committee on comfort women issued a report calling for the creation of a relief fund instead of individual compensation. Nevertheless, the Diet still has not issued an apology. In 1995, the Japanese government created the "Asian Women's Fund" comprised of donations from private sources, offering the equivalent of approximately $18,000 to $20,000 to former comfort women who can document their cases. Many victims have refused to accept compensation from private sources because they want the Japanese government to acknowledge its accountability. The Japanese government created a government-funded reparations plan paying Filipina comfort women approximately $9,300, but this plan excludes comfort women from other countries. Eligible victims who have accepted compensation also complain that Japanese welfare agencies are responsible for dispensing reparations, creating a social stigma rather than signaling that the money is just compensation for the government-sanctioned violence committed against them.[35]

A more recent example of the use of reparations to contribute to justice for human rights abuses stemming from World War II involves the case of Swiss banking scandals. Despite Switzerland's status as a "neutral" country, Swiss banks were complicit in Nazi persecution in that they helped finance the Nazi government. Moreover, after the war ended, they refused to give deposited assets to survivors of Nazi persecution. Under pressure from a variety of Jewish and human rights groups as well as the U.S. government, in 1997 the Swiss government agreed to establish a humanitarian fund of $5 billion by selling gold assets.[36] Additionally, several Swiss banks reached a settlement with Holocaust survivors in 1999. As part of this settlement, these banks agreed to pay $1.25 billion in reparations to survivors. The Swiss government has also established a reparations fund providing individual payments to Jewish Holocaust survivors and Roma survivors of Nazi persecution as well as homosexuals, though victims must demonstrate financial need in order to receive compensation.[37]

In addition to the World War II reparations cases, reparations have also been adopted by a number of other countries as a mechanism for promoting justice in the aftermath of widespread human rights abuses. After the collapse of the Pinochet regime in 1990 and based on the findings of a truth commission in Chile, the new Chilean government passed legislation authorizing reparation benefits to the former regime's victims and their families. This law has resulted in thousands of families' receiving approximately $5,000 per year from the Chilean government. Argentina similarly authorized reparation benefits to victims of serious violations of human rights under the former regime. Interestingly, in both the cases of Argentina and Chile, the laws establishing a right to reparations were created in conjunction with the truth commissions in each of those countries. [38]

An interesting and controversial case is the movement for reparations for slavery in the United States. African American groups at the forefront of this movement—for example, the National Coalition of Blacks for Reparations in America—are seeking material compensation for labor and loss of life during the era of slavery in the United States as well as a national public apology. Although the slavery reparations movement has begun to receive more attention recently, it is actually an old movement, with the first calls for reparations made by abolitionists. Indeed, during the Civil War, Congress passed legislation that called for the provision of forty acres of land to freed slaves. According to the legislation, the land for this program was to come from the confiscation of property previously held by slaveholders. Because President Andrew Johnson rescinded this policy and vetoed new legislation calling for the transfer of land from slaveholders to freed slaves, this reparation for slavery was never fully implemented.[39] The reparations movement was essentially dead for decades until civil rights leaders in the 1960s began to make renewed demands for reparations. To date, the reparations movement has not generated widespread public support in the United States. Indeed, in an ABC News poll at the end of the 1990s, two-thirds of European Americans responding opposed a public apology, and 88 percent opposed reparations.[40]

The slavery reparations movement in the United States is demanding reparations not only from the U.S. government but also from corporations that historically profited from slavery. For example, Deadria Farmer-Paellman, a lawyer living in New York, asked the insurance company Aetna to establish a multimillion-dollar trust fund for minority education and businesses after she learned that the company had profited from slavery by insuring Southern farmers against losses through the death of their slaves in the 1850s and 1860s. Arguing that the company is currently committed to diversity and that it already contributes to a variety of funds that benefit minorities, Aetna declined to pay any restitution but did issue an apology for its past policies. Farmer-Paellman has done additional research that demonstrates that a number of other companies profited from slavery.[41] Indeed, proponents of reparations for slavery may increasingly focus their efforts on corporations rather than the government because it may be easier to demonstrate that the corporations profited financially as a result of their policies toward slavery. Thus, calls for corporate reparations may be more compelling, especially because critics of the reparations movement oppose governmental reparations for slavery on the grounds that so many American citizens died in the fight to end slavery during the Civil War.

The push for reparations for slavery in the United States may be gaining momentum. A new California law requires insurance companies to research whether or not they ever insured slaves as property and to report to the state. Although the law does not say anything about reparations, it is possible that such data could be used as the basis for reparations claims in the future. The Oklahoma Commission to Study the Race Riots of 1921 recommended compensation for the destruction of property and the loss of life suffered by African Americans during the riots initiated by European American mobs against African Americans in Oklahoma in 1921. Proponents of reparations are becoming more vocal and better organized, so these isolated cases may be representative of a future trend, but it remains to be seen whether significant reparations for slavery will be made.[42]

Reparations as a response to mass violence and injustice have a number of potential flaws. In practical terms, it may not be realistic to expect governments to voluntarily compensate victims of historical human rights abuses. With the exception of the German case, most countries that have emerged from authoritarianism have passed only limited reparations laws. Even when countries adopt reparations policies, victims often do not actually receive reparations because it is difficult to prove their status in the absence of well-established records of the war crimes and human rights abuses committed. These records commonly are not forthcoming in countries that have made only a tenuous transition to democracy. [43] Governments typically are even more reluctant to provide reparations to victims of human rights abuses when a great deal of time has passed. As Elazar Barkan notes, "This ambivalence is exhibited when the same morality that informs the need for Germany to pay for the crimes of the Holocaust sees discussion of the notion of reparation for slavery as too radical."[44] States inevitably will exercise discretion in providing reparations, thus limiting the extent to which victims of historic cases of human rights abuses will be compensated.

In addition to practical factors limiting the utility of reparations, one of the potential pitfalls of reparations is that the provision of material compensation for victims of mass violence signals that we can "calculate and quantify evil."[45] In reality, no amount of money can genuinely compensate for the loss of life, health, and loved ones suffered by victims of human rights abuses. As a result, many victims remain motivated primarily by a desire to see justice done to the perpetrators of war crimes and human rights abuses rather than by the desire for material compensation. In this way, reparations fall short of fulfilling an ideal of justice for many victims.

While these criticisms suggest that reparations are insufficient from the point of view of victims, other critics oppose reparations from the perspective of perpetrators or their descendants. According to these critics, only individuals directly responsible for perpetrating violence or injustice should bear the costs of compensating victims. In their view, current generations should not be responsible for making reparations for violence and injustice committed in the past. In other words, these critics do not believe that children should be made to pay for the "sins of the fathers." In practice, reparations commonly are made not by the government directly responsible for the atrocities but by a successor government years later. As a result, the individuals in society on behalf of whom the state is apologizing may not have been alive when the human rights abuses in question were perpetrated. When this is the case, reparations may generate resentment among current members of a society who do not believe they are accountable for the injustice of the past.

In these cases, it is technically true that contemporary members of society are not directly responsible for violence or injustice committed in the past. However, this lack of direct responsibility does not necessarily mean that current members of a society do not owe compensation to the victims of human rights abuses in the past or their descendants who continue to suffer as a result of a history of violence and injustice. As Elazar Barkan notes, "the generational question is anything but straightforward. Our identity, who we are, is a result of our history, for better and for worse. We enjoy the riches of our past and therefore supposedly should pay our historical debts."[46] Indeed, a compelling case can be made that members of a society historically built upon exploitation and injustice have some obligation that carries over from generation to generation even if they do not actively perpetrate or condone violence or injustice.

Although individuals who are not directly responsible for human rights abuses are not criminally liable, they may have moral responsibilities. Individuals cannot claim the rights and privileges provided by a society without also accepting its debts and responsibilities. Ultimately, the conception of both privileges and responsibilities as social goods that carry across generations underlies the case for reparations. The consequences of human rights abuses and injustice do not necessarily end just because the initial victims and perpetrators die or are removed from power. As a result, a moral responsibility to make reparations for human rights abuses committed in the past may carry over from generation to generation. Ultimately, a commitment to make reparations may serve to break a cycle of violence and injustice that hinders reconciliation, justice, and peace in societies scarred by historic human rights abuses.

APOLOGIES

As a method for promoting restorative justice in the aftermath of human rights abuses, apologies, simply put, represent "an admission of wrongdoing, a recognition of its effects, and, in some cases, an acceptance of responsibility for those effects and an obligation to its victims."[47] Standing alone, apologies are not sufficient to promote restorative justice. Nevertheless, they can be an important initial step in a larger process of repairing the fabric of a society that has been torn apart by violence. At a very fundamental level, apologies represent an acknowledgment of victims' experience of mass violence, discrimination, and other human rights abuses. Additionally, apologies signal governments' willingness to admit "that their policies were unjust and discriminatory and to negotiate with their victims over morally right and politically feasible solutions."[48] In doing so, apologies can play an important role in creating a historical record of atrocities and injustice. Similarly, apologies signal that a society accepts its collective guilt in perpetrating this violence. In this way, apologies make it difficult for parties to a conflict to deny their complicity. Ideally, a government's official acknowledgment of complicity will be a first step toward atonement and, ultimately, reconciliation.

Several recent examples illustrate the ways in which different international actors have attempted to use apologies to foster reconciliation. In the spring of 1998, the Vatican called for repentance among Roman Catholics who failed to oppose the Holocaust. More recently, during March 1999, Pope John Paul II formally apologized on behalf of the Roman Catholic Church for its complicity in persecution over the years, particularly for its active role in persecution during the Crusades and for its failure to act against the genocide of the Jews during World War II. During a 1998 foreign policy trip through Africa, President Bill Clinton apologized for the historical role of the United States in the slave trade. He also apologized on behalf of the United States for its part in the international community's failure to respond more strongly to genocide in Rwanda. More recently, the U.S. Senate has been considering a resolution that would officially apologize on behalf of the federal government to American Indians for the government's historic abuses against Native American populations.[49]

One potential dilemma posed by reparations and apologies is that they often are made not by the government directly responsible for the atrocities but years later by a successor government. As a result, the individuals in society on behalf of whom the state is apologizing may not have been alive when the violence or injustice in question was perpetrated. As in the case of reparations, these individuals often believe they should not be punished for the "sins of the fathers." In this way, official apologies may generate resentment among current members of a society and may serve to perpetuate rather than resolve fundamental conflicts among groups.

Moreover, some critics argue that apologies, in particular, are empty gestures that cannot bring real justice to the victims of war crimes or human rights abuses. For example, while Pope John Paul II apologized for the Catholic Church's "sins," the Pope notably did not apologize for the behavior of Pope Pius XII, who critics say at best was indifferent to the plight of the Jews and at worst was a direct anti-Semite who consciously failed to aid the Jews. Indeed, the Church hierarchy still recommends that Pope Pius XII should be beatified as a saint.[50] Similarly, critics have said that President Clinton's apology to Rwanda for failing to act to prevent genocide is meaningless when the international community continues to tolerate such atrocities in many places throughout the globe. Apologizing for the failure to act against genocide may not bring much comfort to the surviving victims whose family and friends were decimated by mass violence.

In spite of the limitations of apologies, they may play an important role in building the foundations for justice in societies scarred by violence and injustice. One of the fundamental contributions apologies can make to the pursuit of justice is in acknowledging the truth of victims' claims. Although the acknowledgment of the truth may not provide direct justice to individual victims, it can represent an important step in moving toward collective justice. Indeed, many victims believe that an acknowledgment of culpability is more important than reparations as a means of pursuing justice for human rights abuses. For example, the Korean victims of Japan's sex-slave system during World War II who refused to accept reparations from a private fund, as discussed previously, "did so despite the fact that the money was substantial for the (by then) old women who were for the most part poor. To them the moral offense—the refusal of the Japanese government to acknowledge responsibility—depreciated the economic value of the compensation and made it valueless."[51] With an apology comes an acknowledgment of the atrocities that have been committed by a government or its predecessor. Subsequently, successor regimes and future generations cannot deny these atrocities. In this way, the record of truth that is established may make it more likely that societies in conflict are able to move toward reconciliation, whereas a denial of the truth may foster continued resentment among victims and may contribute to a cycle of hostilities.

Moreover, in some cases, it is possible that apologies may contribute to more direct reparations to victims. Consider the example of a U.S. massacre of civilians during the Korean War. For nearly fifty years, the American government denied that U.S. forces intentionally killed hundreds of civilians under a railroad bridge near Seoul. South Korean survivors have long told a different story. These survivors have said that hundreds of Korean civilians, including women and children, were trapped under a bridge near Seoul and were killed by U.S. forces in the early weeks of the Korean War. They have sought reparations from the U.S. government as well as the South Korean government, both of which have denied the claims and, hence, have not compensated these individuals. The South Korean government rejected survivors' claim for compensation in 1998. Interestingly, in September 1999, twelve American veterans spoke out and affirmed the claims of the South Korean victims.[52] Had the U.S. government acknowledged its actions and issued a formal apology, the victims likely would have been granted some reparations. A government's failure to apologize can also exacerbate long-standing tensions between parties to a conflict. For example, Turkey has never acknowledged its responsibility for perpetrating genocide against Armenians in 1915, and the Turkish government's silence on this issue has contributed to lasting tensions between the two groups. Thus, these cases illustrate the ways in which an apology—or lack of one—might be instrumental in determining whether victims of human rights abuses attain some degree of justice.

Formal apologies for a government's action also prevent states from teaching obviously distorted versions of history. For example, in Croatia, Croatian textbooks now describe Serbs as "murderers" to elementary schoolchildren.[53] Although in a literal sense, it is true that many Serbs did murder both Croats and Bosnian Muslims during the Balkan War, it also is true that Croats "murdered" Serbs and Bosnian Muslims. If the government of Croatia acknowledged its own perpetration of war crimes, it might go far toward establishing a record of the truth and provide a building block for reconciliation.

Given the horrific nature of human rights abuses, it should not be surprising if victims are reluctant to forgive perpetrators. Indeed, victims are under no obligation to accept an apology. Thus, forgiveness and societal reconciliation will not necessarily follow apologies in the aftermath of societal violence and injustice. Nevertheless, apologies at least offer the opportunity to publicly acknowledge and condemn past human rights abuses. In doing so, apologies can help victims, even if victims choose not to forgive, by "transform[ing] the trauma of victimization into a process of mourning."[54] In doing so, apologies ideally will serve as a first step toward reconciliation and sustainable peace in societies emerging from conflict.

CONCLUSIONS

This chapter has explored truth commissions, reparations, and apologies as mechanisms for promoting restorative justice as a response to human rights abuses. Ideally, these mechanisms will promote reconciliation and sustainable peace in societies scarred by violence and injustice. Additionally, these processes are intended to encourage societies to wrestle with their collective responsibility for human rights abuses. In the process, these efforts to seek restorative justice ideally should contribute not only to the historical record of atrocities but also to a greater understanding of the structural and institutional context in which mass violence occurs. Such understanding may help serve the goal of promoting fundamental social reforms necessary for a comprehensive form of justice. Moreover, groups that have been in conflict hopefully will be able to build on this understanding to move toward reconciliation.

Ultimately, truth commissions, reparations, and apologies represent imperfect mechanisms for pursuing justice in societies scarred by violence and injustice. Many victims of violence will continue to prefer punitive justice for perpetrators, and the adoption of measures founded on the objective of restorative justice do not guarantee that reconciliation will follow. Moreover, it should be noted that punitive and restorative justice are not necessarily exclusive goals. It may well be that an ideal form of justice would include both punitive and restorative components. Indeed, Fletcher and Weinstein conclude that both trials and truth commissions are necessary to foster social repair and sustainable peace.[55] Despite their conclusion that both punitive and restorative responses may be necessary in order to promote justice in the aftermath of human rights abuses, they emphasize that truth commissions and other restorative mechanisms can play an especially crucial role in forcing a society to reckon with collective responsibility.

Restorative justice processes may not bring justice to all *individuals.* However, it is important to remember that they are not necessarily designed to promote individualized justice to either the victims or the perpetrators of human rights abuses. Rather, restorative justice mechanisms ultimately are intended to foster *collective* reconciliation, justice, and peace over time. Because restorative justice involves these long-term goals, only time will tell whether this approach to justice represents an effective response to violence and injustice. Truth commissions, reparations, and apologies do not represent the endpoint in efforts to seek justice for human rights abuses. Nevertheless, these restorative justice practices hopefully will serve as an important step toward reconciliation and sustainable peace in societies emerging from conflict.

DISCUSSION QUESTIONS

1. Do truth commissions do a good job of promoting justice for individual perpetrators and victims of war crimes and human rights abuses? Are truth commissions useful for promoting collective justice for societies scarred by war crimes and human rights abuses? Why or why not?

2. Should individuals "found guilty" by truth commissions, which are not bound by the same due process constraints of legal trials, be named? Why or why not?

3. Who has the moral obligation to apologize and/or make reparations for war crimes and human rights abuses? Should individuals be held responsible for war crimes and human rights abuses perpetrated by their forebears? In other words, should individuals be held morally responsible for the "sins of their fathers"? Who has the moral authority to apologize for human rights abuses or war crimes?

4. Do reparations and apologies do a good job of promoting either individual or collective justice?

5. Is restorative justice preferable to punitive justice as a response to human rights abuses? Why or why not?

6. Is individual justice or collective justice more important in the aftermath of human rights abuses? In other words, is it more important to hold an individual war criminal accountable, thereby bringing justice to his or her direct victims, or is it more important to promote reconciliation at the societal level, even if doing so means avoiding prosecutions of individual war criminals?

WEB RESOURCES

Restorative Justice Online (http://www.restorativejustice.org)

Center for Restorative Justice and Peacemaking (http://ssw.che.umn.edu/rjp)

The Centre for Restorative Justice (http://www.sfu.ca/crj)

United States Institute of Peace Truth Commissions Digital Collection (http://www.usip.org/library/truth.html)

Promoting Human Rights
from the Bottom Up

MOBILIZING SUPPORT
FOR HUMAN RIGHTS IN A WORLD
OF SOVEREIGN STATES

Throughout this book, we have seen that state sovereignty remains an essential organizing principle in world politics. We also have learned that sovereignty and human rights are commonly in tension. As a result, we know that the on-going emphasis on state sovereignty in world politics poses a significant challenge to proponents of human rights as universal principles that transcend the boundaries of states. We keep returning to a fundamental quandary. States are the actors that are typically responsible for perpetrating human rights abuses, either by directly violating human rights or by failing to prevent and punish human rights abuses by non-state actors. Yet because of the continued prioritization of state sovereignty in world politics, the international community has failed to create effective mechanisms for enforcing human rights laws within states. As a result, state cooperation is essential if universal human rights norms are ever to become a reality. However, because states frequently justify human rights violations in the name of national interest and because diverse political, economic, cultural, and ideological forces shape each state's conception of its national interest, can we realistically expect sovereign states to take universal human rights seriously?

A cynic might conclude that the answer to this question is an inevitable and resounding "no." And yet, we can look at the history of world politics and see that change does occur. Practices that were once taken for granted, such as slavery, are now widely considered immoral by most states, representing a wide variety of cultures and political ideologies, in the international system. Thus, change *is* possible and typically occurs when states experience shifts in their conceptions of their national interests. With this in mind, the important question becomes, *when* and *how* do states change their perceptions of the national interest to incorporate universal principles such as human rights?

A growing number of scholars, representing a liberal tradition in international relations scholarship, focus on the role of ideas as a way of explaining change in world politics.[1] According to Andrew Moravcsik, a proponent of this school of thought, liberal international relations theory is distinguished by the

> insight that state–society relations—the relationship of states to the domestic and transnational social context in which they are embedded—have a fundamental impact on state behavior in world politics. Societal ideas, interests, and institutions influence state behavior by shaping state preferences, that is, the fundamental social purpose underlying the strategic calculations of governments.[2]

Transnational ideas and universal principles, such as human rights, can shape state preferences. But how does this happen? How do states come to prioritize certain ideas over others? For many scholars of international relations, international law embodies the ideas that shape state behavior. Yet, as we have seen, international law, a body of law created by states, not surprisingly continues to prioritize state sovereignty. So, where do challenges to sovereignty emerge? Another perspective within liberal international relations theory suggests that challenges to state sovereignty emerge from the bottom up rather than from the top down.[3] In other words, normative constraints on state sovereignty arise *internally* rather than *externally*.[4] Rather than looking at international law as the primary challenge to state sovereignty, effective challenges to a rigid notion of state sovereignty are likely to emerge from *within* states.

This perspective on international relations has fundamentally shaped this chapter. Ideas, and not just interests, are a major force shaping world politics. Non-state actors play a crucial role in shaping state behavior by bringing these ideas to the center of policy debates. In terms of human rights, this perspective suggests that non-state actors *must* play a critical role in mobilizing support for universal principles if human rights are ever to become a reality in world politics. The status of state sovereignty can be challenged by human rights norms if states are pressured by non-state actors to conceptualize their interests in ways that incorporate universal principles as important. This chapter begins with an overview of the role of non-state actors in the global struggle for human rights. It highlights the potential of "bottom-up" efforts to promote universal human rights, as well as the obstacles that limit the effectiveness of such efforts, through case studies of multinational corporations and human rights and health and human rights.

NON-STATE ACTORS AND THE GLOBAL STRUGGLE FOR HUMAN RIGHTS

Non-state actors have played a central role in advancing the idea that all human beings deserve access to fundamental human rights. A successful and well-organized transnational antislavery movement initiated in the 1800s led to the eradication of slavery in the West, an institution that had been widely accepted across the globe for thousands of years, within a period of roughly 100 years.[5] Within roughly the same time frame, the women's suffrage movement, which involved non-state actors both within and across states, successfully led to the extension of the franchise to women in most Western countries within the first few decades of the twentieth century.[6] As we saw in Chapter 2, the creation of human rights norms in the aftermath of World War II proceeded rapidly. Non-state actors played an essential role in mobilizing international support for the emerging body of international human rights norms.[7] These historical examples demonstrate that ideas can lead to the transformation of seemingly entrenched practices and that non-state actors can successfully challenge the absolute sovereignty of states. These examples also suggest that further advances in human rights norms will require extensive involvement by active and committed nongovernmental organizations dedicated to the global struggle for human rights.

In their seminal work on transnational advocacy networks—the label they apply to networks of activists organized around important ideas or values—Margaret E. Keck and Kathryn Sikkink explain how non-state actors can foment change in a world of sovereign states:

> Where the powerful impose forgetfulness, networks can provide alternative channels of communication. Voices that are suppressed in their own societies may find that networks can project and amplify their concerns into an international arena, which in turn can echo back into their own countries. Transnational networks multiply the voices that are heard in international and domestic policies. These voices argue, persuade, strategize, document, lobby, pressure, and complain. The multiplication of voices is imperfect and selective—for every voice that is amplified, many others are ignored—but in a world where the voices of states have predominated, networks open channels for bringing alternative visions and information into the international debate.[8]

Simply put, transnational advocacy networks mobilize support for human rights by gathering and disseminating information about human rights abuses, lobbying governments, educating the public about human rights issues, and providing services to the victims of human rights abuses.[9] The political support for human rights can lead to pressure on states to implement human rights norms internally. When domestic political activism is violently suppressed within particular countries, transnational advocacy networks based in other countries can still generate external pressure on repressive governments by encouraging other states to adopt foreign policies consistent with human rights norms that exert pressure on human-rights-abusing governments. Keck and Sikkink stress that advocacy networks do not always succeed in their goals. Moreover, advocacy networks do not always form around an issue that might deserve international support. Nevertheless, transnational advocacy networks are often a source for important changes in international norms. Thus, transnational advocacy networks will need to play an essential role in creating pressure on states to implement human rights norms both domestically and internationally.

Human rights advocacy groups and human rights relief or development agencies are the most visible non-state actors involved in the global struggle for human rights.[10] Human rights advocacy groups focus on the creation and implementation of international human rights norms. At present, approximately 250 nongovernmental organizations (NGOs) are organized for the purpose of human rights advocacy.[11] Amnesty International is perhaps the best known of this type of human rights organization. Other prominent human rights NGOs include Human Rights Watch, Physicians for Human Rights, the International Federation of Human Rights, and Helsinki Watch.[12] Human rights advocacy groups can be further broken down into organizations that promote human rights in general, such as Amnesty International and Human Rights Watch, and groups that focus on specific human rights issues—for instance, the Human Rights Campaign, an organization dedicated to the promotion of human rights for gay, lesbian, bisexual, and transgendered individuals. Additionally, it is important to note that non-state actors that have *not* been organized primarily for the purpose of promoting human rights, such as churches, labor unions, or ethnic organizations, nonetheless may become involved in human rights advocacy.[13]

Relief and development agencies are organized for the purpose of providing economic, legal, medical, and humanitarian aid to the victims of human rights abuses and humanitarian disasters. A prominent example of this type of human rights NGO is the International Committee of the Red Cross, an organization dedicated to providing aid to victims of war and other "manmade" disasters.[14] Médecins Sans Frontières (Doctors Without Borders), a group that provides medical care to victims of war and humanitarian crises, is another example of this type of human rights NGO. Typically, relief and development agencies work in conjunction with governments and international organizations to provide aid to victims of human rights abuses and to promote economic development within countries. Human rights NGOs devoted to providing relief to victims of human rights abuses and humanitarian disasters must negotiate with governments and other groups involved in civil or international conflicts in order to gain access to victims.[15] Moreover, relief and development agencies typically rely on donations from states to conduct their work.[16] In this regard, relief and development agencies are less likely to challenge state sovereignty than are human rights advocacy organizations and, instead, typically have to cooperate with states in order to pursue their objectives. As a result, relief and development agencies are not as likely to advance human rights norms as principles that fundamentally challenge state sovereignty in the long term. Yet they play a crucial rule in providing immediate relief to victims and in ameliorating human suffering in the short term.

When scholars discuss the role of non-state actors in the global struggle for human rights, they typically have in mind these human rights advocacy or relief organizations. However, militarized groups representing victims of human rights abuses are another prominent type of non-state actor actively involved in the global struggle for human rights. The prominent role often played by militarized groups in political conflicts involving human rights violations raises the controversial question of whether violence is ever an appropriate method for responding to human rights abuses. As a general rule, the human rights advocacy groups discussed in this chapter engage in nonviolent political activities designed to further the international implementation of human rights norms. However, victimized groups have often embraced violence as a valid response to repressive governments.

Indeed, one of the central problems in cases involving systematic state violations of human rights is that violence often begets violence. When a state violently represses the human rights of particular groups, these groups often seek to fight back with violent means. In response, the state points to civil violence as a justification for restricting fundamental human rights in the name of national security. Thus, a cycle of violence is initiated that is often difficult to break. However, in the absence of political support from external actors, repressed groups sometimes perceive that they have no alternative but to engage in violence to assert their basic rights. Unfortunately, when non-state actors use violence in response to human rights abuses, they often resort to repressive tactics that violate basic human rights of individuals in opposing ethnic, religious, political, or ideological groups.[17]

Resolving this important ethical dilemma is beyond the scope of this chapter. What can be said, briefly, is that victimized groups historically have used both nonviolence and violence in response to repressive governments, with varying degrees of success regardless of the tactics used. In the case of the Indian campaign for independence from British rule, the nonviolent direct action advocated by Mahatma Gandhi proved to be an effective mechanism for promoting human rights.[18] In South Africa, what began as a nonviolent campaign against apartheid ultimately adopted violent tactics as part of the larger struggle for equality and human rights.[19] Ultimately, it is difficult to determine the extent to which the eventual demise of apartheid rule resulted from nonviolent political activities, violent tactics, international pressure, or, as is likely, some combination thereof. In any case, what this controversy illustrates is that non-state actors involved in the global struggle for human rights include not only transnational human rights advocacy and relief groups that typically embrace nonviolence as a response to human rights abuses but also militarized groups within states that employ violence as a response to state violations of human rights.

While human rights advocates commonly view human rights NGOs as the best hope for promoting universal principles in a world of sovereign states, critics are sometimes skeptical about the motivations and impact of human rights advocacy. One of the most important criticisms of human rights organizations is that they are most often organized within "Western" states by "Western" elites. As a result, critics charge, human rights NGOs may represent a form of cultural imperialism. Worse, some critics charge that the human rights principles promoted by these groups often mask underlying Western interests and, thus, that NGOs either willingly or unwittingly engage in promoting the national interests of Western states. The historical case of the antislavery movement is instructive. The antislavery movement was driven by religious Christian abolitionists who not only believed that slavery was morally repugnant but also "believed that imperialism would spread Christianity, Westernization, and the benefits of trade, and ingenuously saw no contradiction among these principles."[20] As discussed in Chapter 3, the effects of imperialism in Africa were devastating in terms of human rights. Thus, the antislavery movement was simultaneously involved in promoting human rights by contributing to the end of slavery in the West and in supporting human rights abuses committed as a result of British imperialism. Yet, as Keck and Sikkink note, "The frequent inability of reformers to transcend their historical setting, however, does not undermine the significance of the challenges they made to dominant social and political orders or their contributions to political transformation."[21]

The charge that NGOs engage in cultural imperialism brings us back to a philosophical dilemma considered in Chapter 3. No universally accepted philosophical justification for human rights exists. Relativist critics of the concept of human rights argue that, despite its secular language, international human rights law is fundamentally shaped by Christian doctrine and values. As a result, they believe it is often inconsistent with political and cultural realities in many non-Western settings. In their view, well-meaning human rights advocates may disrupt the social stability of communities that traditional cultural values provide in non-Western societies by promoting ostensibly universal principles. They also fear that the universalizing language of human rights is too often used by Western elites to justify the commission of violence in non-Western states. In the end, they believe that efforts to promote universal human rights across the globe may end up undermining the values that the human rights movement purports to endorse. A careful analysis of both historical and contemporary human rights advocacy does show that religious views often, though not always, have been a motivating force underlying human rights movements. As Keck and Sikkink point out, "religious belief has been one of the main sources of the idea that action outside the borders of one's home countries was not only licit, but necessary." In many cases, human rights activists are "propelled by a belief in a higher law that trumps the laws of nation-states."[22]

Critics also note that NGOs are not necessarily membership organizations. Even when NGOs do have open membership, they are not necessarily organized according to democratic principles. As a result, NGOs may not be accountable to the individuals and groups within civil society that they claim to represent.[23] These facts leave NGOs vulnerable to the charge that they are not necessarily representative bodies with the authority to make legitimate claims on behalf of victims of human rights abuses. In other words, critics contend that human rights NGOs, which ostensibly represent close grassroots connections with individuals and groups, do not necessarily put forth genuinely "bottom-up" perspectives on human rights.

What are students of human rights to make of these criticisms? Do they undermine the legitimacy of human rights as *universal* principles? Do these criticisms support the argument that efforts to promote international human rights norms, even when organized by non-state actors, represent unjust attempts to interfere in other states and cultures? Unfortunately, there are no easy answers to this question. Nevertheless, one can say that the criticism is less valid when human rights movements involve individuals and groups from *within* states who are advocating for human rights on their own behalf or for others within their own culture. Increasingly, human rights movements connect activists from states across the globe representing both Western and non-Western societies. At times, religious values may unite these activists, a reflection of the reality that religious identity transcends political borders. Other times, they are brought together simply by a shared commitment to human rights as a secular principle, a commitment that again crosses state boundaries. In either case, these movements cannot be dismissed as a form of cultural imperialism from the outside when they involve significant numbers of individuals from within non-Western societies. Regardless of the force that mobilizes human rights activism, the truth is that NGOs often give voice to the voiceless by representing the interests of victims whose political speech and participation are repressed by human-rights-abusing governments.

CASE STUDY: TRANSNATIONAL CORPORATIONS AND HUMAN RIGHTS

At the end of the Cold War, optimism about a pending "New World Order" was based in large part on the widely held belief that the triumph of capitalism over communism would ultimately lead to the advancement of civil and political as well as economic and social rights across the globe. This belief is founded in a liberal economic assumption that economic liberalization will eventually lead to political liberalization and that free trade is not only consistent with but also necessary for the advancement of fundamental human rights. Although the post–Cold War era has not ushered in a new age of peace and prosperity, as evidenced by persistent violence and poverty across the globe, there is evidence that basic human rights are positively correlated with the adoption of liberal economic models in the long term.[24] Thus, this analytical framework suggests that transnational corporations (TNCs), as engines of free trade, can play a fundamental role in advancing universal human rights in a world of sovereign states.

In contrast to this optimistic assessment of their long-term role in the advancement of global human rights norms, transnational corporations perpetrate human rights abuses in a variety of ways in the short term. Most obviously, transnational corporations are complicit in human rights abuses when they cooperate with repressive governments in countries where they do business, thereby reinforcing repressive rule.[25] Most transnational corporations want to avoid doing business in politically unstable countries because political instability threatens the security of their economic investments. Notably, political stability does *not* necessarily coincide with good human rights records, at least in the short term. As a result, transnational corporations have a long history of supporting repressive governments in the interest of their bottom line. TNCs contribute to human rights violations in other ways as well, such as when banks provide loans to repressive governments, when they fail to comply with international sanctions against repressive governments, when they comply with discriminatory regulations in countries where they operate, and when technology and security companies sell security equipment, such as riot gas and shock batons, to human-rights-abusing governments that use such equipment as instruments of torture and political repression.[26]

In recent years, the most common charges of human rights violations by TNCs have involved the payment of "abysmally low wages, use of child labor, mistreatment of female workers, and the suppression of labor unions."[27] Accordingly, human rights advocacy groups have emphasized these issues in their efforts to put pressure on transnational corporations. When TNCs take action in support of human rights, they are typically responding to political pressure from human rights advocacy groups and networks. In other words, they consider human rights principles when doing so is deemed to benefit their bottom line. Recent high-profile human rights campaigns targeted at TNCs include the movement against the use of sweatshop labor, the campaign for the payment of living wages, and the drive to eliminate workplace discrimination.[28] A large number of companies, including the Gap, Starbucks, Nike, and Reebok, have changed company policies and adopted voluntary codes of conduct in response to pressure from human rights groups and consumers.[29] However, it ultimately remains difficult to regulate TNCs because they are powerful political actors within states. Moreover, in an increasingly globalized world, TNCs have a great deal of institutional and financial mobility. As a result, they can avoid regulations in one country simply by relocating operations to another country with less stringent regulations.[30]

A few examples illustrate the mixed success of efforts to pressure TNCs to actively support and promote human rights. In the 1980s, the International Baby Food Action Network (IBFAN) organized a global boycott of Nestlé Corporation in response to the company's policy of aggressively marketing infant formula to new mothers. This marketing strategy was especially problematic in developing countries where many mothers who had foregone breastfeeding in favor of formula feeding ultimately could not afford the cost of formula. Thus, they began to dilute it with water from frequently unsafe sources. As a result, many babies became ill and died. According to UNICEF, bottle-fed babies are twenty-five times more likely to die than breastfed babies when mothers do not have reliable access to safe water.[31] In 1984, Nestlé pledged to operate under a new World Health Organization (WHO) code for marketing infant formula. This code prohibits advertising to the general public; the distribution of free samples or promotional gifts to pregnant women, mothers, or their families; and point-of-sale advertising such as special displays or discount coupons.[32] The IBFAN resumed the boycott against Nestlé in 1990 amid charges that Nestlé was not living up to its pledge.[33] The IBFAN continues its boycott against Nestlé at present for failing to live up to WHO standards on the marketing of infant formula. Nevertheless, the network's efforts have been successful in that twenty countries have implemented most of the WHO marketing code.[34]

The response of the Gap, Incorporated, to human rights advocacy on the issue of sweatshop labor also illustrates the difficulties of relying on corporate actors to promote human rights norms. Gap has adopted a code of conduct that requires basic human rights standards for its contractors in other countries. When one of its contractors in El Salvador fired more than 300 workers for forming a union in 1995, Gap agreed to allow independent monitoring of this factory and a few additional foreign contractors.[35] Other retailers who had contracts with the factory in El Salvador, including J.C. Penney and Dayton Hudson, terminated their relationship with the factory after the incident. However, Gap agreed to stay after factory workers begged the company to save their jobs.[36] The independent monitoring arrangement led to basic improvements in working conditions, including regular breaks, improvements to the facility, and a formalized complaint procedure for workers. Yet wage increases have been negligible, and factory owners and Salvadoran government officials have complained that the monitoring process is biased.

This example illustrates that TNCs do not shoulder the entire blame for the fact that transnational economic activities may sustain human rights abuses. In this case, the government of El Salvador and the owners of the factory in question have continued to resist external efforts to "impose" human rights norms. Moreover, consumers are driven by their own bottom line to purchase the most affordable products without thinking of the human rights issues often implicated in the manufacturing and marketing of these goods. In sum, "the lesson from Gap's experience is that competing interests among factory owners, government officials, American managers and middle-class consumers—all with their eyes on the lowest possible cost—make it difficult to achieve even basic standards, and even harder to maintain them."[37]

Critics of the idea that transnational corporations have an ethical obligation to promote human rights argue that they are poorly suited for playing an active role in asserting pressure on repressive governments. Consider the example of the Shell petroleum company in Nigeria. In response to pressure from human rights and environmental advocacy groups that have criticized the impact of its operations on local populations, Shell has implemented development programs, including the construction of schools and medical clinics, in the areas where it drills for oil. Despite these efforts, Shell continues to be criticized by human rights groups for complicity with the repressive Nigerian government. Much of this criticism is unquestionably warranted. Shell and other oil companies have not traditionally considered the interests or needs of local populations when they engage in drilling in their communities. More critically, evidence suggests that Shell not only condoned political repression but also actively funded certain Nigerian efforts to repress political dissent that challenged its right to drill for oil in the country, and Shell maintains a cozy relationship with the Nigerian government.[38]

Nevertheless, one critic argues that human rights advocates may be holding Shell to a standard it simply is not capable of fulfilling: "No matter what it does, Shell cannot pacify its Nigerian and international critics, because what they want is beyond any single actor's capacity to deliver: a democratic, decentralized, efficient Nigeria, respectful of human rights and the environment."[39] Of course, Shell could eliminate its complicity with oppression in Nigeria by ceasing its operations there altogether, but this option is not terribly realistic. Even if it were, critics charge, it is not clear that the flight of international oil companies from repressive countries such as Nigeria would advance the cause of human rights—the repressive Nigerian government would still be in place, and a major source of national revenue would be gone.[40] Although human rights activists do not want revenue flowing to repressive governments, it is difficult to enthusiastically embrace an alternative that leaves a repressive government in place while depriving it of potential resources for meeting the basic needs of its population.

As this section has shown, the relationship between transnational corporations and human rights is fraught with tension. On the one hand, proponents of free trade view transnational corporations as an engine for expanding economic and, eventually, political liberalization across the globe in the long term. On the other hand, the historical record suggests that TNCs are more than willing to accept, if not actively support, violations of human rights if doing so protects the corporate bottom line. Even when TNCs demonstrate a willingness to adopt codes of conduct consistent with human rights norms, they are confronted by the reality that principled economic policies are resisted by other political and economic actors. Ultimately, successful integration of human rights norms into the corporate policies of TNCs will depend upon the willingness of consumers and investors to demand that their purchases and investments be consistent with global human rights norms.

CASE STUDY:
HEALTH AND HUMAN RIGHTS ADVOCACY

Human rights groups focusing on promoting health as a human right engage in several types of advocacy. First, human rights advocacy groups promote the idea that health in and of itself is a fundamental human right. Article 12 of the International Covenant on Economic, Social, and Cultural Rights proclaims "the right of everyone to the enjoyment of the highest attainable standard of physical and mental health" as a basic human right. Human rights advocacy groups focusing on health as a human right emphasize the objective of expanding the access of all human beings to basic health care, lifesaving medications, adequate nutrition, and a standard of life necessary for enjoying basic standards of health. Second, some human rights advocacy groups frame specific human rights norms as health issues. Finally, human rights advocacy groups focusing on health emphasize the ways in which human rights in general are fundamentally connected to health.

Physicians for Human Rights is a prime example of a human rights NGO dedicated to promoting health as a basic human right. This group engages both in advocacy of health as a human right and in advocacy for general human rights norms as a means of ensuring health for all human beings. For example, Physicians for Human Rights asserts that not only access to basic health care but also the rights to "education, food and shelter; to freedom from discrimination and persecution; to information; and to the benefits of science" are necessary for guaranteeing human access to health as a human right."[41] This organization also identifies other violations of fundamental human rights, including repression of freedom of expression, harm to civilian populations resulting from war, torture, inhumane working conditions, and the repression of women as basic threats to human health. In short, Physicians for Human Rights treats various categories of human rights, including civil and political as well as economic and social rights, as fundamentally interconnected. This NGO highlights the connections among these categories by illustrating the way in which violations of rights in both categories seriously affect human health.

Doctors Without Borders (Médecins Sans Frontières) is another prominent example of a human rights NGO involved in the promotion of health as a human right. Because Doctors Without Borders focuses more on providing emergency medical care to victims of military violence and humanitarian crises as well as individuals in remote locations who lack access to basic health care, it is helpful to conceive of this NGO as a human rights relief organization rather than an advocacy group. Doctors Without Borders was created in 1971 by a group of French physicians "who believed that all people have the right to medical care regardless of race, religion, creed or political affiliation, and that the needs of these people supersede respect for national borders. It was the first non-governmental organization to both provide emergency medical assistance and publicly bear witness to the plight of the populations they served."[42] Because its primary objective is to work with vulnerable populations, especially in war-torn societies, Doctors Without Borders must cooperate with states and other non-state actors involved in military conflicts in order to gain access to these groups. Thus, Doctors Without Borders emphasizes medical treatment as a means of promoting health rather than political advocacy for health as a human right. Although it emphasizes emergency medical care, Doctors Without Borders also sponsors long-term programs designed to treat chronic illness and other endemic health problems in impoverished communities throughout the developing world. The organization also seeks to train local medical personnel and to strengthen local medical infrastructure as a way of promoting health as a human right in the long term.[43]

The case of the transnational campaign to eradicate female genital mutilation or "female circumcision" (see Chapter 3) illustrates the way in which human rights advocates can frame human rights norms as health issues in an effort to challenge entrenched cultural practices that threaten fundamental human rights. In the case of female genital mutilation (FGM), human rights campaigns that have emphasized the negative health implications of the practice have been far more successful than approaches that challenge its morality or legality.[44] Campaigns against FGM that focus on its health implications have been better received in many target communities because they are not perceived as culturally biased in the way that moral condemnations often are. Anti-FGM campaigns based on health have been especially effective in challenging the validity of the most extreme forms of the practice that pose the greatest threat to women's health.[45]

Although the strategy of framing FGM as a health issue has had some success, the transnational campaign to eradicate female genital mutilation also demonstrates the potential pitfalls and limitations of framing human rights norms as health issues. In Egypt, for example, the effect of efforts to frame FGM as a health issue has been to sanitize rather than eliminate the practice. Instead of being performed by traditional female "cutters," the procedure is now more likely to be performed by largely male physicians in hospitals. Although this development makes it less likely that women undergoing the procedure will experience infections and other detrimental health consequences, it does nothing to advance other human rights norms, such as the right to bodily integrity and sexual liberty, threatened by FGM. (See Chapter 3 for a more detailed discussion of FGM.) Indeed, the "medicalization" of FGM has undermined a traditional source of power and status for women who served as "cutters" and transferred this power to largely male physicians, a development that raises a different set of human rights issues regarding gender equity.[46]

As the case of transnational campaigns against FGM illustrates, human rights advocacy that frames controversial human rights issues in terms of health implications may avoid some of the political and cultural pitfalls of campaigns that bring morality to the center of the debate. At the same time, the case also shows that framing human rights norms in terms of health does not provide a perfect solution and, indeed, may generate new problems involving different sets of human rights. The complexity illustrated by this case suggests that various strategies may be called for in different contexts. In some cases, framing human rights norms as health issues may be very effective while in other cases doing so may be highly problematic. Despite the fact that it is not a workable solution for all contexts, nongovernmental activism focusing on the promotion of health as a human right illustrates the ways in which nonviolent, grassroots mobilization has the potential to appeal to a universal commitment to human health while remaining sensitive to cultural differences. In doing so, transnational campaigns framing health as a human right demonstrate the way in which "bottom-up" efforts to promote global human rights may be more successful in many cases than efforts to forcefully impose human rights from the top down.

CONCLUSIONS

Human rights NGOs have been a major impetus driving fundamental challenges to state sovereignty and advances in universal principles over interests in world politics. Although human rights groups cannot directly implement human rights norms, they play an essential role in pressuring states to accept and apply human rights principles by mobilizing support for human rights within and across states. Their primary tools in this endeavor are gathering and disseminating information about human rights abuses, lobbying governments, educating the public about human rights issues, and providing services to the victims of human rights abuses. Because states ultimately must be persuaded to uphold human rights for these norms to be meaningful, human rights advocacy groups must negotiate a fine balance between confrontation and cooperation with states.

Critics charge that human rights advocacy often represents a form of cultural imperialism that masks the underlying strategic and economic interests of powerful Western states. This chapter has questioned the validity of this criticism, especially when human rights advocacy groups involve proponents of human rights from within non-Western societies. Nevertheless, the charge that human rights advocacy may represent a form of cultural imperialism reminds us that it is appropriate to critically examine claims by non-state actors that they are acting in the name of human rights. From the point of view of an advocate of human rights, healthy skepticism can ensure that genuinely principled concerns for human rights and not underlying strategic or economic interests motivate human rights advocacy. Moreover, such skepticism can lead human rights groups to be very conscientious in making sure that their activism responds to the real needs of the individuals and groups they are trying to help and does not have the unintended consequence of fostering more human suffering than it prevents.

Significant political obstacles hinder global efforts to promote universal human rights from the bottom up. Individuals typically feel powerless in the face of such obstacles. Yet principled change has marked the evolution of world politics in many cases. When dramatic changes in the principles governing world politics have occurred, grassroots movements, non-state actors, and individuals have typically been at the forefront of the struggles precipitating these transformations. At times, weak and vulnerable individuals and groups only have the moral language of human rights to use against powerful states and non-state actors responsible for their repression or suffering. Words and ideas, no matter how morally compelling, appear to be weak weapons when they are used against actors armed with guns and other tools of violence. Yet the moral language of human rights can be a powerful force, especially when it is embraced by large numbers of people. When embraced by sufficient numbers, the idea of human rights can change the political calculus, ideologies, and principles that shape states' perceptions of their national interests and, ultimately, their policies.

DISCUSSION QUESTIONS

1. How does the promotion of human rights from the bottom up differ from top-down efforts to promote human rights as discussed in Chapter 8? Are there any similarities between these two approaches to human rights?

2. Are "bottom-up" approaches to human rights implementation more appropriate than "top-down" approaches? Why or why not?

3. What are the main criticisms of transnational human rights advocacy? Do these criticisms support the argument that efforts to promote international human rights norms, even when organized by non-state actors, represent unjust attempts to interfere in other states and cultures?

4. Do criticisms of human rights advocacy as a form of cultural imperialism have merit? Why or why not?

5. Does the fact that a great deal of human rights activism is motivated by religious underpinnings undermine the legitimacy of human rights as *universal* principles? Why or why not?

6. Do individuals or groups have a right to use violence against governments that are violating their fundamental human rights? Why or why not? If so, what types of human rights violations justify the use of violence by repressed groups?

7. Do transnational corporations have a responsibility to promote and protect international human rights in countries where they conduct business? Why or why not?

8. Do consumers have a moral obligation to consider the human rights implications of their purchasing decisions? Similarly, do investors have a moral obligation to consider the human rights implications of their financial investments? Why or why not?

9. When human rights advocacy groups frame human rights issues as health concerns, their campaigns are sometimes perceived as less threatening to target communities. Why? What does this suggest about the strategies that human rights advocacy groups should use in their efforts to promote global human rights? In addition to health, are there other ways that human rights groups could frame controversial human rights issues in an effort to generate cross-cultural consensus on human rights norms?

WEB RESOURCES

Amnesty International (http://www.amnesty.org)

Center for Economic and Social Rights (http://www.cesr.org)

Doctors Without Borders (http://www.doctorswithoutborders.org)

Global Lawyers and Physicians Working Together for Human Rights (http://www.glphr.org)

Human Rights Campaign: Working for Lesbian, Gay, Bisexual and Transgender Equal Rights (http://www.hrc.org)

Human Rights Watch (http://www.hrw.org)

Inter-Faith Center on Corporate Responsibility: Global Corporate Accountability (http://www.iccr.org/index.php)

International Commission of Jurists (http://www.icj.org)

International Committee of the Red Cross (http://www.icrc.org)

International Gay and Lesbian Human Rights Commission (http://www.iglhrc.org)

International Helsinki Federation for Human Rights (http://www.ihf-hr.org)

International Rescue Committee (http://www.theirc.org)

International Women's Rights Action Watch (http://iwraw.igc.org)

Lawyers Without Borders (http://www.lawyerswithoutborders.org)

Oxfam (http://www.oxfam.org)

Physicians for Human Rights (http://phrusa.org)

Sweatshop Watch (http://www.sweatshopwatch.org)

Conclusions

The history of human rights is, at a very basic level, the history of world politics. This history has been rife with civil and international conflicts, ideological disputes over the proper role of government and the place of individuals in society, and interactions reflecting clashing cultures. All of these things involve fundamental questions of human rights. The civil and international conflicts that regularly erupt in world politics have often been based on conflicting conceptions of human rights, even if historically the language of human rights has not been explicitly used to describe these conflicts. Today, the language of human rights has become a prominent tool used by states, international organizations, nongovernmental organizations, and individuals in their global interactions, and these actors increasingly frame their disputes using this language. Ultimately, the very forces and events that have shaped world politics reflect an evolving conception of human rights.

Because contested ideas over human rights have been central to world politics, the study of human rights sheds great light on world history. It should not be surprising that a professor who writes and teaches about human rights would put forth this proposition. However, a student might be left asking, What is the lesson? Exactly what does the study of human rights teach us about world politics? This book's overview of human rights contains a great deal of information that might engender cynicism among students. Despite growing global endorsement of a large body of human rights norms, states continue to violate human rights in the name of state sovereignty. When states do employ the rhetoric of human rights, they often manipulate this rhetoric for cynical, self-interested reasons. Torture, political repression, genocide, abject poverty, discrimination, and inequality continue to be standard features of life for vast numbers of human beings across the globe. This book highlights these themes again and again. Thus, it would be easy for students to sink into despair or indifference on the grounds that there is nothing they can do.

That is not the intended lesson of this book. An equally important theme that appears throughout the book is that human rights, at a fundamental level, are about politics. This political reality means that students as individuals are in a position to try to shape the global struggle for human rights in a positive way. My hope is that many of the themes and examples presented in the book will inspire anger and passion about the pressing need for universal human rights rather than despair or indifference. Ultimately, I hope that students will be inspired to take sides and to become involved in the global struggle for human rights from the bottom up.

While my hope is that students will be inspired to take sides and to engage in politics as a way of struggling for global human rights, I do not want them to do so with blind idealism. This book is based on the premise that human rights *should* be universal in principle, even if the current reality of world politics suggests that they are not universal in practice. Nevertheless, the book is not intended to suggest that a universal perspective on human rights is without flaws. The principle of state sovereignty, which has been used and exploited in ways that are often damaging to global human rights, in theory can also serve to protect important values in world politics—namely, security, stability, and peace. To this end, state sovereignty should not be dismissed lightly, and criticisms of human rights based on the premise that universal principles can threaten these values need to be taken seriously. Similarly, the assertion of universal values by nation-states has been used to justify intervention in the internal affairs of other states for cynical, self-interested reasons. As a result, relativist critiques of universal human rights also need to be considered carefully.

When I say that I want students to take sides in the global struggle for human rights, I want them to do so in a deliberate and thoughtful way in which they carefully scrutinize the politics of all of the actors involved in the debate over global human rights—from states to human rights activists. Students who are aware of the political dynamics that historically have shaped the struggle for human rights will be more likely to evaluate the intentions motivating states when they claim that they are acting in the name of universal principles. Similarly, they will be more likely to consider the consequences, intended or unintended, of policies designed to promote global human rights, whether such policies are proposed by states or human rights activists. Students who are aware of the historical way in which human rights have been abused in the name of universal principles will carefully evaluate the merits of proposed humanitarian policies. In the same way, they will remain sensitive to concerns that emerge from within cultures about the ways in which even well-meaning humanitarian policies can fail if political and cultural realities in particular cases are ignored.

Ultimately, my hope is that students who engage in the political struggle for global human rights will do so with a critical eye that will help them remain open to persuasive arguments made by critics. As a result of this openness, I hope students will seek creative responses to human rights problems that are sensitive to the values represented by both state sovereignty and culture relativism rather than simply adopting polarizing and rigid rhetoric in the name of human rights. In the end, proponents of human rights who adopt rigid, if principled, positions may accomplish little if they offend the people they are ostensibly trying to help and if they blatantly threaten the state and cultural elites whose cooperation will ultimately be necessary if global human rights are ever to become a reality.

This book does not pretend that there are easy answers. Not only can universal human rights conflict with other values such as state sovereignty, but universal human rights claims can also be in tension. Collective rights may threaten certain individual rights, and vice versa. At times, certain collective rights compete with other collective rights, as when one religious community claims rights that threaten the rights of another religious community. In a similar vein, some individual rights can be in tension with other individual rights, such as when the right to freedom of speech threatens the right of a minority group to be free from discrimination. The potential conflicts between different sets of rights are seemingly endless and can lead students of human rights to want to throw out the baby with the bathwater. However, I hope that students do not do this. Very few things in life that are worth fighting for involve easy answers.

Thus, although easy answers may not be forthcoming, the quest for global human rights remains essential. At the end of the day, my hope is that students who read this book will come to care deeply about morality in world politics. This book is based on a vision of world politics as something that is close to the lives of individuals everywhere—not something conducted from a distance solely by state elites with the necessary expertise and knowledge in foreign affairs. We all make choices—from the purchases we make as consumers to the policies we support as citizens—that affect the basic human rights of other individuals across the globe. Similarly, our own ability to fully enjoy basic human rights is shaped not only by governments across the globe but also by the citizens of other nation-states. Recognition of this reality should encourage us to think of world politics in terms of principle and not just power.

Ultimately, my hope is that all of us who consider ourselves ongoing students of human rights will make choices as consumers and citizens that are informed by considerations of morality and not mere interests. Integrating morality into the choices we make as citizens and consumers does not guarantee that the promise of universal human rights will be fulfilled, but it at least ensures that we will consider our potential impact on human rights. Even individuals who believe that the ideal of a world in which all human beings are fully able to enjoy fundamental human rights represents an unlikely utopia might be inspired to try to make choices that "do no harm" and that will minimize the experience of human rights abuses across the globe. The idea of human rights is a human creation, and individuals can and should play a key role in striving to make this idea a political reality for more human beings across the globe.

After the Holocaust, commentators and political elites became fond of repeating the refrain "Never again." The harsh truth is that the Holocaust was neither the first nor the last incidence of systematic violence and killing in the twentieth century, even though the scale of violence and killing in the Holocaust remains truly staggering. Sadly, gross violations of human rights and war crimes were a hallmark of the twentieth century, from the Armenian genocide early in the century to the genocide in Rwanda toward the century's end. Genocidal violence in the Sudan continues as I write this conclusion, an indication that gross violations of human rights are continuing into the twenty-first century. The human degradation represented by the prevalence of vast poverty across the globe challenges the notion that a global commitment to universal human rights exists. To date, the international community has been largely unable or, perhaps more accurately, unwilling to prevent human rights abuses, war crimes, genocide, and poverty. Yet political activists and idealistic politicians continue to employ the rhetoric of human rights and to seek innovative solutions to the problems of war, human rights abuses, and human suffering in general. Will the refrain "Never again" become a reality in the twenty-first century? History suggests otherwise. Nevertheless, hope and humanity require that concerned global citizens at least struggle to make this refrain speak the truth. This book represents an effort to contribute to this struggle.

Notes

INTRODUCTION

1. Michael P. Scharf, *Balkan Justice* (Durham, NC: Carolina Academic Press, 1997), xi–xii.
2. Amnesty International, "Torture as Policy," in *Human Rights in the World Community,* 2nd ed., ed. Richard Pierre Claude and Burns H. Weston (Philadelphia: University of Pennsylvania Press, 1992), 85.
3. This story was told in *War Photographer*, the 2001 Academy Award–nominated documentary by photojournalist James Nachtwey.
4. Fauziya Kassindja with Layli Miller Bashir, *Do They Hear You When You Cry?* (New York: Delta, 1999).
5. This "story" was captured in a Pulitzer Prize–winning photograph in 1993; reproduced in Joshua Goldstein, *International Relations,* 5th ed. (New York: Longman, 2004), 478.
6. William R. Slomanson, *Fundamental Perspectives on International Law* (New York: West, 1995), 195.
7. Louis Henkin, *The Age of Rights* (New York: Columbia University Press, 1990), x.
8. Ibid.
9. Tzvetan Todorov, "In Search of Lost Crime," *New Republic*, 29 January 2001, 29.
10. Judith Goldstein and Robert O. Keohane, "Ideas and Foreign Policy: An Analytical Framework," in *Ideas and Foreign Policy: Beliefs, Institutions, and Political Change,* ed. Goldstein and Keohane (Ithaca, NY: Cornell University Press, 1993); Kathryn Sikkink, *Ideas and Institutions: Developmentalism in Brazil and Argentina* (Ithaca, NY: Cornell University Press, 1991).
11. Peter Maass, "Dirty War," *New Republic,* 11 November 2002, 18–21.
12. Seymour M. Hersh, "Torture at Abu Ghraib," *New Yorker*, 10 May 2004.

CHAPTER 1

1. Jack Donnelly, *Universal Human Rights in Theory and Practice* (Ithaca, NY: Cornell University Press, 2003), 7.
2. Jack Donnelly, *International Human Rights*, 2nd ed. (Boulder, CO: Westview Press, 1998), 20.
3. Jerome J. Shestack, "The Philosophic Foundations of Human Rights," *Human Rights Quarterly* 20, no. 2 (1998): 203.
4. Ibid., 205–206.
5. Ibid.
6. John Locke, *Second Treatise of Government.*
7. Ibid.
8. Shestack, 213.
9. Ibid., 209.
10. Peter R. Baehr, *Human Rights: Universality in Practice* (Houndmills, Basingstoke, Hampshire, UK: Palgrave, 2001), 7.
11. Edmond Cahn, *The Sense of Injustice: An Anthropocentric View of Law* (New York: New York University Press, 1949), 13.
12. Richard Rorty, "Human Rights, Rationality, and Sentimentality," in *On Human Rights: The Oxford Amnesty Lectures 1993,* ed. S. Shute and S. Hurley (New York: Basic Books, 1993), 118–119.

CHAPTER 2

1. Geoffrey Robertson, *Crimes Against Humanity: The Struggle for Global Justice* (New York: New Press, 1999), 13.
2. Ibid., 15.
3. Ibid.
4. *Treaty of Peace with Turkey,* signed at Lausanne July 24, 1923, available at http://www.lib.byu.edu/~rdh/wwi/1918p/lausanne.html
5. *The Armenian Genocide* at http://www.theforgotten.org
6. David Forsythe, *Human Rights in International Relations* (Cambridge: Cambridge University Press, 2000), 35.
7. For an overview of the discussion among legal scholars regarding the status of the UDHR under international law, see Henry J. Steiner and Philip Alston, eds., *International Human Rights in Context: Law, Politics, Morals* (Oxford: Clarendon Press, 1996), 136–147.
8. It should be noted that the lack of enforcement mechanisms and an emphasis on state sovereignty are not unique to international human rights law but characterize international law as a whole.
9. The Office of the High Commissioner for Human Rights, *The Nature of States Parties Obligations (Art. 2, par. 1): 14/12/90. CESCR General Comment 3,* http://www.unhchr.ch/tbs/doc.nsf/(symbol)/CESCR+General+comment+3.En?OpenDocument
10. Robertson, 167.
11. Ibid., 171.
12. Ibid., 171–172.
13. The Lieber Code of 1863 at http://222.civilwarhome.com/liebercode.htm
14. Robertson, 172.
15. Ibid.
16. Ibid.
17. Hague Convention Respecting the Laws and Customs of War on Land available at http://222.lib.byu.edu/~rdh/wwi/hague/hague5.html
18. Robertson, 177.
19. Gayle Binion, "Human Rights: A Feminist Perspective," *Human Rights Quarterly* 17 (1995): 525.
20. Debra L. DeLaet, "Don't Ask, Don't Tell: Where Is the Protection Against Sexual Orientation Discrimination in International Human Rights Law?" *Law and Sexuality* 7 (1997): 36–43.
21. Forsythe, 12–17.

CHAPTER 3

1. Jack Donnelly, *International Human Rights,* 2nd ed. (Boulder, CO: Westview Press, 1998), 33.
2. United Nations, Doc. A/CONF. 157/22 (1993), cited in Seyom Brown, *Human Rights in World Politics* (New York: Longman, 2000), 38.
3. United Nations, Doc. A/CONF. 157/PC/59, cited in Brown, 38–39.
4. Fernando Téson, "International Human Rights and Cultural Relativism," in *Human Rights in the World Community,* 2nd ed., ed. Pierre Claude and Burns H. Weston (Philadelphia: University of Pennsylvania Press, 1992), 47.
5. Alison Dundes Renteln, *International Human Rights: Universalism Versus Relativism* (Newbury Park, CA: Sage, 1990).
6. Téson, 43.
7. American Anthropological Association, "Statement on Human Rights," *American Anthropologist* 49, no. 4 (October–December 1947): 540–541.
8. Adam Hochschild, *King Leopold's Ghost* (New York: Houghton Mifflin, 1998), 38.
9. Richard A. Wilson, "Human Rights, Culture and Context: An Introduction," in *Human Rights, Culture, and Context: Anthropological Perspectives,* ed. Richard A. Wilson (London: Pluto Press, 1997), 6.
10. Amartya Sen, "Human Rights and Asian Values," *New Republic,* 14 and 21 July 1997, 34–35.
11. Ibid., 36.
12. Ibid.
13. Ibid., 38.
14. Téson, 47–50.
15. Rhoda Howard, "Cultural Absolutism and the Nostalgia for Community," *Human Rights Quarterly* 15 (1993): 315, 327.
16. Arati Rao, "The Politics of Gender and Culture in International Human Rights Discourse," in *Women's Rights, Human Rights: International Feminist Perspectives,* ed. Julie Peters and An-

drea Wolper (New York: Routledge, 1995), 169–170.
17. Ibid., 174.
18. Gayle Binion, "Human Rights: A Feminist Perspective," *Human Rights Quarterly* 17 (1995): 509, 521.
19. Ann Elizabeth Mayer, "Cultural Particularism as a Bar to Women's Rights: Reflections on the Middle Eastern Experience, in *Women's Rights, Human Rights: International Feminist Perspectives,* ed. Julie Peters and Andrea Wolper (New York: Routledge, 1995), 176–188; Rao, 167–175.
20. Arvonne S. Fraser, "Becoming Human: The Origins and Development of Women's Human Rights," *Human Rights Quarterly* 21, no. 4 (1999): 853–906.
21. V. Spike Peterson, "Whose Rights? A Critique of the 'Givens' in Human Rights Discourse," *Alternatives* 15 (1990): 303, 315–324.
22. Camelia Entekhabi-Fard, "Behind the Veil," *Mother Jones,* July/August 2001, 72.
23. Alison T. Slack, "Female Circumcision: A Critical Appraisal," *Human Rights Quarterly* 10 (1988): 441.
24. Ibid., 441–442.
25. Ibid.
26. Nahid Toubia, *Female Genital Mutilation: A Call for Global Action* (Women Ink, 1993), 21.
27. Slack, 445–446.
28. Ibid.
29. Ibid., 447.
30. Toubia, 21.
31. Kevin H. Ellsworth, "Universal Human Rights in Discourse and Practice: The Culture of Circumcision in U.S. Foreign and Domestic Policy" (paper presented at the annual meeting of the Western Political Science Association Conference, March 1999), 2–3.
32. Toubia, 21.
33. Slack, 442.
34. Ibid., 450–455.
35. Ibid., 448.

36. Ibid., 463.
37. Ibid.
38. Ibid., 479–481.
39. Gerry Mackie, "Ending Footbinding and Infibulation," *American Sociological Review* 61 (1996): 1015, cited in Ellen Gruenbaum, *The Female Circumcision Controversy: An Anthropological Perspective* (Philadelphia: University of Pennsylvania Press, 2001), 176.
40. Office of the High Commissioner for Human Rights, "Fact Sheet No. 23: Harmful Traditional Practices Affecting the Health of Women and Children," available online at http://www.unhchr.ch/html/menu6/2/fs23.htm
41. Arif Bhimji, M.D., "Infant Male Circumcision: A Violation of the Canadian Charter of Rights and Freedoms" (unpublished paper, 1 January 2000), 1.
42. Ibid., 3.
43. *Infant Male Circumcision Fact Sheet* available online at http://www.eskimoc.om/~gburlin/mgm/facts.html
44. Ellsworth, 2, 13–14.
45. *Infant Male Circumcision Fact Sheet.*
46. Ellsworth, 13–14.
47. Ibid., 15; Bhimji, 29.
48. Ellsworth, 17–18.
49. Bhimji, 3.
50. Ibid., 30; Ellsworth, 20–22.
51. Bhimji, 4.
52. Ellsworth, 23–24.
53. Bhimji, 7.
54. Ibid., 23.
55. Thomas E. Wiswell, M.D., "Circumcision Circumspection," *New England Journal of Medicine* 336, no. 17 (24 April 1997): 1244–1245.
56. Ellsworth, 5–6.
57. Mackie, 1015, in reference to female circumcision.
58. Slack, 479–481.
59. I am grateful to R. Charli Carpenter for this insight.

CHAPTER 4

1. Herbert C. Kelman, "The Social Context of Torture: Policy Process and Authority Structure," in *The Politics of Pain: Torturers and Their Masters,* ed. Ronald D. Crelinsten and Alex P. Schmid (Boulder, CO: Westview Press, 1995), 26–28.
2. Jack Donnelly, *International Human Rights,* 2nd ed. (Boulder, CO: Westview Press, 1998), 40.
3. Ibid., 41–42.
4. John Simpson and Jana Bennett, *The Disappeared: Voices from a Secret War* (London: Robson Books, 1985), 225, cited in Donnelly, 41.
5. Walter Laqueur, "Terror's New Face: The Radicalization and Escalation of Modern Terrorism," in *The Global Agenda: Issues and Perspectives,* 6th ed., ed. Charles W. Kegley, Jr. and Eugene R. Wittkopf (Boston: McGraw-Hill, 2001), 82–84.
6. Catherine Taylor, "Israel's 'Arbitrary' Detention of Palestinians Condemned," *Christian Science Monitor,* 26 July 2002, 7.
7. Ibid.
8. James Bennet, "New Law Raises Obstacles to Israeli–Palestinian Marriage," *New York Times,* 1 August 2003.
9. Taylor, 7.
10. John Kifner, "Israeli Court Upholds Blowing Up Houses," *New York Times,* 7 August 2002.
11. Bruce Hoffman, "The Logic of Suicide Terrorism," *Atlantic Monthly,* June 2003, 42.
12. Ibid.
13. Ibid., 45.
14. Adam Liptak, Neil A. Lewis, and Benjamin Weiser, "After Sept. 11, a Legal Battle Over Limits of Civil Liberty," *New York Times,* 4 August 2002.
15. Ibid.
16. Ibid.
17. Linda Greenhouse, "Justices Affirm Legal Rights of 'Enemy Combatants,'" *New York Times,* 29 June 2004.
18. Thomas L. Friedman, "Bush's Shame," *New York Times,* 4 August 2002.

19. Todd S. Purdum, "U.S. to Resume Aid to Train Indonesia's Military Forces," *New York Times,* 3 August 2002.

20. Faye Bowers, "U.S. Ships Al Qaeda Suspects to Arab States," *Christian Science Monitor,* 26 July 2002, 1.

21. Peter Maas, "Dirty War: How America's Friends Really Fight Terrorism," *New Republic,* 11 November 2002, 18.

22. Ibid., 19.

23. Seymour Hersh, "Torture at Abu Ghraib," *New Yorker,* 14 June 2004.

24. Ibid.

25. David Johnston and James Risen, "Aides Say Memo Backed Coercion for Qaeda Cases," *New York Times,* 27 June 2004.

26. "Torture Policy," Editorial, *Washington Post,* 21 June 2004.

27. Dana Priest and Bradley Graham, "U.S. Struggled Over How Far to Push Tactics," *Washington Post,* 24 June 2004.

28. John A. Scanlan and O.T. Kent, "The Force of Moral Arguments for a Just Immigration Policy in a Hobbesian Universe: The Contemporary American Example," in *Open Borders? Closed Societies? The Ethical and Political Issues,* ed. Mark Gibney (New York: Greenwood Press, 1988), 68; Frederick G. Whelan, "Citizenship and Freedom of Movement: An Open Admission Policy?" in *Open Borders? Closed Societies? The Ethical and Political Issues,* ed. Mark Gibney (New York: Greenwood Press, 1988), 6–16.

29. Scanlan and Kent, 68–74; Whelan, 23–24.

30. Debra L. DeLaet, *U.S. Immigration Policy in an Age of Rights* (Westport, CT: Praeger, 2000), 9–15.

31. Ruben Navarrette, Jr., "Constitutional Slights: Chandler's I.N.S. Sweep Another Black Mark in Valley's Treatment of Latinos," *Arizona Republic,* 31 August 1997, H1.

32. John Crewdson, *The Tarnished Door* (New York: Times Books, 1983).

33. Edwin Harwood, *In Liberty's Shadow: Illegal Aliens and Immigration Law Enforcement* (Stanford, CA: Hoover Institution Press, 1986).

34. Human Rights First, *In Liberty's Shadow: U.S. Detention of Asylum Seekers in the Era of Homeland Security* (New York: Author, 2004).

35. Eric Schmitt, "Immigrant Advocates Cite Problems with New Deportation Powers," *New York Times,* 15 August 2001.

36. American Civil Liberties Union, "In Second Victory for Immigrants' Rights, High Court Says INS Cannot Indefinitely Jail Immigrants," ACLU Press Release, 28 June 2001.

CHAPTER 5

1. Jack Donnelly, *Universal Human Rights in Theory and Practice* (Ithaca, NY: Cornell University Press, 2003), 222–223.

2. Office of the High Commissioner for Human Rights, *The Right to Self-Determination of Peoples (Art. 1): 13/03/84. CCPR General Comment 12,* available at http://www.unhchr.ch/tbs/doc.nsf/(symbol)/CCPR+General+comment+12.En?OpenDocument

3. Peter R. Baehr, *Human Rights: Universality in Practice* (Houndmills, Basingstoke, Hampshire, UK: Palgrave, 2001), 52.

4. Hurst Hannum, "Self-Determination as a Human Right," in *Human Rights in the World Community: Issues and Action,* 2nd ed., ed. Richard Pierre Claude and Burns H. Weston (Philadelphia: University of Pennsylvania Press, 1992), 175–178.

5. Cited in Hannum, 175.

6. Ibid, 176–177.

7. Cited in Hannum, 179.

8. Seyom Brown, *Human Rights in World Politics* (New York: Longman, 2000), 37.

9. Baehr, 52.

10. Ibid., 52–53.

11. Brown, 38.
12. Christian Bay, "Human Rights on the Periphery: No Room in the Ark for the Yanomami?" in *Human Rights in the World Community,* 2nd ed., ed. Richard Pierre Claude and Burns H. Weston (Philadelphia: University of Pennsylvania Press, 1992), 127.
13. Ibid.
14. Norman Cigar, *Genocide in Bosnia: The Policy of "Ethnic Cleansing"* (College Station: Texas A & M University Press, 1995), 22–46.
15. Ibid., 40.
16. Ibid., 38–46, 166–180.
17. Samantha Power, *"A Problem in Hell": America and the Age of Genocide* (New York: Basic Books, 2002), 247–327.
18. Baehr, 53.
19. Steven Lee Myers, "Female Suicide Bombers Unnerve Russians," *New York Times,* 7 August 2003.
20. Human Rights Watch, *Web Reports on Russia and Chechnya,* available at http://www.hrw.org/europe/russia.php
21. Donnelly, 223.
22. Leo Kuper, *The Prevention of Genocide* (New Haven, CT: Yale University Press, 1985), 8.
23. Power, 1–16.
24. Cited in Power, 17.
25. Ibid., 29.
26. Ibid., 42.
27. Ibid., 57.
28. William Shawcross, *Deliver Us from Evil: Peacekeepers, Warlords and a World of Endless Conflict* (New York: Simon and Schuster, 2000), 146–192.
29. Ibid., 188.
30. Ibid., 124–145.
31. Philip Gourevitch, *We Wish to Inform You That Tomorrow We Will Be Killed with Our Families: Stories from Rwanda* (New York: Farrar, Straus and Giroux, 1998).
32. Power, 333.
33. Ibid., 366–370.
34. Ibid., 334.
35. Ibid., 358–364.
36. Ibid., 386.
37. Ibid., 380.
38. Cited in Gourevitch, 325.
39. Ibid., 169.

CHAPTER 6

1. R. J. Rummel, *Death by Government* (New Brunswick, NJ: Transaction, 1994), 1–28.
2. World Health Organization, "Reducing Mortality from Major Killers of Children," Fact Sheet 178, available on WHO Web site at http://www.who.int/inf-fs/en/fact178.html
3. Héctor Gros Espiell, "The Right to Development as a Human Right," in *Human Rights in the World Community: Issues and Action,* 2nd ed., ed. Richard Pierre Claude and Burns H. Weston (Philadelphia: University of Pennsylvania Press, 1992), 168.
4. Ibid., 169–170.
5. United Nations Development Programme, "What Is Human Development?" available on UNDP Web site at http://hdr.undp.org
6. The Office of the High Commissioner for Human Rights, *The Nature of States Parties Obligations (Art. 2,* par. 1): 14/12/90. CESCR *General Comment 3,* available at http://www.unhchr.ch/tbs/doc.nsf/(symbol)/CESCR+General+comment+3.En?OpenDocument
7. William F. Felice, *The Global New Deal: Economic and Social Human Rights in World Politics* (Lanham, MD: Rowman & Littlefield, 2003), 53–54.
8. Asborn Eide, "Realization of Social and Economic Rights and the Minimum Threshold Approach," in *Human Rights in the World Community: Issues and Action,* 2nd ed., ed. Richard Pierre Claude and Burns H. Weston (Philadelphia: University of Pennsylvania Press, 1992), 158–161.
9. Jack Donnelly, "Human Rights, Democracy, and Development," *Human Rights Quarterly* 21, no. 3 (1999): 610.
10. Ibid.
11. Eide, 159.

12. Donnelly, 623.
13. United Nations Development Programme, "Human Development," 2.
14. Ibid., 2–3.
15. Felice, 5.
16. Ibid.
17. United Nations Development Programme, "Millennium Development Goals: A Compact Among Nations to End Human Poverty, *Human Development Report 2003,* available online at http://www.undp.org/hdr2003/, 77.
18. Felice, 127–183.
19. Ibid., 34–35.
20. Ibid.
21. United Nations Development Programme, "Human Development," 3.
22. United Nations Development Programme, "Development Goals," 2.
23. Ibid., 3.
24. World Health Organization, "Reducing Mortality from Major Killers of Children."
25. Liz Marmanides, "Untold Story: Wiping out Measles—One Child at a Time," *Interdependent* 29, no. 1 (Spring 2003): 21.
26. United Nations Development Programme, "Development Goals," 9.
27. Ibid., 8.
28. Ibid., 9.
29. Audrey Chapman, "The Defeat of Comprehensive Health Care Reform," in *The United States and Human Rights: Looking Inward and Outward,* ed. David P. Forsythe (Lincoln:

University of Nebraska Press, 2000), 5–7.
30. Jonathan Cohn, "Ill Treatment," *New Republic,* 2 and 9 December 2002, 13.
31. Ibid.
32. United Nations Development Programme, "Development Goals," 8.
33. Sarah Joseph, "Pharmaceutical Corporations and Access to Drugs: The 'Fourth Wave' of Corporate Human Rights Scrutiny," *Human Rights Quarterly* 25, no. 2 (2003): 428–431.
34. Ibid., 431.
35. Ibid., 432–434.
36. Ibid., 440.
37. Ibid., 436.
38. Felice, 6.
39. Elizabeth Becker, "Poor Nations Can Purchase Cheap Drugs Under Accord," *New York Times,* 31 August 2003.
40. World Health Organization, "Health and Human Rights," available on WHO Web site at http://www.who.int/hhr/en/
41. World Health Organization, "Reducing Mortality."
42. Felice, 7.
43. Donnelly, 608–609.
44. Ibid., 627.
45. Ed Susman, "Cuba's AIDS policy offers lessons," *UPI Science News,* 16 February 2003, available online at http://www.upi.com/view.cfm?StoryID=20030216-024746-8359r

CHAPTER 7

1. Hilary Charlesworth, "Human Rights as Men's Rights," in *Women's Rights Human Rights: International Feminist Perspectives,* ed. Julie Peters and Andrea Wolper (New York: Routledge, 1995), 104–106.
2. Donna Sullivan, "The Public/Private Distinction in International Human Rights Law," in *Women's Rights Human Rights: International Feminist Perspectives,* ed. Julie Peters and Andrea Wolper (New York: Routledge, 1995), 126–134.
3. Charlesworth, 107.
4. Ibid., 105.
5. *Convention on the Elimination of Discrimination Against Women,* Article 4, paragraph 1, available online at http://www.un.org/womenwatch/daw/cedaw/econvention.htm
6. Ibid., Article 5.
7. Sheila Dauer, "Indivisible or Invisible: Women's Human Rights in the Public and Private Sphere," in *Women, Gender, and Human Rights,* ed. Marjorie Agosín (New Brunswick,

NJ: Rutgers University Press, 2001), 66, 70–73.

8. Ibid., 70.

9. Indira Jaising, "Violence Against Women: The Indian Perspective," in *Women's Rights Human Rights: International Feminist Perspectives,* ed. Julie Peters and Andrea Wolper (New York: Routledge, 1995), 53.

10. Mala Sen, *Death by Fire: Sati, Dowry Death, and Female Infanticide in Modern India* (New Brunswick, NJ: Rutgers University Press, 2001).

11. Ibid., 73.

12. Ibid., 74.

13. Sullivan, 129.

14. Rebecca J. Cook, "State Responsibility for Violations of Women's Human Rights," *Harvard Human Rights Journal* 7 (1994): 125–175.

15. Sally Engle Merry, "Women, Violence, and the Human Rights System," in *Women, Gender, and Human Rights,* ed. Marjorie Agosín (New Brunswick, NJ: Rutgers University Press, 2001), 87.

16. Julie Mertus, "State Discriminatory Family Law and Customary Abuses," in *Women's Rights Human Rights: International Feminist Perspectives,* ed. Julie Peters and Andrea Wolper (New York: Routledge, 1995), 140–141.

17. Hnin Hnin Pyne, "AIDS and Gender Violence: The Enslavement of Burmese Women in the Thai Sex Industry," in *Women's Rights Human Rights: International Feminist Perspectives,* ed. Julie Peters and Andrea Wolper (New York: Routledge, 1995), 215–223.

18. Codou Bop, "Women in Conflicts, Their Gains and Their Losses," in *The Aftermath: Women in Post-Conflict Transformation,* ed. Sheila Meintjes, Anu Pillay, and Meredeth Turshen (London: Zed Books, 2001), 29.

19. Ibid., 26–27.

20. Tina Sideris, "Rape in War and Peace: Social Context, Gender, Power, and Identity," in *The Aftermath: Women in Post-Conflict Transformation,* ed. Sheila Meintjes, Anu Pillay, and Meredeth Turshen (London: Zed Books, 2001), 147.

21. Meredeth Turshen, "Engendering Relations of State to Society in the Aftermath," in *The Aftermath: Women in Post-Conflict Transformation,* ed. Sheila Meintjes, Anu Pillay, and Meredeth Turshen (London: Zed Books, 2001), 84.

22. Bop, 27–30.

23. Charli Carpenter, "'Women and Children First': Gender Norms and Humanitarian Evacuation in the Balkans 1991–1995," *International Organization* 57, no. 4 (Fall 2003): 661–694.

24. Adam Jones, "Gendercide and Genocide," *Journal of Genocide Research* 2, no. 2 (2000): 185–211.

25. Dubravka Zarkov, "The Body of the Other Man: Sexual Violence and the Construction of Masculinity, Sexuality, and Ethnicity in Croatian Media," in *Victims, Perpetrators, or Actors? Gender, Armed Conflict and Political Violence,* ed. Caroline O. N. Moser and Fiona Clark (Zed Books: 2001), 69–82.

26. Nicole La Violette and Sandra Whitworth, "No Safe Haven: Sexuality as Universal Human Right and Gay and Lesbian Activism in International Politics," *Millenium* 23 (1994): 575.

27. Ibid., 564–568.

28. Douglas Sanders, "Getting Lesbian and Gay Issues on the International Human Rights Agenda," *Human Rights Quarterly* 18 (1996): 71.

29. La Violette and Whitworth, 566.

30. Debra L. DeLaet, "Don't Ask, Don't Tell: Where Is the Protection Against Sexual Orientation Discrimination in International Human Rights Law? *Law and Sexuality* 7 (1997): 36–43.

31. Julie Dorf and Gloria Careaga Pérez, "Discrimination and the Tolerance of Difference: International Lesbian Human Rights," in *Women's Rights Human Rights: International Feminist Perspectives,* ed. Julie Peters and Andrea Wolper (New York: Routledge, 1995), 324–325.

32. La Violette and Whitworth, 575.

33. Yossi Klein Halevi, "Refugee Status," *New Republic,* 19 and 26 August 2002, 12–14.

34. Country information on Israel and Palestine at GayMiddleEast.Com at http://www.gaymiddleeast.com

35. Halevi, 12–14.
36. Ibid.
37. Ibid., 12.
38. Sanders, 67, 88.
39. Ibid., 89.
40. United Nations Development Programme, *Human Development Report 2003,* available online at http://www.undp.org/hdr2003/
41. Sanders, 91.
42. Statement of Michael Heflin, Director of Amnesty International USA's OUTfront Program, on the Question of the Resolution on Sexual Orientation and Human Rights, 2003 United Nations Commission on Human Rights, Geneva, 29 April 2003, available online at http://www.amnestyusa.org/news/2003/usa04292003.html

CHAPTER 8

1. Jack Donnelly, *International Human Rights,* 2nd ed. (Boulder, CO: Westview Press, 1998), 52.
2. Nigel D. White, *The United Nations System: Toward International Justice* (Boulder, CO: Lynne Rienner, 2002), 157.
3. Ibid., 223.
4. Samantha Power, *"A Problem in Hell": America and the Age of Genocide* (New York: Basic Books, 2002), 244.
5. White, 224.
6. Office of the High Commissioner for Human Rights, "United Nations Human Rights Programme," available online at http://www.unhchr.ch/html/abo-intr.htm
7. Seyom Brown, *Human Rights in World Politics* (New York: Longman, 2000), 97.
8. White, 229.
9. *Antti Vuolanne v. Finland* (No. 265/1987), Selected Decisions of the Human Rights Committee under the Optional Protocol, Vol. 3, Thirty-third to Thirty-ninth Session (July 1988–July 1990), available online at http://222.ohchr.org/english/about/publications/docs/sdecisions.rtf
10. Office of the High Commissioner for Human Rights, "Fact Sheet No. 16 (Rev. 1), The Committee on Economic, Social, and Cultural Rights," available online at http://www.unhchr.ch/html/menu6/2/fs16.htm.
11. White, 227.
12. Ibid., 225.
13. Ibid., 232.
14. Donnelly, 69.
15. Ibid., 69–70.
16. Burns H. Weston, Robin Ann Lukes, and Kelly M. Hnatt, "Regional Human Rights Regimes: A Comparison and Appraisal," in *Human Rights in the World Community: Issues and Action,* 2nd ed., ed. Richard Pierre Claude and Burns H. Weston (Philadelphia: University of Pennsylvania Press, 1992), 247.
17. David P. Forsythe, *Human Rights in International Relations* (Cambridge: Cambridge University Press, 2000), 119.
18. Donnelly, 69–70.
19. Ibid., 71.
20. Ibid.
21. Ibid.
22. Ibid., 72.
23. Peter R. Baehr, *Human Rights: Universality in Practice* (Houndmills/Basingstoke, Hampshire, UK: Palgrave, 2001), 79.
24. Donnelly, 77.
25. Ibid., 77–78.
26. Ibid., 87.
27. Forsythe, 140, 148–149.
28. Paul Christopher, *The Ethics of War and Peace: An Introduction to Legal and Moral Issues,* 2nd ed. (Upper Saddle River, NJ: Prentice Hall), 193.
29. Brown, 138.
30. Baehr, 98–100.
31. Ibid.
32. Power, 516.
33. Christopher, 199–202.
34. Noel Malcom, *Kosovo: A Short History* (New York: Harper Perennial, 1999), 334–356.
35. Ibid.

36. Ibid.
37. Power, 449.
38. Geoffrey Robertson, *Crimes Against Humanity: The Struggle for Global Justice* (New York: New Press, 1999), 414–415.

39. Power, 450.
40. Ibid., 460–463.
41. Robertson, 414–415.
42. Power, 460.

CHAPTER 9

1. Gary Jonathan Bass, *Stay the Hand of Vengeance: The Politics of War Crimes Tribunals* (Princeton, NJ: Princeton University Press, 2000), 5.
2. Ibid., 37–39.
3. Ibid., 59.
4. Ibid.
5. Ibid., 104–105.
6. Ibid., 106.
7. Ibid., 124–125.
8. Ibid., 126.
9. Ibid., 128–130.
10. Geoffrey Robertson, *Crimes Against Humanity: The Struggle for Global Justice* (New York: New Press, 1999), 221.
11. Tim Maga, *Judgment at Tokyo: The Japanese War Crimes Trials* (Lexington: University of Kentucky Press, 2001), 134–135.
12. Bass, 159.
13. Ibid., 174.
14. Ibid.
15. Ibid., 204.
16. David Cohen, "Beyond Nuremberg: Individual Responsibility for War Crimes," in *Human Rights in Political Transitions: Gettysburg to Bosnia,* ed. Carla Hesse and Robert Post (New York: Zone Books, 1999), 60.
17. Ibid., 62–64.
18. Ibid., 53.
19. Robertson, 214.
20. George Hicks, "The Comfort Women Redress Movement," in *When Sorry Isn't Enough,* ed. Roy L. Brooks (New York: New York University Press, 1999), 113.
21. Samantha Power, *"A Problem from Hell": America and the Age of Genocide* (New York: Basic Books, 2002), 49.
22. For a comprehensive overview of the criticisms of international war crimes prosecutions and a defense of such prosecutions, see Mark J. Osiel, "Why Prosecute? Critics of Punishment for Mass Atrocity," *Human Rights Quarterly* 22, no. 1 (2000): 118–147.
23. Bass, 257.
24. Richard Holbrooke, *To End a War* (New York: Modern Library, 1999), 107.
25. Ibid., 147.
26. Ibid., 321–322.
27. The ICTY at a Glance, "Fact Sheet on ICTY Proceedings," http://www.un.org/icty/glance/index.html
28. Ibid.
29. Samantha Power, "Mute Justice," *New Republic,* 17 and 24 April 2000, 20–24.
30. International Criminal Tribunal for Rwanda, "General Information: Achievements of the ICTR," http://www.ictr.org/
31. Ibid.
32. Power, *"A Problem from Hell,"* 32.
33. Samantha Power, "The Stages of Justice," a review of *Mass Atrocity, Collective Memory, and the Law* by Mark Osiel, *New Republic,* 2 March 1998, 32–38.
34. Danna Harman, "Rwanda Turns to Its Past for Justice," *Christian Science Monitor,* 30, January 2002, 9.
35. Elizabeth Neuffer, "It Takes a Village," *New Republic,* 10 April 2000, 18–20.
36. Jeremy Sarkin, "The Necessity and Challenges of Establishing a Truth and Reconciliation Commission in Rwanda," *Human Rights Quarterly* 21, no. 3 (1999): 796–798.
37. Tom J. Farer, "Restraining the Barbarians: Can International Criminal Law Help?" *Human Rights Quarterly* 22, no. 1 (2000): 93.
38. Harman, 9.
39. Neuffer, 18–20.

40. Harman, 9.
41. Ibid.
42. Jamie Mayerfield, "Who Shall Be Judge? The United States, the International Criminal Court, and the Global Enforcement of Human Rights," *Human Rights Quarterly* 25 (2003): 104.
43. Ibid., 98.
44. Ibid.
45. Ibid., 95.
46. Ibid.
47. Ibid., 118.
48. Ibid., 105.
49. Carroll Bogert, "Calling for Justice," *Interdependent,* Summer 2004, 24–25.
50. For additional background information on the ICC, see Ved P. Nanda, "The Establishment of a Permanent International Criminal Court: Challenges Ahead," *Human Rights Quarterly* 20 (1998): 413–428.
51. For a detailed discussion of this case, see Richard J. Wilson, "Prosecuting Pinochet: International Crimes in Spanish Domestic Law," *Human Rights Quarterly* 21, no. 4 (1999): 927–979.

52. Marc Cooper, "Ballots and Bones," *Mother Jones,* March/April 2000, 70–77.
53. Mayerfield, 104.
54. Elisabeth Rosenthal, "Wartime Slaves Use U.S. Law to Sue Japanese," *New York Times,* 2 October 2000, A1.
55. Hicks, 113–125.
56. Mayerfield, 113.
57. Andrew Rigby, *Justice and Reconciliation: After the Violence* (Boulder, CO: Lynne Rienner, 2001), 39.
58. Norbert Frei, *Adenauer's Germany and the Nazi Past: The Politics of Amnesty and Integration* (New York: Columbia University Press, 2003).
59. Rigby, 15–38.
60. Bass, 158.
61. Ibid., 159.
62. Ibid., 297.
63. Ibid., 284.
64. Daniel Jonah Goldhagen, *Hitler's Willing Executioners: Ordinary Germans and the Holocaust* (New York: Knopf, 1996).
65. Bass, 300.
66. Ibid., 285.
67. Rigby, 18–24.

CHAPTER 10

1. Isabelle Allende, *The House of the Spirits* (New York: Bantam Books, 1986), 432.
2. Howard Zehr, "Restorative Justice," in *Peacebuilding: A Field Guide,* ed. Luc Reychler and Thania Paffenholz (Boulder, CO: Lynne Rienner, 2001), 330–331.
3. Jennifer Llewellyn, "Restorative Justice in Transitions and Beyond: The Justice Potential of Truth Commissions for Post-Peace–Accord Societies," in *Telling the Truths: Truth Telling and Peacebuilding in Post-Conflict Societies,* ed. Tristan A. Borer (Notre Dame, IN: University of Notre Dame Press, 2005).
4. Laurel E. Fletcher and Harvey M. Weinstein, "Violence and Social Repair: Rethinking the Contribution of Justice to Reconciliation," *Human Rights Quarterly* 24 (2002): 601.

5. Robert I. Rotberg, "Truth Commissions and the Provision of Truth, Justice, and Reconciliation," in *Truth v. Justice: The Morality of Truth Commissions,* ed. Robert I. Rotberg and Dennis Thompson (Princeton NJ: Princeton University Press, 2000), 3.
6. Priscilla Hayner, *Unspeakable Truths: Confronting State Terror and Atrocity* (New York: Routledge, 2001), 14.
7. Juan E. Mendez, "Accountability for Past Abuses," *Human Rights Quarterly* 19 (1997): 268.
8. Hayner, 32–49.
9. Ibid, 43–44.
10. Mendez, 255–282.
11. Ibid., 274.
12. Ibid., 269.
13. Ibid., 277.
14. Eric K. Yamamoto and Susan K. Serrano, "Healing Racial Wounds? The Final Report of South Africa's

Truth and Reconciliation Commis-
sion," in *When Sorry Isn't Enough,* ed.
Roy L. Brooks (New York: New
York University Press, 1999), 494.

15. Ibid.

16. Peter Ford, "Serbs Begin to Deal
with Their Past," *Christian Science
Monitor,* 11 February 2002, 7.

17. Hayner, 79–80.

18. Cited in Tina Sideris, "Problems of
Identity, Solidarity and Reconcilia-
tion," in *The Aftermath: Women in Post-
Conflict Transformation,* ed. Sheila
Meintjes, Anu Pillay, and Meredeth
Turshen (London: Zed Books, 2001),
57–58.

19. Tina Sideris, "Rape in War and
Peace: Social Context, Gender,
Power, and Identity," in *The Aftermath:
Women in Post-Conflict Transformation,*
ed. Sheila Meintjes, Anu Pillay, and
Meredeth Turshen (London: Zed
Books, 2001), 157.

20. Beth Goldblatt and Sheila Meintjes,
"South African Women Demand the
Truth," in *What Women Do in Wartime:
Gender and Conflict in Africa,* ed.
Meredeth Turshen and Clotilde
Twagiramariya (London: Zed Books,
1998), 27–61.

21. Ibid., 36–37.

22. Judith Herman, M.D., *Trauma and
Recovery* (New York: Basic Books,
1992).

23. Cited in Emily H. McCarthy, "Will
the Amnesty Process Foster Reconciliation among South Africans?" in
When Sorry Isn't Enough, ed. Roy L.
Brooks (New York: New York University Press, 1999), 487.

24. Wilhelm Verwoerd, "Justice after
Apartheid? Reflections on the South
African TRC," in *When Sorry Isn't
Enough,* ed. Roy L. Brooks (New
York: New York University Press,
1999), 483.

25. Roy L. Brooks, "The Age of Apol-
ogy," in *When Sorry Isn't Enough,* ed.
Roy L. Brooks (New York: New
York University Press, 1999), 9.

26. Elazar Barkan, *The Guilt of Nations:
Restitution and Negotiating Historical
Injustices* (New York: Norton, 2000),
xxvii.

27. Ibid., xxii–xxiii.

28. Ibid., 27.

29. Ron Nixon, "Peculiar Profits,"
Mother Jones, July/August 2000,
17–19.

30. Hubert Kim, "German Reparations:
Institutionalized Insufficiency," in
When Sorry Isn't Enough, ed. Roy L.
Brooks (New York: New York Uni-
versity Press, 1999), 77–80.

31. Barkan, 13–14.

32. Ibid., 24–25.

33. Roger Daniels, "Redress Achieved,
1983–1990," in *When Sorry Isn't
Enough,* ed. Roy L. Brooks (New
York: New York University Press,
1999), 189.

34. Barkan, 31.

35. George Hicks, "The Comfort
Women Redress Movement," in
When Sorry Isn't Enough, ed. Roy L.
Brooks (New York: New York Uni-
versity Press, 1999): 124.

36. Barkan, xv.

37. Kim, 79.

38. Theo van Boven, "Study Concerning
the Right to Restitution, Compensation and Rehabilitation for Victims
of Gross Violations of Human Rights
and Fundamental Freedoms," in
*Transitional Justice: How Emerging
Democracies Reckon with Former Regimes: Volume 1. General Considerations,*
ed. Neil J. Kritz (Washington, DC:
United States Institute of Peace,
1995), 536–542.

39. Barkan, 284.

40. Joe R. Feagin and Eileen O'Brien,
"The Growing Movement for Reparations," in *When Sorry Isn't Enough,*
ed. Roy L. Brooks (New York: New
York University Press, 1999), 341–
344.

41. Nixon, 17–19.

42. van Boven, 536–542.

43. Ibid., 542–543.

44. Barkan, 344.

45. Ibid., xl.

46. Ibid., 344.

47. Ibid., xix.

48. Ibid., 319.

49. "The Long Trail to Apology," Editorial, *New York Times,* 28 June 2004.

50. John Cornwell, *Hitler's Pope: The
Secret History of Pius XII* (New York:
Penguin Books, 1999).

51. Barkan, 324.
52. "G.I.'s Tell of a U.S. Massacre in Korean War," *New York Times,* 30 September 1999.

53. March Champion, "On Edge," *New Republic,* 29 December 1997, 15–16.
54. Barkan, 323.
55. Fletcher and Weinstein, 601–603.

CHAPTER 11

1. Judith Goldstein and Robert O. Keohane, "Ideas and Foreign Policy: An Analytical Framework," in *Ideas and Foreign Policy: Beliefs, Institutions, and Political Change,* ed. Judith Goldstein and Robert O. Keohane (Ithaca, NY: Cornell University Press, 1993).
2. Andrew Moravcsik, "Taking Preferences Seriously: A Liberal Theory of International Politics," *International Organization* 51, no. 4 (Autumn 1997): 513.
3. Ibid., 517.
4. Debra L. DeLaet, *U.S. Immigration Policy in an Age of Rights* (Westport, CT: Praeger, 2000), 8.
5. Margaret E. Keck and Kathryn Sikkink, *Activists Beyond Borders: Advocacy Networks in International Politics* (Ithaca, NY: Cornell University Press, 1998), 41.
6. Ibid., 58.
7. Ibid., 80–84.
8. Ibid., x.
9. David P. Forsythe, *Human Rights in International Relations* (Cambridge: Cambridge University Press, 2000), 166–172.
10. Ibid., 163.
11. Jackie Smith and Ron Pagnucco with George A. Lopez, "Globalizing Human Rights: The Work of Transnational Human Rights NGOs in the 1990s," *Human Rights Quarterly* 20, no. 2 (May 1998): 379–412.
12. Forsythe, 164.
13. Ibid., 164-165.
14. Ibid., 180.
15. Ibid., 180–181.
16. Ibid., 179.
17. Seyom Brown, *Human Rights in World Politics* (New York: Longman, 2000), 108.
18. Ibid., 107.
19. Ibid., 110–122.

20. Keck and Sikkink, 77–78.
21. Ibid.
22. Ibid., 76.
23. Peter R. Baehr, *Human Rights: Universality in Practice* (Houndmills/Basingstoke, Hampshire, UK: Palgrave, 2001), 119–122.
24. Forsythe, 199.
25. Ibid., 196–197.
26. Matthew Lippman, "Transnational Corporations and Human Rights," in *Human Rights in the World Community: Issues and Action,* 2nd ed., ed. Richard Pierre Claude and Burns H. Weston (Philadelphia: University of Pennsylvania Press, 1992), 394–396.
27. Gary Gereffi, Ronie Garcia-Johnson, and Erika Sasser, "The NGO–Industrial Complex," *Foreign Policy,* July/August 2001, 58.
28. Ibid.
29. Forsythe, 198.
30. Forsythe, 193–194.
31. International Baby Food Action Network, "Bottle Feeding Can Kill," http://www.ibfan.org/english/issue/overview01.html#1
32. The International Code of Marketing of Breast-Milk Substitutes available at http://www.who.int/nut/documents/code_english.PDF
33. Chadwick Alger, "Actual and Potential Roles for NGOs in Worldwide Movements for the Attainment of Human Rights," *Transnational Associations* 6 (1992): 323–324.
34. International Baby Food Action Network, "History of the Campaign," http://www.ibfan.org/english/issue/history01.html
35. Gereffi, Garcia-Johnson, and Sasser, 62.
36. Leslie Kaufman and David Gonzalez, "Labor Standards Clash with Global Reality," *New York Times,* 24 April 2001.

37. Ibid.
38. Forsythe, 197.
39. Marina Ottaway, "Reluctant Missionaries," *Foreign Policy,* July/August 2001, 47.
40. Ibid., 48–49.
41. Physicians for Human Rights, "The Link between Health and Human Rights," online at http://www.phrusa.org/healthrights/link.html
42. Doctors Without Borders, "What Is Doctors Without Borders/Médecins Sans Frontières (MSF)?" available online at http://www.doctorswithoutborders.org/about/
43. Ibid.
44. Alison T. Slack, "Female Circumcision: A Critical Appraisal," *Human Rights Quarterly* 10 (1988): 479–481.
45. Ibid.
46. I am grateful to Charli Carpenter for her insights about the potential downside to framing FGM primarily as a health issue.

Index